OXFORD STUDIES IN AFRICAN AFFAIRS

———

THE AFRICAN CHURCHES
AMONG THE YORUBA

THE AFRICAN CHURCHES
AMONG THE YORUBA
1888 – 1922

BY

JAMES BERTIN WEBSTER

Fellow of the Institute of African Studies
University of Ibadan

CLARENDON PRESS · OXFORD
1964

Oxford University Press, Amen House, London E.C.4

GLASGOW NEW YORK TORONTO MELBOURNE WELLINGTON
BOMBAY CALCUTTA MADRAS KARACHI LAHORE DACCA
CAPE TOWN SALISBURY NAIROBI IBADAN ACCRA
KUALA LUMPUR HONG KONG

*Printed in Great Britain by Richard Clay and Company, Ltd.,
Bungay, Suffolk*

TO LIL

ACKNOWLEDGEMENTS

In a study such as this one is almost entirely dependent upon the co-operation of Nigerians, in this case chiefly Yorubas, for both written and oral source material. To the people of Western Nigeria who took me into their confidence after very short acquaintance I owe whatever merit this work may possess.

I am particularly indebted to Chief Adekunle Coker; the Most Rev. E. M. Olulode, the Rev. Supt. J. O. Okusanya, the Rev. C. F. Roberson, Mrs. Grace Campbell, the late Most Rev. G. A. Oke and the late Bishop N. B. Iyalla for generously permitting me the use of their family papers and other collections in their possession. I also wish to acknowledge their assistance in criticizing my manuscript, while at the same time absolving them from all responsibility for my mistakes and omissions.

Among the other Nigerians who provided me with assistance and hospitality the following deserve special mention: the Most Rev. A. Aboyade-Cole, the Coates family, Oyebode Coker, J. O. Dipeolu, Bishop V. Ayo Falkner, A. O. Glover, Charles Ijaoye, Bishop D. D. Iyadola, O. T. Jibowu, A. K. Lamilisa, Bishop M. F. Lijadu, W. F. Oduntan, Gen. Supt. J. F. Ogunko, J. F. Olanipekun, J. O. Olatunbosun, Othniel Taylor, Jacob M. Thomas, the G. A. Williams and F. E. Williams families, N. A. Winfunke, and S. O. Wright.

I am also indebted to the staff (especially Miss Wood, Librarian, and Miss Keen, Archivist) of the Church Missionary Society headquarters at Salisbury Square; Miss Wolfendale of the Methodist Archives, Marylebone Road, London; L. C. Guam and the staff of the Nigerian National Archives, Ibadan, and the staff of the Baptist Seminary, Ogbomoso.

For financial and other material assistance my thanks are due to the Canada Council, which financed two years of my research, the University of Ibadan, which provided housing and other amenities, and the Institute of African Studies (University of Ibadan), which allowed me study leave to prepare the manuscript for publication. None of these bodies in any way dictated the direction of my work, and they are totally absolved from responsibility for the attitudes expressed, which are entirely my own. Finally, it would be ingratitude to neglect to mention the financial sacrifices which my mother has made towards these years of research.

For encouragement, academic guidance, and intellectual stimulation I am indebted to Professor Roland Oliver of the School of Oriental and African Studies, London; Professor A. C. Cooke of the University of British Columbia, Canada; and Professor J. F. A. Ajayi of the History Department, University of Ibadan, Nigeria.

Finally, to my wife I owe the deepest debt of gratitude for the hours she has spent sorting papers, taking notes, and typing drafts. The dedication of this book acknowledges her as my sharpest and most sympathetic critic. In a very real sense this work is ours rather than mine.

Department of History
University of Ibadan   J. B. W.

CONTENTS

LIST OF ILLUSTRATIONS

INTRODUCTION

THERE is at present a small but growing body of literature available
on the activities of the Christian church in West Africa. But in view
of its multiple forms and manifest activities in every sphere of African
life it is surprising how little serious attention the Christian church
has received. Foreign missionary societies have produced a sizeable
body of published material which frequently confines itself to the
activities of their alien personnel. One may search and fail to find the
smallest account of the life of the church that the missionary society
fathered. There is a grave danger in the belief that because one is
familiar with the missionary society one automatically understands
the offspring church. This attitude is too facile. The controlling hand α
in the missionary society has been alien, while the dominant force in
the church has been indigenous.

If the neglect of the church produced by foreign enterprise is a
reality, how much more are churches created solely by Africans
ignored? The African churches of Yorubaland in Western Nigeria
(the subject of this study) have been referred to twice in publications
which reach the international world: Geoffrey Parrinder's *Religion
in an African City* (1953) and J. S. Coleman's *Nigeria: Background to
Nationalism* (1958). This is all the more peculiar when, as the bibliography shows, the African churches have published a remarkable
amount of material about themselves. It is unlikely that any other
movement prior to 1940 has produced such a quantity of literature of
African origin. On the other hand, the African churches have never
sought to publicize themselves among Europeans. Their reports,
pamphlets, and periodicals have been directed towards the African
community. This is not to say that African churchmen have not been
irritated by their neglect.

The significance of this neglect is more profound than mere pique.
Within the last few decades the Christian church has begun to create
an international structure, an international voice to project the universal church and the values to which all its denominational parts
adhere. This activity parallels similar developments in other fields of
international endeavour. But African churchmen are excluded from
this international body. No Christian organization in Africa begun
and wholly operated by Africans free of foreign affiliation has been

granted international recognition. On the other hand, Africans witness their statesmen participating on international political and economic bodies, their trade unions wooed by world organizations, their women's clubs, sporting bodies, in fact almost any organization deserving the name sought after by the international world. Only the universal Christian church continues to discriminate. The only Africans privileged to sit on international Christian bodies are those who have maintained their affiliation with a denomination in Europe or America.

To what do African churchmen attribute this discrimination? Is it the lack of foreign affiliation? Certainly it is not doctrine, for the African churches are at least as orthodox as the Anglicans or Methodists and much more orthodox than the Pentecostals. Churchmen believe that the reasons are mainly two, one of which is the fault of the universal church, the other due to their own shortcomings. In the first instance they believe that the international church is dominated by the concepts and modes of thought against which they have struggled for half a century or more in Africa, a struggle which this study attempts to record and analyse. Secondly, churchmen are aware of their own shortcomings. They are belatedly discovering that it is not enough to propagate the gospel in their own local sphere, to worship in spirit and in truth, to lift the fallen, tend the sick, minister to the poor. They must also—to use a nasty modernism—project their image. Their failure to do so is now resulting in active international hostility towards the indigenous representatives of Christianity in Africa. At least partly for this reason, the following study was welcomed and generously supported by the African churches.

Some clarification appears advisable as to classification and the nomenclature applied to the various expressions of the Christian church in Africa. Efforts at present are being made towards standardization. Thus the African Churches of Western Nigeria are classified as 'Ethiopian'. For the purpose of this study the nomenclature used and understood by African churchmen themselves has been used. Ethiopianism has no meaning for them. If it has, it refers to a denomination, the Ethiopian Communion, which holds views and tenets that place it outside the African church Movement. Occasionally it is associated with groups which paint the devil white and colour the angels black, a philosophy which rightly or wrongly has overtones and connotations that are far removed from the philosophy of the African churches.

In Western Nigeria four major Christian groups can be identified: (1) the nineteenth-century missions, occasionally called 'the historic churches', including Roman Catholics, Anglicans, Methodists, and Baptists; (2) the African churches; (3) the twentieth-century missions, frequently fundamentalist in nature; (4) the Aladura—Apostolics who emphasize prayer and faith healing ('Aladura' is a Yoruba word meaning 'the praying people'). These churches have drawn extensively upon African culture for their symbolism and ritual.

Even a cursory glance indicates the heterogeneous nature of the groupings. With the exception of the African churches which possess marked affinities, they all contain extremes as divergent as the Roman Catholics and Baptists. On the other hand, except during very recent years, there was more possibility of intra-group co-operation between Catholics and Baptists than there was of inter-group activity between Anglicans and the African church Incorporated, whose doctrinal positions, rites, rituals, and hierarchical organization were almost identical. This has been the sad tragedy of Yoruba Christianity. Those denominations most closely akin in essentials have frequently been the bitterest enemies. The unpleasant truth is that Catholics and Baptists share a bond which appears stronger than all others—white leadership. Conversely, the bitterness between the white-led Anglicans and black-led African church has in the past created an unbridgeable gulf. It is significant that where an Anglican diocese is headed by an African bishop there have been quiet, unpublicized, almost furtive joint services with the local African church. This is one of the major reasons why Africans continue to demand that expatriates be totally removed from positions of power and authority. Much has been written about the ill effects of denominational differences in Africa. Most of it totally misses the chief point. Where differences are fundamental full African control may witness their intensification. Where they are trivial expatriates and their overseas connexions are often rightly accused of perpetuating them.

Of the four major groups there is less diversity among the African churches (in doctrine, ritual, hymnology, and to a lesser extent organization) than in any other. One could say at the risk of oversimplification that in doctrine and ritual they resemble evangelical Anglicanism, while in organization they combine an Anglican-type hierarchy with Methodist-type congregationalism. Their hymns are a mixture of traditional Victorian and original African composition. The African churches maintain that they are the fulfilment of missionary policies pursued in the middle nineteenth century. They were brought into being as a revolt against new policies and practices introduced by the missions to meet the situation created by the penetration, partition, and subjugation of Africa by imperial European forces.

The African churches maintain that their greatest contribution to Christendom is the attitude they have adopted towards polygamy. Whether they 'tolerate' or 'accept' the custom, they believe that their policy stands up to biblical practice, conforms to the spirit of Christ's teaching, provides flexibility in a changing society, is based upon honesty, and faces the reality of Yoruba family life today. In addition, churchmen believe that this policy is the greatest of all steps towards indigenization. Consequently, there has been a marked lack of interest in those externals of identification with Africa that are now agitating members of the mission churches—African colour symbolism, synthesizing African ancestor worship with the European doctrine of the saints, or fusing pagan and Christian festivals. Churchmen's reactions to these mission preoccupations range from accusations of cultism to indifference. Peculiarly enough, although churchmen pride themselves on the enlightenment of their policy towards polygamy, it has been the major point of interdenominational friction inside the movement. Dogmatic positions are taken up on whether to merely 'tolerate' or whether to 'accept' polygamy.

The African churches of Yorubaland are not, and never have been, what might be called cultist, syncretist, or separatist. They disapprove of such groups whether they originate overseas or in Africa. They may or may not be mission schismatics. Of the six organizations more or less intensely studied in this work, three were mission schismatics, three were not. They were not the creation of one man, nor do they revere one founder. They do not emphasize one section of the Bible at the expense of another. They are neither dreamers and visionaries nor prophets and diviners. They can neither be accused of being loosely organized nor confined to a particular segment of Yoruba society. In short, they do not conform to commonly held preconceptions.

In Western Nigeria the African church Movement did not influence the Roman Catholics, for complex reasons. The lack of dynamic expansion, and Catholic emphasis upon the Yorubas who returned from Brazil (involving the subsequent identification with Yoruba-

Brazilian culture) played their part. In much the same way the Yorubas who returned from Sierra Leone remained loyal to their Protestant mission affiliations. In addition, there had been no Catholic teaching of a self-supporting, self-propagating, and self-governing church. There was no indigenous clergy. Finally, the less-than-close relationship with the imperial power prevented Catholic identification with the penetration of Yorubaland during the scramble for and partition of Africa.

Frequently, when it is dealing with a topic such as this one, research is directed towards understanding the 'peculiar phenomena' of the African churches, treating them as a deviation from the 'normal'—the mission societies. Such research aims to assist the missions to adapt themselves to their African environment. This was not the presumption nor purpose of this study, which operated from the premiss that the missions are the 'peculiar phenomena' and the African churches the 'normal'. This is closer to the mid-nineteenth-century philosophy of evangelism upon which the African churches were built.

In addition, this study endeavours to show the influence of economic and social activities on religious attitudes. It would be unfortunate if the results were to expose churchmen to the criticism that their religious behaviour was based, to any greater degree than that of people elsewhere in the world, upon secondary and mercenary ends. This study tries to give due prominence to the ideological views for which they often sacrificed their economic and social status. African church membership was never the path to the top among the Yoruba people. For the first generation at least, it took outward courage coupled with inner conviction and spirituality—attributes of the truly sincere Christian.

B

PART I

The Settlement of 1894

... there are times when it is more helpful that a people should be called upon to take up their responsibilities, struggle with and conquer their difficulty than that they should be in the position of vessels taken in tow, and that for West African Christianity, this is the time.

JAMES JOHNSON, 19 July 1892

A DISCUSSION of Christianity in West Africa must begin with Sierra Leone. Not only was the colony of Sierra Leone the first field of modern missionary enterprise on the West Coast but it also provided numerous black missionaries who fostered the growth of the church in all the coastal cities. Furthermore, because it was the first to receive the gospel, Sierra Leone led West Africa in church organization, in submerging the European-controlled mission, and in creating an African-controlled church.

The colony of Sierra Leone was founded by a philanthropic company as a home for repatriated slaves. In 1789 the first freed slaves arrived from England. In 1792 over one thousand black loyalists arrived from Nova Scotia, and in 1800 further New World repatriates, the Maroons, came from Jamaica. By 1808 the colony had proved too great a financial undertaking for the Sierra Leone Company and became a Crown Colony. After the Act of Abolition in 1807 the British Government attempted to put an end to the slave trade. The British West African Squadron patrolled the West Coast, intercepting slave ships and forcing them into Freetown, where the slaves became freemen.

The Church Missionary Society (C.M.S.) was founded in 1799 by men who had been active in the Sierra Leone Company.[1] It was not surprising that Sierra Leone should be one of the first areas of interest. Missionaries were sent out in 1804. The mission proved both a challenge and an opportunity for the C.M.S. The challenge lay in the

[1] E. G. Ingham (Bishop of Sierra Leone, 1883-96), *Sierra Leone After a Hundred Years*, London, 1894, p. 193.

climatic unsuitability of the Coast for Europeans and in the lack of modern precedent in missionary methods. The opportunity was the ability to reach a significant number of Africans who were uprooted from their tribal surroundings and who represented a variety of ethnic groups.

The missionaries organized the Colony into parishes, and provided education culminating in training colleges for boys (Fourah Bay College) and for girls (Annie Walsh Training Institution). Because of the heavy mortality of Europeans an African Ministry was trained early, and carried the greatest burden of the work of the church. In 1852, late in the mission's history,[1] the Diocese of Sierra Leone was established with a European bishop at its head. This enabled African clergy to be ordained without taking the long voyage to England. In 1873 an independent pastorate was organized. This meant that the African clergy and laity could now control the local administration of the church through their parish committees and church council. The bishop, who took an oath of allegiance to the Archbishop of Canterbury, was the supreme authority in the Colony in matters of doctrine. The clergy held their licences from the bishop and were responsible to him.

Before the slave trade was completely abolished many ex-slaves of Freetown in the 1840s began for various reasons to migrate to cities all along the coast from the Gambia to Calabar in what is now Eastern Nigeria. Some returned to their tribes, others searched for their relatives, and some settled in other cities for the sake of the trading opportunities available. By 1860 there existed small communities of Christian ex-slaves, or Sierra Leonians as they were called, in all the cities along the coast and as far as three hundred miles inland. The missionaries in Sierra Leone were called to begin Christian work in these towns.

The largest migration flowed back to Lagos and its hinterland, the Yoruba country, and especially to Abeokuta, capital of the Yoruba Egba Kingdom. Both Anglican and Methodist missionaries responded to the call of the Christian Egbas and began missionary activities in Abeokuta in 1846. In 1851 the British Government forced the closing of the slave markets in Lagos and placed a consul there to prevent illicit smuggling of slaves. The missionaries came to Lagos

---

[1] 'Had the Church of England been as much alive to her ecclesiastical responsibilities, as her handmaid (the C.M.S.) had been in her own *evangelistic* department, Sierra Leone would not have had to wait so long, to her loss, for this necessary development.' Ingham, *Sierra Leone After a Hundred Years*, p. 198.

immediately. For geographic, commercial, and political reasons
Lagos attracted a large number of the returning exiles.[1] The Christian church developed rapidly. The history of Sierra Leone was
repeated. The city was divided into parishes, each with its own
church—St. Paul's (Breadfruit), St. John's (Aroloya), Holy Trinity
(Ebute Ero), St. Peter's (Faji), and St. Jude's (Ebute Metta). Christ
Church, where Europeans and the most Europeanized Africans worshipped, was without a parish. Educational institutions similar to
those of Freetown were developed early in Lagos. Again like Freetown, Lagos was organized as soon as the churches were self-supporting into a native pastorate. This organization began in 1876 and was
completed in 1887 after a decade of European missionary opposition.

In Lagos, when the independent pastorate was established, Europeans were no longer in ministerial positions except in Christ Church,
which remained outside the pastorate. A few remained employed in
educational work. The European missionaries concentrated upon the
interior cities of Abeokuta, Ibadan, and Oyo. It was noteworthy that
in Lagos and Freetown the organization stopped short of an African
bishop, both being under the English Bishop of Sierra Leone.

Farther east along the coast, in the Delta and drainage basin of
the Niger, merchants began a profitable trade in palm oil. Since the
Africans efficiently organized the collection of palm oil in the interior
and supervised its transport to the coast, European merchants came
only as far as the Delta to trade. Henry Venn, secretary and leading
spirit in the C.M.S., decided that in this area a new missionary approach should be undertaken. The problems of the method employed
in Freetown and Lagos, arising out of English racialism, might be
avoided if a mission were wholly managed by Africans.

The method used in Lagos and Freetown was for a European missionary to settle in a large city and gather a small Christian congregation. The Christians were taught to read their Bibles. A few who
emerged with greater spirituality and a more intelligent grasp of the
scriptures would be appointed to live as catechists in other wards of
the city or in surrounding villages, preach the gospel, and teach reading. As the number of catechists grew, those who qualified for the
ministry were given further training or sent to a training institution
such as Fourah Bay. If the bishop was satisfied with these men they

[1] The return of the Sierra Leone exiles to Yoruba is fully discussed in Jean F.
Herskovits, 'Liberated Africans and the History of Lagos Colony to 1886',
D.Phil. thesis, Oxford, 1960.

were then ordained and worked directly under the European missionary. When there were sufficient ordained African clergy, congregations large enough to support them, and a school system culminating in a secondary institution, a native pastorate governing a number of churches would be set up. At this point the European missionary should withdraw and settle on the missionary frontier to begin the process all over again. Logically, if proclaimed policy had been carried out, when the pastorate (or two pastorates) ran smoothly and clerical leadership had been given an opportunity to develop, an African bishop should have been appointed. At this stage the mission would disappear and the church fully emerge. As noted above, this last step was not taken in Sierra Leone or Lagos.

Between 1841 and 1872 Henry Venn, general secretary of the C.M.S., formulated the Society's policy virtually single-handed. He believed in planting self-supporting, self-governing, and self-propagating churches overseas. The method so far employed in Freetown and Lagos had not achieved these aims. The greatest difficulty was in the timing of the step-by-step change from mission to church. Africans felt the pace was depressingly slow; Europeans thought it alarmingly fast. Europeans who had, over a lifetime, built a church congregation desired to remain as pastors to the flock they had gathered, and begrudged moving to the frontier in the later years of their lives.[1] Shortage of funds often aggravated this feeling, as the mission society was unable to provide expensive European accommodation in new areas. Sometimes Europeans were left for years in old-established churches, supervising larger and larger areas worked by Africans. African ministers, although they had freedom of action, due to the inability of Europeans to supervise so large an area, did not receive the authority and power which they felt was commensurate with their work. This, coupled with the reluctance of the Society to go the last step and consecrate African bishops, caused friction between mission and church, and had a depressing influence on the Christian work. A situation arose which a mission critic half a century later accurately described:

Those who are seeking to gain authority never agree to wait until those who hold it think that they are sufficiently prepared. The moment arrives only when those who are seeking to gain authority are strong enough to

---

[1] This attitude of European missionaries was discussed by E. C. Stuart in a paper at Bath Church Congress, 1873, quoted in Stock, *History of the Church Missionary Society*, London, 1899, vol. ii, p. 418.

drive those who hold it into concessions, by threats of revolt. The inevitable result of this method is discontent and strife.[1]

Henry Venn was aware of these problems and attempted to secure support for the consecration of Samuel A. Crowther as Bishop of Yorubaland. He met opposition from missionaries anxious that this position should go to one of their own number. When these older missionaries finally accepted Venn's views a younger group of missionaries refused to work under Crowther.[2]

In the 1860s the Niger area presented a new challenge and a new opportunity to Venn. If a European missionary effort was difficult due to the climate, and if one of the problems of the traditional method was a conflict between the mission and church, could not an all-African mission solve these problems. In addition, the cost to the Society would be less, both in salaries and capital outlay. Furthermore, because the returning exiles had been so successful in Yoruba surely they would be as successful on the Niger. On the strength of these arguments Venn persuaded the Archbishop to consecrate Samuel Crowther as Bishop on the Niger in 1864.

Upon Crowther's consecration the second Diocese of the Anglican Church was established. This diocese was never delimited. It took in vaguely all of West Africa except those areas under British jurisdiction, such as Lagos, Sierra Leone, and the Gambia, which were under the Bishop of Sierra Leone. It was, however, from the mouth of the Niger, three hundred miles inland to Bida where Crowther spent his life. It was in this area where his reputation was to be established.

Much was made by C.M.S. leadership and Anglican periodicals of this mission. It was an experiment which aroused considerable interest. Its expected success was to be an eloquent answer to those who were disparaging the Negro race. The Niger, with its African staff and leadership, was to prove that educated Africans could carry the gospel successfully to the interior of the continent.

The difficulties faced by Crowther in the Niger Diocese have been fully discussed elsewhere,[3] but must be briefly reviewed here. Four

[1] Roland Allen, *The Spontaneous Expansion of the Church*, London, 1949, p. 33.

[2] Townsend, Hinderer, Gollmer, and Smith (pioneer missionaries in Yoruba) petitioned Venn, objecting to the consecration of S. A. Crowther. See J. F. A. Ajayi, 'Christian Missions and the Making of Nigeria, 1841–1891', Ph.D. thesis, London, 1958, pp. 418–19. For opposition from the younger generation of missionaries (Faulkner, Wood, and Maser) see Herskovits, 'Liberated Africans', p. 450.   [3] Ajayi, 'Christian Missions', pp. 555–99.

peculiarities made Crowther's situation unlike that of the Bishop of Sierra Leone. First, there were the long distances over which he had to travel, much of it on foot. On the river transport was irregular, and in the hands of commercial companies who were not interested in the passenger trade. Even after Crowther used his own boat the seasonal flow of the river left the upper Niger without supervision for long periods.

The latter years of Crowther's episcopate were ones of commercial struggle between the European companies, on one hand, and the African coastal tribes and Sierra Leonian merchants, on the other. On the middle Niger, Crowther's African ministers were closely re-lated to, and sympathized with these merchants, and opposed the European trading houses. In the Delta the Christians of Brass and Bonny, along with their pagan neighbours, were the middle men who were being squeezed out of the trade. In this struggle the English missionaries sided with their English compatriots in business.

The Niger area encompassed a wide variety of tribes. There were three distinct groups: the coast people of the Delta, the Ibos of the middle Niger, and the Muslims speaking a variety of languages on the upper Niger. The tribal situation was unlike the Yoruba area, in which the Europeans had been missionaries since the 1840s. In this area there existed a similarity of language and custom, a valuable asset to the missionaries for translation and mobility purposes. An-other outstanding trait of Yorubaland was the large numbers of returning emigrants who provided ready-made Christian communi-ties to welcome and support the missionaries. Trained priests re-turned with the emigrants, many of whom were related to the people. The C.M.S. had Egba ministers to work in Abeokuta, Ijesha minis-ters for Ilesha, and Ibadans for Ibadan.

None of these favourable conditions existed on the Niger. Transla-tion work was extremely complex. There were few emigrant Christian communities or ministers. With the exception of two or three Ibos and one Hausa minister, Crowther had to work the area with Yorubas. These men, like Europeans, had to study the language and adjust to foreign customs. Because of the dialect problems, Crowther could not freely shift his clergy to prevent their close association with the politics of the tribe. Furthermore, on the upper river the Niger clergy were involved with a Muslim population. New methods of evangelization were necessary if Christian congregations were to be gathered from among these people. Lastly, Crowther was not an independent bishop with an established revenue. He was a missionary bishop dependent upon the C.M.S. for his salary and subject to its control. As long as Henry Venn dictated C.M.S. policy, Crowther could rely upon support, not only because of their personal friendship but also because they viewed the missionary problem in much the same way. A change of leadership in the C.M.S., coinciding with a clash of European and African commercial interests on the Niger, seriously weakened Crowther's support in London.

The success or failure of the Niger experiment must be judged against the background of these facts. On the positive side, it can be said that the Niger Mission penetrated farther inland than any other on the West Coast. Crowther was the first to meet Islam advancing from the north. He realized that the chiefs were particularly interested in missionaries for the education they provided. He successfully persuaded them to finance the schools, and so removed a financial burden from the mission funds.

In 1890 work on the upper Niger was still in the pioneer stage and extremely feeble. In the Delta, however, a flourishing church with a cathedral at Bonny had been established. In 1892 the Delta church contributed £748 to its support, a figure which compared favourably with other missions. The Yoruba interior, for example, in 1892 contributed £517.[1]

Between 1880 and 1890 antagonism grew between European and African traders, and between European and African clergy. Exaggerated reports reached London of the low morals of the ministry and laity of the Niger Mission. A number of Europeans were sent throughout the decade to report. Generally these reports were unfavourable to the Africans, but they differed widely and contradicted each other in their recommendations—one reporting that certain clergymen were unsuitable, another the following year praising their work. A type of disguised European supervision was gradually introduced in the 1880s. In the latter years of the decade a large number of Europeans were sent to the Niger, and so began the purge of the mission associated with the names of J. A. Robinson and G. W. Brooke. The issue raised in the purge became involved in the issue of Crowther's successor. If the purge was justified Crowther's episcopate had been a failure, and he should be succeeded by a European. If it was not, the advantages of an African bishop were as strong in 1891 as they had been in 1864.

[1] *C.M.S. Annual Proceedings*, 1893.

The purge of the Niger Mission undertaken by G. W. Brooke and J. A. Robinson in 1890, which resulted in discrediting the Sierra Leonian clergy, was more than simply directed against the African agency. Brooke and Robinson were convinced that the whole missionary approach to the heathen was wrong. They sought to change the traditional West Coast missionary method. They would have been critical of any West Coast or, indeed, of any African mission. Brooke mentioned that the purge of the C.M.S. Niger Mission was only the beginning.

Do not foster the theory that the evils we have unmasked are confined to the Niger and are not to be expected in other C.M.S. circles in Africa, because the other places must also be inspected and purged, where possible of similar wickedness and imposture.[1]

There was a difference. Had Brooke and Robinson attempted their purge in an English-supervised area such as the Yoruba states or Sierra Leone, they would have had their appointments terminated, supposing they had been successful in getting their reports beyond the bishop or mission secretary. The C.M.S. in any case would have ignored them, especially if those in the field had been as unanimous as the Niger agents in their opposition. But the ideas of the anthropologists of African inferiority, so stoutly challenged by Venn and his generation, were beginning to affect the younger members of the C.M.S. committee. Advice of ten Africans no longer equalled the report of one Englishman. The story of the Niger Mission simply cannot be comprehended without a clear understanding of the deep racist feeling of the English embodied in almost all communications to and from the C.M.S. This is the only explanation for the credence which the C.M.S. gave to reports so contradictory, so incomplete, so defamatory to a whole race.

Brooke's plans for the evangelization of Africa were to centre around European missionaries who would adopt African customs. They must dress in Native clothes, eat Native food, live in Native style houses, and teach in Native fashion.[2] The schools were to cease catering to the Sierra Leonian traders, and discontinue the produc-

---

[1] Brooke to Lang, 6 Aug. 1890, *C.M.S.*, G3 A3/O, no. 124. Brooke talked of two great revolutions in the C.M.S.—one on the Niger under his leadership, and one in East Africa under Douglas Hooper. See D. C. Crowther to Lang, 12 Feb. 1892, *C.M.S.*, G3 A3/O, no. 93.

[2] Brooke imitated Muslim Mallams. He sat on his veranda and Muslims came to him and sat at his feet to learn. As he taught he brushed verses of scripture in Arabic on small boards, which he gave to the students when the lesson was over.

tion of clerks for the Niger Company. The curriculum should stress Christianity and crafts. It should prepare children for Native society rather than clerical posts. It should graduate evangelists for the Native society and not of the Sierra Leone type, interested in material benefits.

There is no hope of success until we have first taken down the whole of the past work so that not one stone remains upon another. I mean that the pastors . . . must be changed, the time, mode and place of worship must be changed, the school children must be changed and the course in the schools must be changed.[1]

Graham Wilmot Brooke was an unusual man. His outstanding ability and total consecration to the mission cause greatly impressed the C.M.S. Parent Committee and the Europeans with whom he came in contact. He impressed his fellow missionaries by his devotion and spirituality.[2] On the other hand, Archdeacon Crowther, the son of the bishop, called him a racialist.[3] His letters in both form and content were unique. They were typed in turquoise ink and signed with his full signature in purple. The thick purple pencil was used to underline for emphasis and for decoration.[4] His forceful manner of writing gave the impression of a man intolerant of other points of view. He had a singleness of purpose—dedication to the purge of the Niger and the conquest of the Sudan for Christ.[5]

Brooke was twenty-three years of age, 'hardly out of boyhood',[6] when in 1889 he was accepted as an honorary missionary by the C.M.S. He was not of Anglican background[7] and appeared attracted by ideas current among the Baptists during the 1880s, that the missionary must be free from the control and discipline of a missionary

[1] Brooke to Major-Gen. J. Touch, 5 June, *C.M.S.*, G3 A3/O, no. 93.

[2] Report of J. S. Hill to the Archbishop of Canterbury (hereafter referred to as Hill's Report), 20 Dec. 1892, *C.M.S.*, G3 A3/O, 1893, no. 6.

[3] D. C. Crowther to Lang, 12 Feb. 1892, *C.M.S.*, G3 A3/O, no. 93.

[4] See any of Brooke's letters during 1890–1. For example, Brooke to Lang, 28 May 1891, *C.M.S.*, G3 A3/O, no. 169.

[5] During the year 1891 Brooke became preoccupied with death, seeking it, glorifying it. He gave the C.M.S. instructions in minute detail on how they were to behave in case of his death. See G. W. Brooke, 'Steps to Be Taken in the Event of My Death', n.d. *C.M.S.*, G3 A3/O, no. 103.

[6] S.G.S., 'In Memorium', *The Intelligencer*, May 1892, p. 369. Brooke's father was Lt.-Col. Robert Wilmot Brooke of the Sixtieth Rifles. His mother was the daughter of Sir Duncan Macgregor and sister of the well-known Rob Roy, 'The Sudan Mission Band', *The Christian Workers*, April 1890, pp. 112–13, *C.M.S.*, F4/6.

[7] *Intelligencer*, Feb. 1889, pp. 123–4, and *C.M.S. Register*, no. 1148.

society. His views had been confirmed by Baptist missionaries in the Congo.[1] Brooke finally achieved his aim. He was permitted to join the C.M.S. as an honorary missionary, supported by a special committee organized in Manchester, which printed and distributed monthly leaflets written by Brooke.[2]

Even from a casual perusal of his private papers, it was obvious that Brooke was peculiar. He boasted that the passengers on the ship to West Africa not only thought him odd but hated him intensely.[3] He recorded his finances in embarrassing detail and kept a meticulous chart of his correspondence. His letters indicated a preoccupation with the political affairs of the Niger.[4] He possessed a strong military feeling and looked forward with anticipation to participating in the defence of Lokoja against the Nupes, even though conscious that this was contrary to the spirit of his missionary vocation.[5]

In religion he leaned towards fanaticism. There was much oral confessing in his company.[6] He admired the Moravians, who voluntarily became lepers, and told the Niger Company that if he became destitute in the Sudan he would willingly sell himself as a slave to tend camels or labour in the garden.[7] His Journal noted such items as nude wrestling and reading novels which he later described as 'disobedient folly' and 'drinking poison'.[8] He maintained a most unhealthy relationship with his few African disciples from whom he demanded complete submission.[9]

Brooke discredited his reports from the West Coast by recording

---

[1] Brooke to Leonard Shaw, 13 Oct. 1887, Stanley Pool, Congo, *C.M.S.*, F5, bdle 2, also Brooke to his father, 22 Aug. 1887, Congo Hotel, Banana, *C.M.S.*, F5, bdle 2.

[2] The first *Monthly Leaflet* was published for Jan. 1890, see *C.M.S.*, F4/6. The last one, no. 20, was written by Dr. Battersby Mar.–Apr. 1892 after Brooke had died, *C.M.S.*, F4/8.

[3] Brooke to M.G.B. (on boat to Congo), n.d., and Brooke to M.G.B., n.d., *C.M.S.*, F5/1.

[4] Brooke to Callender, Oct. 1891, 'The State of Lokoja Politically', Private and Confidential, *C.M.S.*, F5/1.

[5] Brooke to his father, 12 Feb. 1892, Lokoja, *C.M.S.*, F5/1. Brooke decided to become a missionary after failing 'under rather peculiar circumstances in an army examination', 'The Soudan Mission Band', *The Christian Worker*, Apr. 1890, pp. 112–13, *C.M.S.*, F4/6.

[6] Brooke's Journal, Feb. 1890, pp. 180–1, *C.M.S.*, F4/7 (hereafter noted as 'Journal').

[7] Brooke in conversation with Flint, Journal, p. 52.

[8] Journal, pp. 53, 87.

[9] Brooke's formal dismissal of Salim C. Wilson as his 'working companion', 17 Apr. 1888, *C.M.S.*, F5/1.

his sources of information. In no single instance does he report a conversation with anyone sympathetic to the Christian community. A Hausa officer gave him the 'facts' about Lagos Christians. G. Rose, who had broken from the Anglican Church and was then, like Brooke, an independent missionary, informed Brooke on the Niger and Sierra Leone. Brooke said of Rose that although 'his manner was nervous (somewhat) with that anxiety not to give offence which is rather too prominent in West Coasters', yet, 'I watched him for suspicious signs but I certainly believe the man was genuine'. The conversation which followed was a rare example of subtlety on the part of Rose. He carefully drew out from Brooke his attitude, and then supplied the examples from the Christian life of West Africa to confirm what Brooke wanted to hear. At one point Rose strayed but Brooke led him back by a question which suggested its own answer.[1]

Throughout his journals, letters, and reports, Brooke never once substantiated by reasonable evidence his charge against the Africans. His descriptions were loaded with phrases which indicate a profound antipathy to the Black race. Sierra Leone was a 'den of thieves' and Sierra Leonians the 'very worst on the coast', being 'crafty traders', 'depraved Coast Negroes', 'with rascally-looking faces', who made a 'clever assumption of child-like simplicity'.[2]

The Niger mission, too, was a 'den of thieves' and the Niger clergy were inmates fit for the den: Macaulay was 'painfully obsequious', Johnson, 'untruthful and overbearing', Coker had 'a most sinister unpleasing expression', Smart was 'a fat man with a most repulsively soapy manner', Peters was 'unutterably idle' and 'oily', Grant was a 'Sierra Leone rascal'.[3]

[1] Journal, May 1889, p. 74.
[2] Journal, 31 Mar. 1889, p. 18, and 3 Apr. 1889, p. 22, also Brooke to his father, 22 Aug. 1887, *C.M.S.*, F5/2 and Leaflet no. 6, July 1890, *C.M.S.*, F5/5. H. H. Dobinson, a Niger missionary, who like Brooke, stopped for short periods in Freetown, analysed why many Europeans who had contact with Sierra Leone disliked the people. He admitted of having picked up a prejudice from these Europeans. 'The fact is, the Englishman has to behave himself in Sierra Leone. He cannot swagger, and curse, and kick the natives to his heart's content as is too often the case elsewhere. In Freetown the Natives can get quick and sure redress, for it is a well-known fact that the Courts are almost always inclined here to give every case in favour of the Native. So our blustering fellow-countrymen have to be careful.' His sister, *Letters of Henry Hughes Dobinson* (hereafter, Dobinson, *His Letters*), London, 1899, letter dated Mar. 1896, from Freetown, pp. 193–4.
[3] Brooke to his father, 24 Feb. 1889, *C.M.S.*, F5/5, Journal, pp. 46, 67, 80, 116, 118, 120.

Brooke was intolerant of any material progress of the church on the Niger. He complained that one house costing two hundred pounds and good enough for white ladies was inhabited by an African who would be happy in one costing five or ten pounds. He made fun of Bishop Crowther because he would not allow one of his clergymen to move into a house costing twenty-five pounds because it had no iron roof or plank floor. And again, this house was fit for Europeans.[1] The church at Bonny he described as a credit to its European builder and a disgrace to the Africans who secured the funds for its construction.[2]

The redeeming of slaves he described as disguised slavery, but soon was complaining that these slaves would not leave the Christians and that the schools were only serving the Christian slave-children. On the other hand, when Robinson redeemed a slave, Brooke wrote a long defence of domestic slavery.[3]

When Brooke was confronted with large and regular congregations he observed that 'their continual attendance is proof that sin is not exposed ...'. He constantly criticized clergymen for their choice of texts for sermon. When Archdeacon Crowther preached on the Christian's need of a sanctuary, a rather apt text for small bands of Christians in the Pagan Niger, Brooke poked fun at it.[4]

It did not take Brooke long to remedy the situation in his own station—Lokoja. He called a conference of the Native agents at Lokoja, heard their advice, and then completely overruled them. He accused all the Christians of fornication, closed the class books 'with a bang', and excommunicated the entire membership by a public pronouncement. He demanded a public confession of sin before members were reinstated. He drew a scarlet line in the church which separated the saints from the sinners and refused to allow the sinners to contribute to the Sunday offertories.[5]

---

[1] Journal, pp. 39 and 67. The first mission houses on the Niger for Europeans were built at Onitsha. The total cost of two such houses was £2,600. Dobinson in mentioning this commented, 'we are very costly and expensive usefulness; our accommodation, passage, and allowances eat up far more than two thirds of the mission expenses at present'. Dobinson, *His Letters*, p. 178.

[2] Journal, p. 77.

[3] Journal, pp. 59, 81; Leaflet no. 5, Aug. 1890, *C.M.S.*, F4/6.

[4] Journal, p. 82.

[5] 'Conference as to Steps to be taken on Evil Lives of Christians', Lokoja, 29 June 1890, J. A. Robinson's Journal, pp. 270–1, *C.M.S.*, F5/4; Leaflet no. 6, July 1890, *C.M.S.*, F5/4 and Brooke's Journal, p. 273, *C.M.S.*, F4/7.

In the face of these measures the Christian community, both White and Black, stood firm. The church emptied and never filled again. Brooke preached to his own mission staff, who publicly confessed, presumably to hold their jobs. Brooke expressed surprise that the Christians thought that an empty church would force him to leave.[1] Later he complained that he was unable to get acquainted with the Christian community, an unconscious admission that his purge of the Lokoja church had been undertaken before he became acquainted with the congregation.

Brooke introduced a congregational form of government whereby the membership (his mission staff) plus the European missionaries voted for the admission of new members. Disputes arose immediately among the missionaries as to whether applicants for membership were converted and some missionaries refused to sit on the council.[2]

The Parent Committee of the C.M.S., acting on Brooke's instructions, disconnected the African clergy on the Niger. Only the bishop had the power to withdraw licences, and this Crowther declined to do until he had been informed of the charge against his clergy. The Parent Committee refused to reveal these charges. Thus the dismissed clergy were free to seek positions outside the C.M.S. but within the Church of England; in the independent pastorates of Sierra Leone, Lagos, and the newly formed Delta.[3]

Brooke interpreted the reluctance of the Parent Committee to press charges as a lack of confidence in himself. He threatened the C.M.S. by stating he would go to Cambridge and expose their methods and the corruption of their missions, not only on the Niger but everywhere in Africa.

We are one and all convinced that the subscribers confidence in the Society's method of administering its missions in this continent is utterly

[1] Leaflet no. 7, Jan. 1891, *C.M.S.*, F4/8. This leaflet was written by J. A. Robinson, and is in the form of a defence of the severe discipline which had been introduced into the church at Lokoja. The Black members could only show their hostility by absenting themselves from services, but the White members possessed more formidable weapons. The Niger Company officials slighted the missionaries socially, and sent their complaints to Flint, until Brooke and Robinson were forced to back down. Brooke's Journal, pp. 274, 286.

[2] Journal, pp. 272, 277.

[3] A Pastorate resembling that in Lagos and Sierra Leone was being hurriedly organized to frustrate English control extending to the Delta area of the Niger Mission.

misplaced, and it is our duty either to inform them of the fact and of our reasons for our belief, or to see that method radically changed.[1]

Brooke arrived on the Niger in April 1889 as an independent missionary. After a six-month tour of inspection he returned to England. While on board ship he drew up a memorandum of the problems he faced in urging the C.M.S. to reform. He felt that he had best remain in England as a 'commentator'.[2] He decided that there was a 'party of reform' at Salisbury Square which would be too cautious to challenge the elder members who were sympathetic to Bishop Crowther. In fact, the Bishop he saw as the most formidable reactionary because of his wide influence in England. He knew that J. B. Whiting would fight against him. Originally he had classed Eugene Stock as a possible reform leader in the Committee, but Stock had questioned some of Brooke's more vociferous statements and accused him of insincerity.[3] He now dismissed Stock as a 'diplomatic temporizer' and far too cautious a reformer to suit his purpose. Brooke feared that Robinson, 'who has a lurking awe of dignitaries', would back down because the Bishop's case 'will seem so strong'. Brooke had no idea which side Cust would take, but felt it was important to influence him to the side of reform. Brooke finally decided he was the natural leader. 'I think I can infuse vigour, and unanimity into them. . . .' He then decided that his policy would be to recommend sending Crowther as an adviser to the Bishop of Yoruba and that Henry Johnson must go. This he would make an absolute point of principle, 'Johnson is fit for nothing but to be cast out, I cannot conscientiously withdraw this'. He was convinced that should the Bishop and Johnson be removed, 'all the other points would be carried with a rush'.[4]

The reform party at Salisbury Square was to be assisted by a public attack on the Niger Mission launched at Cambridge 'to promote speedy action'.[5] Should the reform party succeed, Brooke was willing to join the C.M.S. as honorary missionary to the Niger, he and his party supported by a Committee in Manchester.

[1] Brooke to Lang, 28 May 1891, *C.M.S.*, G3 A3/O, no. 169, Brooke was reported as having said that he would not hesitate to invite the Baptist to take over the Niger because he did not approve of C.M.S. methods. See D. C. Crowther to Lang, 12 Feb. 1892, *C.M.S.*, G3 A3/O, no. 93.
[2] Journal, pp. 148–9.
[3] Brooke to Lang, 16 July 1889, *C.M.S.*, G3 A3/O, 1889, no. 114.
[4] Journal, pp. 148–9.
[5] Brooke to Lang, Lokoja, 16 July 1889, *C.M.S.*, G3 A3/O, 1889, no. 114.

Brooke's movements in England are unknown, but two things become clear by his subsequent actions. He must have felt the reform party was in control of the Parent Committee, for he offered and was accepted as an honorary missionary before returning to the Niger. Secondly, the reform party at Salisbury Square was hampered in its object by the inconsistency of the various reports from the Niger Mission. When Brooke returned to Africa he set out to remedy this situation.

Brooke returned to Africa in February 1890. In July he called the Niger missionaries together at Lokoja for an informal meeting. Here the previous reports on the Niger Mission were read and the report then being framed was harmonized with the older reports to make it 'as powerful a weapon as possible'. Individual missionary reports were read out and amended to prevent conflicting evidence. Further-more, it was decided that each missionary should write to as many members of the Parent Committee as possible, insisting that all com-munications from the Niger Mission be read out in full Committee.[1]

From this Lokoja meeting the missionaries proceeded to the famous Onitsha Finance Committee Meeting with Bishop Crowther and his African clergy. Charges were brought against the Niger clergy. The pastors, plus Archdeacon Crowther, were suspended, and the Bishop resigned from the Committee.[2] The Onitsha meeting brought the whole issue of the Niger before the public in England and in Africa. Within a month Brooke was again on his way to England.

Brooke's purge of the Niger, which dismissed the African agency, was accompanied by an influx of Europeans. During the 1880s there had been an average of one European missionary a year in the mis-sion. In 1891 there appeared eight Europeans on the Niger. In 1894 only one was left, the remainder including Brooke having died or been invalided home. In 1895 nine new Europeans who fell back upon the traditional missionary method began work on the Niger.[3] By 1895 Venn's experiment of an African agency, and Brooke's plans for the evangelization of Africa, were abandoned and discredited.

It would seem unfortunate that the C.M.S. should have allowed its agents to destroy one another on the Niger when immense areas of Africa were unevangelized. Two missionary methods, both of them unique, both containing admirable qualities were discredited by being in such close proximity. Both methods might have pointed the way to

---

[1] Journal, pp. 285–6, 296.   [2] Ajayi, Christian Missions.
[3] C.M.S., *Annual Proceedings* for the various years 1891–5.

C

new avenues of approach in Africa. But because they came into conflict neither was given an opportunity to prove itself. Both were
abandoned and destroyed.

In 1894 Henry H. Dobinson, secretary of the Mission, was the
only European on the Niger. He was assisted by a skeleton staff of
Africans: one ordained minister, three catechists, and two teachers.
Many stations formerly occupied and possessing mission houses were
closed for lack of workers. Dobinson had been an enthusiastic supporter of Brooke's mission of young purifiers. Now alone on the
Niger, he gradually acquainted himself with the African staff and
admitted to a complete change of views.

Dobinson belatedly realized the value of the African agents. They
were the ones who did the work, even if supervised by Europeans.
Supervision at this point was of secondary importance, for many of
the stations were closed. He appealed for more Sierra Leonian
workers and insisted that Europeans were a nuisance and should not
be sent out until sufficient Africans were employed to teach them.[1]
The C.M.S. informed Dobinson that it did not intend to introduce
Sierra Leonians to the Niger again. The regulations were framed in
such a manner that they would find it undesirable to work there.[2]

Dobinson protested. He questioned how the Niger Mission was to
be carried forward in the next fifteen years before indigenous catechists could be trained.[3] Dobinson's letters over the period of the
seven years he was connected with the Niger were an excellent study
in the change which can come over an expatriate as he gradually
becomes familiar with the indigenous people and culture. In 1890,
after his visit to Brooke, Dobinson claimed he had learned a few
lessons at Lokoja. When he returned he excommunicated the entire
membership of the Onitsha church. His Native workers, including his
interpreter, abandoned him, leaving him helpless.

When Brooke had left and Dobinson was alone on the Niger he
underwent a complete change of attitude. Six years later he was
called the friend of the African and was warmly received by African
congregations.[4] Dobinson was one of those rare individuals who not
only could change his mind but could openly admit his former error.
This admission he made not only to the C.M.S. authorities at Salis-

---

[1] Dobinson to Baylis, 26 Feb. and 29 Mar. 1894, *C.M.S.*, G3 A3/O, nos. 47, 60.
[2] Dobinson to Baylis, 7 June 1894, *C.M.S.*, G3 A3/O, no. 76.
[3] Dobinson to Baylis, 7 June, 1894, *C.M.S.*, G3 A3/O, no. 76.
[4] Dobinson, *His Letters*, pp. 62, 66, 195.

BISHOP JAMES JOHNSON

bury Square, which was relatively easy, but also to the congregations of West Africa. It was undoubtedly this open repentance and apology which turned Dobinson from one of the hated Niger purgers to the African's friend in the space of six years. There is little question that the quick return to normal fellowship on the Niger, as compared with Lagos, was greatly assisted by the change of attitude of Dobinson. He admitted to the C.M.S. that in the early years of Brooke and Robinson, 'I was hurried along in unknown depths of a fierce-flowing river. . . .' He refused to preach in St. Stephens Cathedral, Bonny, because of the shame he felt for his past actions, and in Sierra Leone he apologized before the church for 'the sad events of 1890, when many men were misjudged, and had greatly suffered in consequence'. He admitted that upon arrival he despised Native custom but was now convinced 'that the people have wonderfully adapted themselves to their surroundings, and do everything for a reason of their own, and not just haphazard as it seems'.[1]

Dobinson's contrition was sincere. He became the African's great defender. The mission agents he described as isolated and lonely, who struggle against fearful odds, working for seven to nine years without leave. They bore the brunt of the battle, while the missionary after a fitful eighteen months returned to England. The white missionary was one of their greatest trials for he was 'hasty and impatient and over-bearing'. 'The climate has much to do with it, but our pride has more, I think.' The missionaries he called a 'costly usefulness' and 'unintentional oppressors'. Upon his death in May 1897 one of his African subordinates paid him one of the finest tributes any missionary could receive.[2]

The most obvious feature of the Niger purge was the dismissal of ordained and lay agents. However much dispute there might be about other aspects of this release of clergymen, there could be no questioning its thoroughness. Of the fifteen ordained Africans who worked on the Niger between 1880 and 1890, twelve were either disconnected or recommended for disconnexion.[3] In 1895 there remained one Sierra Leonian clergyman employed by the C.M.S. Five of the Niger clergy returned to the ministry in Sierra Leone, five

[1] Dobinson, *His Letters*, pp. 167, 195, 216, 217, 224.
[2] Ibid., pp. 171, 176–8, 224.
[3] Brooke gives the total who left the Niger as fifteen and the causes as follows: 3 adultery; 1 theft; 5 incorrigible lying; 2 incorrigible idleness; 2 resigned (shady); 2 resigned in ill health. Brooke to his father, 21 Oct. 1890, *C.M.S.*, F4/5, bdle 5.

joined the Niger Delta Pastorate, and four disappeared from the
records. Of the twelve clergy released, eight were recommended for
disconnexion during Brooke and Robinson's purge in 1890. Of the
eleven lay agents known to have been employed, only three survived
the purge. Thus ended the remarkable missionary effort of the church
of Sierra Leone to the Niger.

On the Niger in 1890 Brooke and Robinson sent their recommendations for disconnexion directly to the Parent Committee.
Neither Bishop Crowther nor members of the Finance Committee
knew the charges upon which the disconnexions were based. Robinson further complicated the situation by personally suspending Archdeacon Crowther, the bishop's son. The Society admitted that this
action was illegal, and an apology was sent to the Archdeacon.

Bishop Crowther stood on firm ground when he refused to cancel
the clergymen's licences until the Society laid the secret charges before him.[1] Although he did not officially know the substance of the
charges, there circulated rumours emanating from Europeans as to
their nature.[2] Shortly before his death he wrote a defence of his clergy
in which he pointed out the strenuous nature of the work on the
Niger. He mentioned that the agents had to learn the vernacular,
take up its translation, and deliver sermons in it twice on Sunday.
They were expected to teach the day school five hours, five days a
week, prepare classes of catechumens, candidates for baptism, and
communicants three afternoons a week. They must hear and settle
disputes between converts, visit in the towns daily, and spend a certain time itinerating. Over and above this, they were to manoeuvre
their own canoes when journeying on the river. 'Failing to do this
[they are] pronounced unfit to be retained in the employ of the
Society.'[3]

Lagos Anglicans were determined either to force the C.M.S. to
prove the charges or drop them. They neither objected to dismissals
nor desired unworthy men in the ministry. Dismissals were not unknown. They had taken place in Sierra Leone, Lagos, and Yoruba,
but never before in this fashion. The disconnected agents were not
told their faults nor given a chance to improve. They had not been

[1] D. C. Crowther and J. Boyle to Hill, 29 Nov. 1892, *C.M.S.*, G3 A3/O, 1893,
no. 11.
[2] H. Johnson to Hill, 26 Nov. 1892, *C.M.S.*, G3 A3/O, 1893, no. 8.
[3] Crowther on Agents to Be Dismissed, n.d., received 21 Jan. 1892, *C.M.S.*,
G3 A3/O, no. 16.

formally charged, given a trial nor an opportunity for defence. The accusers were their juniors in age, service, and experience, and strangers to the country and people. This treatment was compared with that meted out to Europeans who were similarly charged, and with New Testament usage.[1]

It was also pointed out to the C.M.S. the damaging effect of the unproved charges and attendant rumours to personal character. The secretiveness was tantamount to a proved charge of immorality,[2] and encouraged slander. Many of those charged were left without means of livelihood. They had families to support, but were too old to learn a trade. Teaching, a monopoly of the church, was not open to them.[3] In this atmosphere of slander and speculation rumours began to circulate privately and in the Press that European missionaries were involved in misuse of Niger finances.[4] Europeans in Lagos pointed out that the rumours and speculation were more disastrous to church harmony than any revelations of individual misdemeanour.[5] They believed that the African clergy were guilty, that the C.M.S. had only to prove it and the Africans would accept it.[6] Similarly, the missionaries believed the Europeans were not guilty and that the C.M.S. should clear their names.[7]

A Commission of Inquiry to sit in Africa was requested by Lagos and the Delta in order that the disconnected Niger agents might defend themselves.[8] The Delta churches promised to submit to its findings.[9] Henry Johnson petitioned the Committee for a Commission;

[1] James Johnson to Wigram, 25 Sept. 1891; Lagos Memorial, 7 Dec. 1892, *C.M.S.*, G3 A2/O, nos. 156, 13; D. C. Crowther and J. Boyle to Hill, 29 Nov. 1892; Hill's Report, 20 Dec. 1892, *C.M.S.*, G3 A3/O, nos. 11, 6.

[2] Hill's Report, 20 Dec. 1892.

[3] J. Johnson to Wigram, 25 Sept. 1891, *C.M.S.*, G3 A2/O, no. 156.

[4] *Lagos Weekly Record*, 15 Aug. 1891. See also W. H. Roberts to Lang, 27 May 1891, *C.M.S.*, G3 A3/O, no. 166.

[5] Tugwell to Fenn, 19 Aug. 1891, *C.M.S.*, G3 A2/O, no. 143.

[6] Tugwell to Wigram, 17 Aug. 1891, also Tugwell to Lang, 23 May 1892 (Private), *C.M.S.*, G3 A2/O, nos. 143, 146.

[7] W. H. Roberts to Lang, 27 May 1891, *C.M.S.*, G3 A3/O, no. 166. Vernal to Hamilton, 14 May 1891, and Tugwell to Fenn, 19 Aug. 1891, *C.M.S.*, G3 A2/O, nos. 101, 139.

[8] In a Memorial in 1890 Lagos asked that the disconnected agents who desired it be given an opportunity of defence. 'The opportunity was not granted and the several disconnections were left to become a settled matter. Our views have not undergone any change.' Lagos Memorial to Hill, 7 Dec. 1892, *C.M.S.*, G3 A2/O, 1893, no. 13.

[9] D. C. Crowther and J. Boyle to Hill, 29 Nov. 1892, *C.M.S.*, G3 A3/O, 1893, no. 11.

went to England to plead with the Society, and promised that he would not go to court for damages if the Commission found him innocent.[1]

Joseph Sydney Hill, a special emissary from the Archbishop of Canterbury, visited West Africa to advise on the situation, and found that the main issue, which had to be settled quickly in order to bring peace to the church, was the issue of the disconnexions. The clergy must be proved guilty or cleared. He strongly recommended that a Commission of Inquiry sit in the Niger Mission to try those men ready to defend themselves.

Hill placed the C.M.S. in an unenviable position. He had in his possession the charges against the agents, and the evidence collected by Brooke and Robinson. Although, like the other Europeans, he believed the accused were guilty, he claimed that even if all the evidence he possessed were substantiated by witnesses, no judge was likely to condemn the agents on the strength of it.[2] Furthermore, Brooke, Robinson, and Crowther, the main witnesses, had died in 1891–2. The Society was further embarrassed to find that the rumours of European misdemeanour were true.[3] Hill, bishop-designate of the Niger, was aware that his success as bishop would depend largely on his ability to settle this question. He and his assistant Oluwole used all their influence to secure employment elsewhere for the agents.[4]

It would seem peculiar that today, seventy years later, the charges against the clergy upon which so much hinged in this critical decision in mission history cannot be produced. Except for Brooke's brief list quoted in footnote 3 on p. 17, they are still not available. Until they are produced the interpretation given here is the only one possible for the unbiased. It would seem that the charges were used as a mask behind which the mission was determined to choke the trend to African leadership. Whether the charges were true or not was never the real question. Any move to assert African leadership usually brought forth the same charge of adultery against the leaders of the revolt. It was again employed to discredit the schismatics of 1901.

[1] H. Johnson to Hill, 26 Nov. 1892, *C.M.S.*, G3 A3/O, 1893, no. 8.
[2] Hill's Report, 20 Dec. 1892.
[3] Ajayi, Christian Missions.
[4] Hill to Lang, 25 June 1892, *C.M.S.*, G3 A3/O, no. 148; also Dr. Oluwole to C.M.S., 27 June 1893, and J. S. Hill to C.M.S., 24 Oct. 1893, *C.M.S.*, G3 M (1893–1904).

A kind of justice prevailed in the end. One agent died uncleared, but all the others were finally re-employed (the last in 1898) by the churches in Sierra Leone and the Delta. Had the C.M.S. wished to clear itself and restore maximum confidence in Lagos and the Delta, it should have forthrightly apologized to its African agents as Hill recommended in his report. But the fact that it did not do so, coupled with its attempt to keep Sierra Leonians from working in the Niger Mission, gave the impression that although it could not prove the charges, it believed them. The C.M.S. was merely postponing the difficulties.

The Africans were not entirely helpless in the face of these disconnexions. Little could be done on the middle Niger, for work still remained in the pioneer stage. The clergy depended upon the Society for financial support because congregations were small and membership practically non-existent. In the Delta the church was in a healthier state. The Delta church was the most outstanding example of Bishop Crowther's labours. Christian work was begun by the bishop at Bonny on 29 April 1865. In the short period 1865–90 Christianity had expanded more extensively than in the whole of Yoruba, excluding Lagos and Abeokuta. The four main clergymen in the Delta, D. C. Crowther, James Boyle, John D. Garrick, and Walter E. Carew, had been associated with the work almost from the beginning. These men were intimately connected with the Delta church; had witnessed its phenomenal growth, and were unlikely to stand aside and watch the English step in and 'tear it down'.

It was this desire to 'pull down' the mission which prompted Bishop Crowther to plan a Native pastorate in the Delta resembling that prevailing in Lagos, so that the people and clergy with a minimum of outside interference could control the affairs of the Delta. When questioned by the C.M.S. regarding this hasty action, the bishop replied that it had been forced on him by the English expression 'we cannot build unless we pull down'. Crowther felt this 'pulling down' was approved by the C.M.S. One of its periodicals had commented 'we cannot help supporting them' [the Europeans]. Crowther replied: 'This being the case I determined that this pulling down should not extend to the Delta Mission.'[1]

Bishop Crowther was deeply and painfully hurt by the European behaviour and appeared to lose confidence in the C.M.S., chiefly because of expressions in the *Intelligencer* which had pronounced the

[1] Bishop Crowther to Lang, 1 Dec. 1891, *C.M.S.*, G3 A3/O, 1893, no. 15.

Niger Mission a failure.[1] Acting upon pressure from the clergy of the
Delta, Lagos, and Sierra Leone, Bishop Crowther drew up the Niger
Delta Pastorate scheme on 8 May 1891 to be inaugurated in January
1892. He informed the C.M.S. that Lagos and Sierra Leone were
unhappy with the introduction of English supervision on the Niger,
and were offering financial assistance until the Delta was self-
supporting.

I feel convinced that the suggestion of the churches of the Native
Pastorate of Lagos and Sierra Leone is providential, that the Delta district should be made a Native Pastorate, to be worked entirely through
Native agency toward the expenses of which they resolve to contribute a
supplement.[2]

The church in Sierra Leone became active in the cause of the Delta
church through the efforts of Archdeacon D. C. Crowther, who spent
part of 1891 on furlough there. The men prominent in the movement
to support the Delta were a denominationally mixed group. They
wrote to Bishop Crowther in March 1891 offering financial assistance
for 'the spread of the gospel and elevation of the race'.[3] In October a
canvassing committee was formed which had collected £600 by the
beginning of December.[4]

European observers in Sierra Leone felt that little or no financial
assistance would come from Sierra Leone, as the church there was
not self-supporting. However, when the money was raised they said
it was because 'the matter had been treated as a race question' and
coercion used.

. . . pecuniary help has been given by not a few, not because they approve the plan, but because they are forced to do so, to avoid being boycotted or otherwise persecuted.[5]

As early as March the Sierra Leone committee appealed to Lagos
to assist the Delta. Lagos formed a Delta Finance Committee in
April under the chairmanship of James Johnson and supported by
prominent members of the Lagos Pastorate. The committee noted

[1] Allen to Wigram, 22 Dec. 1891, *C.M.S.*, G3 A3/O, no. 18.
[2] Crowther to Lang, 1 Dec. 1891, *C.M.S.*, G3 A3/O, no. 15, 1892.
[3] Sawyer, Betts, Thomas to Bishop Crowther, 17 Mar. 1891, *C.M.S.*, G3
A3/O, no. 137.
[4] Humphrey to Archdeacon Hamilton, 20 Oct. 1891; Allen to Wigram, 8 Dec.
1891, *C.M.S.*, G3 A3/O, nos. 251, 304.
[5] Bishop of Sierra Leone to Wigram, 7 Aug. 1891; Humphrey to Hamilton,
20 Oct. 1891; Allen to Wigram, 8 Dec. 1891, *C.M.S.*, G3 A3/O, nos. 202, 251,
304.

that the Delta required £700 from external sources, and passed a resolution that it would raise £350, and thereafter for five years a gradually decreasing amount. They justified this action on the assumption that European supervision was 'calculated to prevent the healthy growth of self-reliance and manly independence'.[1]

The £350 was not raised by public subscription as in Sierra Leone, but was guaranteed by a few prominent men, mainly members of Christ Church.[2] Although Johnson convened the first meeting of the committee, J. A. O. Payne was the inspiration behind the movement to challenge C.M.S. control in the Delta.[3] Popular opinion wanted a pastorate fashioned upon the Lagos pattern; a majority desired Europeans employed in educational work, and a minority pressed for the total exclusion of Europeans from the Delta. A few wished to set up an independent undenominational church.[4]

The deputation (William Allen and Archdeacon J. Hamilton) sent to investigate for the C.M.S. took the peculiar view that James Johnson had convinced some of the desirability of a Native Pastorate, and persuaded the others to keep quiet.[5] They repeatedly referred to Isaac Oluwole,[6] principal of the Lagos Grammar School, as the man representing the soundest views in Lagos. He was rewarded by the C.M.S. and earned an unpopularity in Lagos which was one of the main causes of schism in 1901.

The man with the influence to impose a settlement on the Delta, acceptable to Lagos, was James Johnson. The C.M.S. were not unaware of his feelings. He wrote to the Society in September 1891 outlining not only why he supported a pastorate for the Delta but also setting forth his theory of missions. He favoured the scheme because he felt the Delta had reached the point where the people were able to contribute to the Native agency. He pointed out that he had presented a memorandum to the Society in which he expressed the belief

---

[1] James Johnson to Bishop Crowther, 21 Apr. 1891, *C.M.S.*, G3 A3/O, no. 137.

[2] Tugwell to Fenn, 19 Aug. 1891, *C.M.S.*, G3 A2/O, no. 139. Christ Church, where the European community and the most-Europeanized Africans of Lagos worshipped, was directly under the C.M.S. and a European clergyman, and did not come under the pastorate like the other churches of Lagos.

[3] Tugwell to Lang, 13 Nov. 1891, *C.M.S.*, G3 A2/O, no. 179.

[4] Tugwell to Fenn, 19 Aug. 1891, *C.M.S.*, G3 A2/O, no. 139.

[5] Report of the Deputation to the Niger (hereafter, Deputation Report), Mar. 1892, *C.M.S.*, G3 A3/O, no. 87.

[6] The deputation interviewed Bishop Crowther and J. Johnson once, and Isaac Oluwole three times. See Hamilton, Narrative of Visit to West Africa, n.d., *C.M.S.*, G3 A3/O, 1892, no. 76.

that the Society had been ill-advised in not transferring financial responsibility more rapidly. He recommended that self-support be introduced much earlier while the people still remembered the zeal and self-reliance 'they had maintained and exhibited in and toward heathenism'.[1] Lagos and Sierra Leone had been dependent so long upon foreign support that they had come to that stage where it was difficult to maintain racial harmony. Prejudice had arisen on both sides. There was a want of confidence between the races and a temptation to distrust each other's motives.

Johnson assured the C.M.S. that no one in Lagos contemplated severance from the Society, nor did they desire action in which the Society did not take part. He was sure some assistance would still be welcomed from Europeans in the Delta. The Society would lose that control 'which comes of financial dependence', but would have the moral influence such as existed between a child and its parent. He asked the Society if they would have objected had the usual grant-in-aid system been used. He said that he saw little difference and much to commend '. . . the supply of grants-in-aid by members of sister Native churches and others who sympathize with the cause instead of the Society. . . .'[2]

In August 1891 Herbert Tugwell, the English pastor in charge of Christ Church, Lagos, called a meeting of the congregation. After hearing the views expressed, he wrote to the C.M.S. asking them to take the African public into its confidence. He was sure the public would be loyal if all the issues were placed before it.

My experience with the African character is that when treated with confidence and when persuaded of the integrity of his advisers' motives he is loyal and true.[3]

Tugwell recommended that a deputation be sent from the C.M.S. to the Niger and suggested that two Lagos residents join it. In November the Society acted on his advice. The C.M.S. dispatched a telegram to Bishop Crowther requesting that he delay the inauguration of the Delta Pastorate for three months to await a deputation immediately leaving England.[4] The Parent Committee sent a letter to the West African churches calculated to reach the coast at the same time as the deputation. It was not the type of letter to soothe irri-

[1] J. Johnson to Wigram, 25 Sept. 1891, *C.M.S.*, G3 A3/O, no. 156.
[2] Loc. cit.
[3] Tugwell to Fenn, 19 Aug. 1891, *C.M.S.*, G3 A2/O, no. 139.
[4] D. C. Crowther to Lang, 12 Feb. 1892, *C.M.S.*, G3 A3/O, no. 93.

tated African feelings. It spoke of the 'ripened Christianity' which twelve centuries had given Englishmen, and 'which can scarcely be looked for except in European teachers'.[1]

The Hamilton–Allen Deputation which arrived in Freetown 7 December 1891 was not intended to inquire into the feasibility of the Niger Delta Pastorate, but rather to prevent its inauguration. The deputation knew that the Parent Committee was convinced of the inability of the African to run a church organization.

As things stand you are chiefly surrounded just now by those who take a strongly anti-African view of the situation.[2]

Furthermore, their instructions forbade the recommendation of anything that tended 'to recognize and perpetuate a severance between the African and European spheres of work which would probably be premature and undesirable'.[3] European missionaries on the coast with whom they resided during their visit were not likely to challenge the views which they already held.

Brooke took for granted that the Native Delta Pastorate would come into existence and advised that it be prevented from raising subscriptions in England.[4] Battersby, another Niger missionary, said Europeans in Lagos and Sierra Leone were united in opposing the Native Delta Pastorate. He advised the C.M.S. not to give in to Archdeacon Crowther, for money would not be forthcoming from Lagos or Sierra Leone, and, furthermore, the Delta people did not desire to be under Crowther.[5] The Bishop of Sierra Leone confirmed the general opinion that Lagos and Sierra Leone subscriptions would lessen as the excitement abated, and submitted a plan to stop the scheme. The Diocese of Sierra Leone was chartered to extend over all Her Majesty's possessions on the West Coast of Africa, while Crowther's diocese included the area outside British control. The Delta had recently been declared a British protectorate. The Bishop of Sierra Leone thought the Delta was now under his jurisdiction. He wrote:

. . . may I not claim this Delta as my diocese, and so prevent the establishment of a native church there except under my personal or delegated superintendence.[6]

[1] 'Letter to the West African Churches', *Intelligencer*, 14 Nov. 1892, p. 61.
[2] Allen to Wigram, 1 Jan. 1892, *C.M.S.*, G3 A3/O, no. 47.
[3] Deputation Report, Mar. 1892.
[4] Brooke to Wigram, 1 Aug. 1891, *C.M.S.*, G3 A3/O, no. 214.
[5] C. F. Hartford-Battersby to Wigram, 14 Apr. 1892, *C.M.S.*, G3 A3/O, no. 125.
[6] Bishop of Sierra Leone to Wigram, 7 Aug. 1891, *C.M.S.*, G3 A3/O, no. 202.

Among the missionaries, only Herbert Tugwell felt that opposition was futile; if the Delta was prepared to support its own pastors and accept the guidance of the C.M.S. he saw no reason to oppose it.[1] Claude Macdonald, Consul-General of the Oil Rivers Protectorate, came unexpectedly to the defence of the Africans. Strictly from a political point of view, Macdonald favoured African clergy because of their assistance to the Government in tribal matters.[2] Macdonald claimed no intention of interfering in the dispute between the Delta church and the C.M.S.,[3] yet he chose this delicate moment to accept the position of patron of the Native Delta Pastorate, and to offer Archdeacon Crowther £200 per year for industrial training in the Delta schools.[4]

Hamilton and Allen could hardly be expected to consider the African point of view with impartiality, considering their instructions and the influence of European opinion on the coast. They were confident of preventing the inauguration of the Native Delta Pastorate on the strength of three powerful arguments: the C.M.S. controlled the salaries of the clergy; they owned the land and buildings in the Delta, and they could influence the Archbishop to reject an African successor to Bishop Crowther.

The question of finance was vital. If the Delta could not support its clergy the pastorate was impossible.[5] When the deputation discovered that the needed money had been raised it discounted this in two ways. First, it was unlikely that the external support would be maintained over the five years, the time estimated to achieve self-support in the Delta. Second, the part of the funds subscribed by dissenters was unacceptable.[6]

The question of property ownership was almost as vital as finances.[7] Hamilton and Allen found that this land had been given

[1] Tugwell to Fenn, 19 Aug. 1891, *C.M.S.*, G3 A2/O, no. 139.

[2] Bishop of Sierra Leone to Wigram, 7 Aug. 1891, *C.M.S.*, G3 A3/O, no. 202.

[3] Macdonald to D. C. Crowther, 6 July 1892, *Lambeth*, Benson, I, 11g, 1892 For.

[4] Macdonald to Archdeacon Crowther, 15 July 1892, *Lambeth*, Benson, I, 11g, 1892 For. J. B. Whiting, after interviewing Macdonald, asked the Archbishop to talk to him before deciding upon a European successor to Crowther.

[5] 'Even societies which have been most emphatic in the assertion of the theory of independence of Native churches have found in the power of the purse a sure device by which to guard infant churches from lapses or novel experiment.' Dr. A. J. Brown, *I.R.M.*, Oct. 1921, p. 489, in Allen, *Spontaneous Expansion*, p. 58.

[6] Allen to Wigram, 8 Dec. 1891, *C.M.S.*, G3 A3/O, no. 304.

[7] 'I consider your tenure of church property a most valuable safeguard', Bishop of Sierra Leone to Wigram, 7 Aug. 1891, *C.M.S.*, G3 A2/O, no. 202.

before British occupation, and was therefore held under African law. It was not Delta custom to part with land absolutely. The C.M.S. could dismantle the buildings. This was permitted by customary law. But this was morally questionable, since the Society had not contributed to the erection of the Delta churches.

On the issue which had fostered the organization of the Native Delta Pastorate—the disconnexions—the deputation recommended that the C.M.S. have nothing to do with the scheme unless Archdeacon Crowther promised not to employ disconnected agents.[1] The Archdeacon replied that although these agents were disconnected by the C.M.S., they had not lost their licences to administer the sacraments in the Anglican Church. However, Crowther promised to consult with the committee in Lagos and to submit to the findings of a Commission of Inquiry.[2]

In the deputation report submitted to the C.M.S. in March 1892 it was obvious that Hamilton and Allen were unable to give logical arguments why the Native Delta Pastorate should not be encouraged. In one part they recommend that the C.M.S. should support the pastorate only if Crowther promised not to employ disconnected agents. In another they stated that the Society should induce the Native Pastorate Committee to abandon the scheme and to convince anyone appointed Bishop of the Niger to delay his assent to its formation.

Unfortunately Bishop Crowther died shortly after the deputation's arrival in Lagos, and the issue of a successor became acute. Hamilton and Allen recommended that a European should succeed him, aided by a Native assistant bishop.[3]

The Hamilton–Allen report was considered by the Committee of Correspondence of the C.M.S. on 5 April 1892. In a lengthy meeting the Committee split into two opposing factions. The majority, led by F. E. Wigram and R. Lang, believed that the experiment on the Niger begun in 1864 must be abandoned. Crowther's episcopate had proved a failure. They feared that the tendency to rupture and schism would be encouraged and spread to Lagos. They resented this shrinking of C.M.S. authority. They opposed an African bishop.[4]

The minority, led by R. N. Cust and J. B. Whiting, were as firmly

[1] Deputation Report, Mar. 1892, and D. C. Crowther to Lang, 12 Feb. 1892, *C.M.S.*, G3 A3/O, no. 93.

[2] D. C. Crowther and J. Boyle to Hill, 29 Nov. 1892, *C.M.S.*, G3 A3/O, no. 11.

[3] Deputation Report, Mar. 1892.

[4] The Archbishop re the Niger, 16 July 1892, *Lambeth*, Benson, I, 11g, 1892.

convinced that Crowther's episcopate had been a success. They desired to advance from the status conferred on Crowther, believing that his successor should be partly or wholly supported from African sources.[1] This would be a step towards making the new bishop a diocesan rather than a missionary bishop and would free him even more from the control of the Society. Cust argued against the whole policy of the C.M.S. He asked how long the Society intended to hold the African church in pupilage. He pleaded for a return to apostolic practice, when each tribe or nation as it became Christian acquired its own indigenous bishops, priests, and deacons. Cust warned that unless a decided policy of extending the historic three orders of the ministry was taken now, 'we shall have a frightful complication in the next century'.[2]

The discussion in the Committee of Correspondence centred around William Allen's letter dated 2 January 1892, from Lagos, in which he recommended the division of the Niger diocese into two; one headed by a European, and one by an African bishop: for

. . . it would be even more than perilous to the interests of church missions in West Africa, if the desire of the Natives for another African bishop were altogether ignored by the C.M.S. . . .[3]

But a letter of 29 January, dated Brass, signed by both Allen and Hamilton recommended that all authority should be vested in a European bishop while the inevitable retrogression should be masked by the appointment of an African assistant bishop.[4] In their formal report dated March 1892 Allen was apparently overwhelmed by Hamilton. They recommended one European bishop.

Wigram and Lang carried the committee with them in passing Resolution XX, which instructed the secretaries 'to seek a suitable European to be nominated as a successor to Bishop Crowther', adding a rider intended to pacify the minority.

. . . that in passing the above resolution the committee affirm their desire that an Assistant African Bishop or Bishops with ultimate prospect of an independent African Bishop should be appointed in West Africa as soon as in the interests of the church there such an appointment appears desirable.[5]

[1] Whiting to the Archbishop, 8 Feb. 1892, *Lambeth*, Benson, I, 11g, 1892, For.
[2] Cust to the Archbishop, 27 Sept. 1892, *Lambeth*, Benson, I, 11g, 1892, For.
[3] Allen to Wigram, 2 Jan. 1892, *C.M.S.*, G3 A3/O, no. 48.
[4] Hamilton and Allen to African secretary, 29 Jan. 1892, *C.M.S.*, G3 A3/O, no. 75.
[5] Correspondence Committee Minutes, 5 Apr. 1892, p. 288.

After the minority unsuccessfully attempted to defeat Resolution XX at a later meeting of the Parent Committee Cust and Whiting resigned. Cust was convinced that the racial arrogance of the English was responsible for the decisions taken on the Niger Mission. This was why missions among five generations of Christians had not yet evolved into churches; why an English curate of little ability was preferred for bishop to godly and outstanding Negroes; why the post of assistant bishop was created for the non-English. 'The difference of treatment is only skin deep, and the reason only extends to the skin.'[1]

The English on the Niger he called 'sensational young missionaries'. He criticized their reports on the moral state of Africa. They knew only one town in Africa, understood no vernacular, and yet presumed to speak about Africa. He questioned whether they had taken a good look at the vices and immoralities of London, where only a minority had been affected by Christianity, 'while the majority are as much heathen in their religious conceptions, and as free from moral restrictions, as our forefathers were in pre-Roman Britain'.[2] Cust blamed the paid secretaries, Wigram and Lang, for taking upon themselves the responsibility for decisions and their execution,

. . . until a promising mission like that in the Niger Delta, is destroyed by the blind and wayward folly of an uninstructed Committee, driven by impulsive secretaries, determined to have their own way.[3]

Cust was the voice of Johnson, Crowther, and Payne in England. He cut through the mass of propaganda with which Wigram's party was able to fill the C.M.S. organs of information. Eugene Stock, another paid secretary and great admirer of Wigram, attempted to make Cust appear an inconsistent aberration in the progressive and enlightened C.M.S. But Cust was eagerly read and applauded by Africans in Lagos and by the Niger missionary, Henry Dobinson.[4]

Upon the resignation of Cust and Whiting, the secretaries complied with Resolution XX and nominated J. S. Hill to the Archbishop

[1] R. N. Cust, *Evangelization of the Non-Christian World*, London, 1894, pp. 188–9, 222.

[2] Ibid., p. 233. Cust's resignation was a protest against the whole trend of missionary policy in the 1890s, but specifically he disapproved of the C.M.S. acting as a tool of imperial penetration in Uganda and the appointment of a European successor to Crowther on the Niger.

[3] Ibid., p. 140.

[4] Stock, *History*, iii, pp. 668–9; Dobinson, *His Letters*, p. 185.

as a successor to Crowther. Because of the publicity given to the unrest in Lagos and the Delta, and because of the split in the C.M.S. Committee, it was doubtful whether the Archbishop would accept Hill's nomination without further inquiry into the causes of the discontent. The Archbishop became a mediator between the two parties within the C.M.S. and between the Society and African Christians.

Joseph Sydney Hill was attached to the majority party. He felt a debt to the C.M.S. for his education and training, and had the closest ties of friendship with Wigram and Lang.[1] Like them, he believed there was an immense danger of encouraging the spirit of dislike towards European control by giving a premium to revolt. Hill was convinced that Whiting and Cust were encouraging the Africans to agitate.[2]

Archbishop Benson accepted Hill as the successor to Crowther. Aware of Hill's relationship to Wigram and Lang, the Archbishop warned him that his duty lay in working out a just and fair solution and not in attempting to please the Society.[3]

The Archbishop laid down the lines of a solution. He suggested that the diocese be divided; that two English bishops be invested with authority and each assisted by an African assistant bishop. He did not consider that the time was ripe for a diocesan African bishop. As to the persons to be consecrated for the position of assistant African bishops, he was willing to have anyone nominated, preferably James Johnson and Archdeacon Crowther. The Archbishop was not prepared to consecrate Hill at the present time. He desired that Hill should go to West Africa as his special emissary with the status of bishop-designate, to report upon the unrest in the Lagos and Delta churches.[4]

The Archbishop's proposals were laid before the C.M.S. on

[1] Hill's Report, 20 Dec. 1892.

[2] Hill to Battersby, 30 Sept. 1892, also Hill to Wigram, 2 Oct. 1893, *C.M.S.*, G3 A3/O, nos. 224, 72.

[3] Edward White Benson, Archbishop 1883–96. Archbishop Benson in the early years of his primacy laid great stress upon the creation of national churches, 'not merely branches of the Church of England working in foreign lands. . . .' He warned against repeating 'the error of the great Boniface, in making not a Teutonic but an Italian church in Germany' (1885). In 1886 he encouraged the Bishop of Japan to establish a Japanese, not an English church. Towards the end of his primacy he did not adopt this liberalism in dealing with the Canadian and Australian churches. His biographer comments upon this contradiction. See A. C. Benson, *The Life of Edward White Benson*, vol. ii, London, 1899, pp. 456, 466, 467, and 484.

[4] Archbishop re the Niger, 16 July 1892.

19 July. The Committee appreciated that Benson had accepted their nominee for bishop, but disliked the idea of assistant bishops because of the 'undesirability of making the experiment of placing an African bishop over European clergymen'.[1] If the Archbishop forced assistant bishops upon them Wigram and Lang were determined it should not be James Johnson or Archdeacon Crowther. They tried to extract a promise from Benson that he would not accept the nomination of these two men. The Archbishop refused. It was quite vital to the success of his plans that Johnson and Crowther be won over to the compromise.[2]

Wigram and Lang were determined. They wanted the consecration of an English bishop, but opposed assistant bishops in general, and Johnson and Crowther in particular. If they could persuade the Archbishop to consecrate Hill immediately they could then put difficulties in the way of future appointments of assistant bishops. Benson, aware of these tactics, was adamant. He would either authorize the consecration of three bishops (Hill and his two African assistants) or none at all. After another interview with Wigram and Lang Benson felt he had 'brought them around to see my mind'.[3] But the Archbishop had forced and not convinced them. Wigram warned Hill not to nominate Johnson or Crowther. Should he do so, Wigram threatened to use his influence in the C.M.S. to make Hill's episcopate in West Africa an unhappy one.[4]

In Lagos the death of Bishop Crowther overshadowed the issue of

[1] Wigram to Archbishop, 13 July 1892, *Lambeth*, Benson, I, 11g, 1892, For.

[2] Correspondence Committee Minutes, 5 Apr. 1892, p. 288, Archbishop re the Niger, 16 July 1892: On 13 July at 9.45 a.m. Archbishop Benson held a 'very long interview' with Wigram and Lang. At 4.10 p.m. he held an interview with Hill, in which he emphasized that assistant bishoprics should be pressed on Johnson and Crowther. 'Nothing could have such effect in winning the coloured dissenters.' Official Diary of Archbishop Benson, *Trinity College Library*, Cambridge, p. 195. Following the interview Wigram wrote the Archbishop (see *Lambeth*, Benson, I, 11g, 1892, For.) strenuously objecting to Johnson and Crowther being offered episcopal positions.

[3] Archbishop re the Niger, 16 July 1892: *Benson's Official Diary*, 22 July 1892, p. 204.

[4] Wigram to the Archbishop, 13 July 1892, *Lambeth*, Benson, I, 11g, 1892, For. The persistent stubbornness of Wigram may have been one of the causes of the Archbishop's public criticism of the mission societies in 1894. He accused them of working independently of the church (especially the C.M.S.) and being unable to handle outstanding men in the overseas churches. Benson possibly had Crowther and Johnson in mind when he said: 'There are no men I more highly esteem than Mr. Tucker (S.P.G.) and Mr. Wigram, but I should like to see what they would do with a Saint Martin!' Stock, *History*, iii, p. 652.

D

the Niger Delta Pastorate and the disconnexion of agents. An African successor to Crowther became the crucial issue. James Johnson saw the importance of this moment to Africa, the Native churches, and African Christianity. He called it a crisis 'that very much for or against ourselves depends on the decision and action we take. . . .'[1]

The subordination of the African agency and later the disconnexion of agents on the Niger was an indication that the C.M.S. had come to the conclusion that Crowther's episcopate was a failure. Equally disturbing was the publicity given to this failure in Anglican and C.M.S. periodicals.[2] Articles in these publications came to the attention of the African public through the West Coast Press. The people knew that the Niger Mission had been found a failure and that this pronouncement had been accepted by a number of leading members of the Parent Committee.[3]

Africans could not afford to allow Crowther's episcopate to be labelled a failure. It had been 'an experiment to prove the capacity of Negroes for evangelizing . . . the African continent . . . without the stimulus of the presence and supervision of Europeans'. Moreover, they were convinced that Crowther's episcopate had been a success, a success which supplied 'a warrant for the continuation of the Native episcopate'.[4] They feared what they called 'the drift of the Society's mind', which had increasingly been evident.[5]

But attempts have been made the last few years on account of moral weakness discovered in some of the infant churches which have been gathered in, and serious faults in some of the agents and the like, to pronounce the experiment a failure and the Negro incapable for a responsible trust and for an independent life; and in spite of the century of training and teaching he has had, unfit still to be set free from his pupilage and the leading strings of European supervision. . . . In our humble opinion the ar-

---

[1] J. Johnson to Cust, 19 July 1892, *Lambeth*, Benson, I, 11g, 1892, For.

[2] *The Rock*, 28 Jan. 1891; *The Record*, 28 Jan. 1891; The *Intelligencer*, Oct. 1890, said it had in its possession some very encouraging reports from the Niger written by the Secretary of the Mission, F. N. Eden. These reports were never published.

[3] The Press also gave publicity to speeches of the members of the Parent Committee and one by the Archbishop 'which is interpreted to mean, that you have already made up your mind upon the subject, and have decided against the Natives, and accepted the opinion of the European missionaries'. Hill's Report. For a warning re the effects of the Press, see Wood to Fenn, 3 Aug. 1891, *C.M.S.*, G3 A2/O, no. 140.

[4] Lagos Memorial to Hill, 7 Dec. 1892.

[5] J. Johnson to Cust, 19 July 1892, *Lambeth*, Benson, I, 11g, 1892, For.

rangement proposed, backed as it seems with the weight of the Archbishop's position, seems to lend sanction to this pronouncement.[1]

The unrest was more than religious. It was also 'patriotic and political'. Africans had come under the spirit of the age. Just as the cry rang out 'Australia for Australians', so in Lagos it was 'Africa for the Africans'. Because racial feeling was rising among English and African, 'the seed of discord [had] fallen into a prepared and congenial ground'.[2] Crowther had become a symbol to Africans of all tribes and creeds of the improving position of the Negro in the world.[3] James Johnson suggested that this racial feeling could be minimized by dividing the diocese; one diocese under a European and worked largely through European agency and the other under an African worked by Africans. This, he claimed, was the only way friction between European missionaries and African church workers could be avoided. This friction had in the past 'exercised a depressing influence upon the work'. He feared the proposal of African Assistant Bishops would not remove but 'rather perpetuate and accentuate the evil'.[4]

Johnson approached the problem from the general theory of missions. He felt, like Cust, that African Christianity had been 'held too long in a state of dependence'. As a result, Christianity after one hundred years was still exotic. In this there was no guarantee of permanence. He pointed to North Africa and Benin as examples of exotic Christianity which passed away.[5] The C.M.S. decision in favour of an English episcopate,

. . . has been its own practical pronouncement of the failure of its own efforts during ninety years to christianize the people and raise up among them independent and self-governing Christian churches.[6]

Hill arrived in Lagos on 5 October 1892 as bishop-designate of the Niger and personal emissary from the Archbishop. He brought with him from the Archbishop a message of peace and a command to report upon the Delta Pastorate, divide the diocese, and choose assistant bishops. Hill's most difficult task was to break the barrier of his own position, a European in succession to Bishop Crowther. He

[1] Lagos Memorial to Hill, 7 Dec. 1892.
[2] Hill's Report, 20 Dec. 1892.
[3] J. Johnson to Cust, 19 July 1892, *Lambeth*, Benson, I, 11g, 1892, For.
[4] Lagos Memorial to Hill, 7 Dec. 1892.
[5] Loc. cit.
[6] J. Johnson to Cust, 19 July 1892, *Lambeth*, Benson, I, 11g, 1892, For.

did this through a genuinely Christian display of deep humility. He
was unwilling to attempt a defence of European actions on the Niger,
even if he was not ready to publicly condemn them. His offer dis-
armed Lagos.

. . . the last thing I would do, is to remain in office if my appointment is
unacceptable to you.[1]

The clergy pointed out that they had asked the C.M.S. to appoint
an African to succeed Crowther, but the Society had appointed a
European. Although their feelings had not changed, because Hill was
the appointed European, the subject was now a delicate one and the
argument closed.[2] The situation and its outcome operated exactly as
the Archbishop expected: if Hill went out as Bishop-designate Lagos
'will be too nervous to assent to what they wish at the time viz. a
coloured bishop'.[3]

The Lagos clergy and laity were still desirous that the Delta be
made a separate diocese and an African appointed there, who would
be a successor to Crowther. Hill attempted to persuade them that to
refuse this request was not a reflection upon the episcopate of
Crowther. It was neither because the C.M.S. wished to recede from
its former position of giving them a Native episcopate nor was it
because there were no suitable Native clergymen available for this
position.[4] It was rather because great extension of the Native church
organization was necessary in the Delta before the Archbishop would
be willing to consecrate an African diocesan bishop. He further encouraged them not to look to the Niger, but rather to Lagos and
Sierra Leone, for an extension of the indigenous episcopate.

It is in those places where the Native church is more exclusively at work,
and where it is most efficiently organized and where its development is
most advanced that Native episcopal supervision would most naturally be
sought.[5]

Hill argued that it was of great importance when the present action
was spoken of as a retrograde step to realize that Crowther had not
been an independent bishop, but a missionary bishop accountable to
the C.M.S. in all his actions. So also the assistant bishops would be

---

[1] Hill, 'Memorandum Prepared before My Interview with the Clergy and
Representative Laymen', Nov. 1892, *C.M.S.*, G3 A2/O, no. 6.
[2] Lagos Memorial to Hill, 7 Dec. 1892.
[3] Archbishop re the Niger, 16 July 1892.
[4] Hill to Wigram, 2 Oct. 1893, *C.M.S.*, G3 A3/O, no. 72.
[5] Hill, Memorandum, Nov. 1892 *C.M.S.*, G3 A2/O, 1893, no. 6.

responsible to a European bishop.[1] The clergy reminded Hill that
there had been no church organization when Crowther had been
consecrated, and yet this was now a prime consideration before his
successor could be appointed. It was only too obvious that the
C.M.S. had lost confidence in African bishops, for while a European
could be appointed without this organization and only on the
strength of an oath of allegiance to the Archbishop, an African
could not.

The clergy and representative laymen of Lagos presented a memorial to Hill in which they set forth their ideas for the future governing of the diocese. It ended:

... should he (the Archbishop) still decide to consecrate none other than
a Native Assistant or Native Assistant Bishops, we shall feel that we have
discharged our responsibility, and would respectfully submit to his better
judgement and decision.[2]

By this 'submission' Lagos gave away its only bargaining point.
The C.M.S., European missionaries, and Hill had moved ever so
cautiously because of the great fear that unless the African point of
view was acted upon there would be a schism embracing the Delta,
Lagos, and Freetown.[3] Hill had won, and was quick to point it out
to the Archbishop.[4] There were possibly three reasons for this 'submission'. It may have been the reaction to Hill's humility and the
belief that by going the extra mile they should persuade the C.M.S.
to do the same. Perhaps they felt that the battle was already lost, and
that it was preferable to submit to their new leader gracefully.
Plausibly it was an attempt to secure unanimity, since the Memorial
was signed by the conservatives as well as the radicals.

The results were far reaching. By submitting to an arrangement
which they were unable to defend before the general laity, the clergy
abdicated their position of leadership. In mission organizations the
hierarchical order was simple and direct from the missionaries at the
top to the parishioners at the bottom. The clergy occupied the potential friction point between the two. They were the employees of the
missions carrying out their directives, as well as the mouthpiece of
the laity. They were both servants and leaders. Normally this gave

[1] Hill, Memorandum, Nov. 1892.
[2] Lagos Memorial to Hill, 7 Dec. 1892.
[3] Wood to Fenn, 3 Aug. 1891, *C.M.S.*, G3 A2/O, no. 140, also Cust to the
Archbishop, 27 Sept. 1892, *Lambeth*, Benson, I, 11g, 1892, For.
[4] Hill's Report, 20 Dec. 1892.

the clergy a degree of influence. The position had now become untenable. The missionaries refused to modify their policy and the parishioners refused to accept it. A compromise was impossible, and the choice was either submission or rebellion.

They chose submission. Partly due to habit and partly because they were conscious of where ultimate authority lay. But it was more than this. The clergy suffered from the chronic disability of the educated African. They admitted that they lost respect for African leadership in the process of an education which was as much the acquiring of English attitudes as it was a familiarization with academic skills. The clergy emerged from their training as sceptical of African leadership as their English counterparts. As a consequence, the clergy in 1888 voted against an African bishop for the Yoruba country. As a result, the African professional class preferred an English clergyman to minister to them at Christ Church. The clergy, along with the professional class of which they formed a part, were as reluctant to work under a black bishop as were the English. Thus Lagos and Freetown agitated for an African bishop for the Delta, but not for themselves. The clergy were acting as the mouthpiece of the laity without a personal conviction that African leadership was really desirable.

Under these conditions Crowther's success on the Niger was more than statistical. In his struggle with the English Crowther was not betrayed by his clergy as James Johnson had been in Abeokuta between 1878 and 1880.[1] Crowther's clergy refused to be tools in missionary hands.

The submission of the clergy was mainly a tragedy for James Johnson, who had chosen to emphasize his position as leader rather than servant. It left him little room to manoeuvre, but he had no intention of abandoning his policy of working towards an African church. In future his advocacy would be considered treasonous to the new arrangement, which was not an 'experiment' and, as such, subject to review, as was Crowther's episcopate. The settlement was to be permanently endowed with a sanctity which made criticism intolerable. The missionaries, realizing how closely they had come to losing control, would in future deal severely with clergy who showed signs of deserting them and espousing the popular cause of African leadership.

After two months in Lagos Hill sent his report[2] to the Archbishop

[1] J. K. Coker, History of the African Church, 1941, *Coker Papers*.
[2] Hill's Report, 20 Dec. 1892.

on 20 December 1892. He recommended the division of the diocese
into three:[1] the Niger Delta under an African bishop; the Niger
under an English bishop, and the Yoruba diocese, to which Lagos
would be transferred, should be under an English bishop, assisted by
two African assistant bishops, one over Ondo and one over Lagos
and Ijebu. For an interim period of two or three years the three
dioceses would remain under one English bishop until the reorgan-
ization could be carried out.

The Delta diocese should be delayed until it was properly organized; present difficulties settled; a suitable man, Johnson or Crowther,
chosen, and an endowment provided. The appointment of a Delta
bishop should not be rushed 'as if these men were agitating for their
own advancement'. Some people might 'look upon it as a premium
given to quiet them'. He suggested, however, that the Archbishop
give a definite promise to consecrate a bishop for the Delta when the
church there was 'doing steady and satisfactory work'.

Hill's choice of assistant bishops was important for the immediate
future if he was to gain the support of the Africans for the major
recommendations of his report. Johnson and Crowther, the obvious
choices, although acceptable to the Archbishop, were not to the
Society. English opinion on the coast opposed both men. It was admitted that Johnson had qualifications which made him suitable for
episcopal office, but 'unfortunately he holds views and adopts
methods in carrying them out which . . . would . . . be the cause of
. . . very serious embarrassment'.[2] Hill did not cease to admire
Johnson, but took on some English attitudes towards him.

> I admire him, I sympathize with him, but he is not liked. . . . He is de-
> cidedly the ablest man we have, and the most crotchety, opinionated, one-
> sided, intolerant, zealous, earnest and powerful.[3]

Missionaries were unanimous that Archdeacon Crowther would
not do. Opposition must not be rewarded. Furthermore, he soured as
he grew older.[4] Hill chose Isaac Oluwole, the principal of the
Grammar School in Lagos, and the Rev. Charles Phillips. Both were

[1] The first division of the diocese occurred in 1919 and the second in 1952.
[2] Wood to Hill, 19 Oct. 1892, *C.M.S.*, G3 A3/O, 1893, no. 7.
[3] Hill's Report, 20 Dec. 1892. I have seen it mentioned in secondary material
that J. Johnson was offered an assistant bishop's position by J. S. Hill, but neither
Hill nor Johnson refer to it in the primary material of this period. See E. M. T.
Epelle, *The Church in the Niger Delta*, Port Harcourt, 1955.
[4] Hill's Report, 20 Dec. 1892, and Wood to Hill, 19 Oct. 1892, *C.M.S.*, G3
A3/O, no. 7.

supported by the missionaries. Oluwole had the reputation of not going beyond his position and causing friction with his superiors. He was reported to be 'most beloved by the clergy and laity of Lagos'.[1] Nothing could be farther from the truth—an example of the lengths to which missionaries would go to get their own way. Phillips was called the most spiritual man among the clergy and an aggressive missionary, an attribute necessary for the pioneer work proposed for him in Ondo. One thing remained clear. The natural leaders were overlooked in favour of men who were acceptable to the English missionaries and to the committee in England. Taken as a whole, Hill's compromise was satisfactory; he did his best with a complicated situation. He risked total rejection in Lagos or London. Had the report been implemented, there is reason to believe it would have satisfied Lagos. It recommended a Commission of Inquiry into the disconnexions.[2] It promised within two or three years to provide a diocesan bishop in the Delta in succession to Bishop Crowther.[3] It requested an apology from the C.M.S. for the behaviour of its English agents on the Niger.

Had this been the entire substance of the report, it would have been totally objectionable to the C.M.S. The interim settlement was acceptable, for it assured English control. Johnson and Crowther were not recommended for assistant bishops. The assistant bishops were given jurisdiction over areas where no Europeans were employed, which overcame Wigram's objection to placing Africans over Englishmen. Hill, aware that the report might be unacceptable, offered his resignation to the Archbishop.[4]

[1] Wood to Hill, 19 Oct. 1892, *C.M.S.*, G3 A3/O, 1893, Hill's only objection to Oluwole was that his wife was too Anglicized. See *Hill's Report*. Allen reported that there would be serious objection in Lagos to the consecration of Oluwole. See Allen to Wigram, 2 Jan. 1892, *C.M.S.*, G3 A3/O, no. 48.

[2] The Parent Committee disconnected one clergyman, H. S. Macaulay, while Hill was in Lagos. Correspondence Committee Minutes, 1 Nov. 1892.

[3] Hill asked the Archbishop to promise an African successor to Crowther in his Report of 20 Dec. 1892. In October Hill changed his mind, possibly under pressure from Wigram. He considered it unwise 'to make any promise, or plan for the future, until we are assured of their fidelity, stability, and spirituality'. See Hill to Wigram, 2 Oct. 1893, *C.M.S.*, G3 A3/O, no. 72. The Archbishop nevertheless made the promise. 'I am ready to take the necessary steps as soon as the development and organization of your church justify such an appointment.' See Archbishop to Delta Pastorate Church, 12 Oct. 1893, *C.M.S.*, G3 A3/O, no. 72.

[4] Hill apologized to Wigram for his criticism of the C.M.S. in his Report. See Hill to Wigram, 21 Dec. 1892, *C.M.S.*, G3 A3/O, 1893, no. 5; Hill's Report, 20 Dec. 1892.

The report was a fair analysis of the situation in the Anglican mission. Had it been carried out in the following decade, it was possible the schism of 1901 might have been avoided. But it was most unlikely that the C.M.S. would have ever allowed its full implementation as long as Wigram and Lang were powers in the Parent Committee. As it happened, Hill only lived long enough to carry out the interim recommendations. Thereafter the Society ignored the body of the report.

Hill, Phillips, and Oluwole were consecrated on 29 June 1893 bishops of the Niger diocese, now renamed the Diocese of Western Equatorial Africa. The date was carefully chosen. It was the twenty-ninth anniversary of Crowther's consecration. What tragic irony for Africans. The new settlement—a blatant reversal of the past—paraded as a forward step in the Venn tradition. It was the ultimate humiliation. In December the three bishops, accompanied by the largest party of English missionaries ever sent forth at one time, arrived on the West Coast.

There was no public welcome in Lagos. The laity, brushing aside their docile clergy, sought among themselves for leaders.[1] If the clergy had been emasculated by their training, many of the laity were not so afflicted. The boycott was total. Lagos was in mourning. Only the pulpits of Christ Church (Tugwell) and St. Johns (N. Johnson) were open to the new bishops. The assistant bishops were in an unenviable position. Never before in Lagos had episcopal authority rested so lightly upon African support and depended so heavily upon English. Bishop Phillips summed it up, '. . . if we do not enjoy the full confidence of the Parent Committee, our position will become most intolerable and difficult'.[2] This was the final mockery. No other African leaders would ever enjoy the stubborn, insistent support which the missionaries gave the assistant bishops. Feted in England and pampered in Africa, they became the symbols of indirect rule within the church—the African façade behind which the English governed.

January 1894 was called 'Black January'. Bishop Hill died on the fifth, his wife hours later, followed by four of the newly arrived missionaries. Considering the health measures common on the coast, it was supposed such a tragedy was impossible in 1894. A wave of sympathy, which surprised the missionaries in its intensity, swept over Anglicans in Lagos. The largest congregation in Lagos history

[1] Tugwell to Baylis, 8 Jan. 1894, C.M.S., G3 A2/O, no. 7.
[2] Bishop Phillips to Wigram, 26 Dec. 1893, C.M.S., G3 A2/O, no. 15.

assembled to mourn at the double funeral for Bishop and Mrs. Hill.
It was a clear indication to the assistant bishops that they were the
major objects of dislike.

The force of this display of divine power was sufficient to convince
one European missionary that the policy was wrong. He changed his
mind entirely, recommending that Europeans pull out of the coastal
areas, leaving them to the care and supervision of African bishops.
They might make errors, but would learn by their mistakes. He called
for a mass C.M.S. exodus from the coast to the interior.[1] The effect
on Africans was the reverse. Black January broke the organized boycott of the new system. It did not change African views, but it gave
the assistant bishops a chance to prove themselves.[2]

Herbert Tugwell was immediately summoned to England and
consecrated Bishop of Western Equatorial Africa on 4 March 1894.
Hill's report was shelved and ignored.

The years 1890–4 were years of crisis for Christianity in West
Africa. The Niger experiment of 1864 of evangelizing Africa by means
of an African agency under the supervision of an African was pronounced a failure in 1890. By 1891 almost the total missionary staff,
clerical and lay, had been recommended for disconnexion. The bishop
and his two archdeacons were subordinated to European supervision.

Bishop Crowther, leader and supervisor of the Niger Mission since
its inception, was discredited in the eyes of the English. Crowther had
been a symbol of the regenerated Africa, of the Negro race rising
through education and Christianity to the highest position in the
African church. To his disparagers, Crowther's supposed failure was
not the failure of one man—it was the failure of the race.

The Black Bishop of the Niger was a symbol particularly to one
small but powerful group on the West Coast of Africa—the educated
and Christian liberated slaves, commonly called the Sierra Leonians.
He was a symbol of this group, upon whom missionary societies depended for the evangelization of Africa; upon whom humanitarians
relied for the carrying of western civilization to the interior; and
upon whom commercial companies counted to bring western goods
to African households.

To discredit Crowther was to discredit the Sierra Leonians. To discredit the Sierra Leonians was to say in effect that Africans, given the
benefit of education and Christianity, would never fully rise to the

[1] Dobinson to Baylis, 25 Jan. 1894, *C.M.S.*, G3 A3/O, no. 36.
[2] Tugwell quoted in the *Intelligencer*, vol. xix, 1894, p. 610.

status of the English. If Crowther, who was admitted to be a scholar and Christian, could not succeed, how sadly would the vast majority fail?

The English did not understand this. Most Africans, on the other hand, could see it in no other way. Looking forward to 1920 or to 1950, it could be said that the Africans saw the issue correctly. For indeed Crowther became not only the symbol of the failure of the Black race but of all non-whites the world over—the *raison d'être* for the all-white episcopacy in the Anglican Church.[1]

The issue of the episcopate was settled. The Settlement of 1894 assured English control of the highest offices in the African mission for the next half century. Sixty years later the Church discovered that while the senior political and administrative posts in the Government were passing into African hands the church lagged behind with an English episcopate. Until 1894 the African had been 'in the habit of looking to the church for a more immediate advance in his social and political power'.[2] After 1894 he searched elsewhere. The hesitation of the missionary societies to entrust the highest position in the Church to Africans created the sharp distinction between Mission churches and African churches. It delayed for sixty years the evolution of the missions into churches. Some men looked to the African churches for outlets for initiative, others turned to politics. By the 1950s those in political activities were realizing their ambitions. The missions belatedly fell into line. There was irony and much truth in an African nationalist slogan 'Seek ye first the political kingdom and everything else shall be added unto you'.[3]

[1] Stephen Neill, *Anglicanism*, London, 1958, p. 341; also Allen, *Spontaneous Expansion*, p. 191; see G. F. S. Gray, *The Anglican Communion*, London, 1958, p. 69.
[2] Hill's Report, 20 Dec. 1892.
[3] On Nkrumah's statue in Accra.

PART II

The Causes of the African Church Movement

That this meeting in humble dependence upon almighty God is of opinion that Africa is to be evangelized and that the foreign agencies at work at the present moment taking into consideration climatic and other influences cannot grasp the situation; resolved that a purely Native African Church be founded for the evangelization and amelioration of our race to be governed by Africans.

W. E. COLE and D. A. GLOSTER, U.N.A. Minutes, 14 Aug. 1891

DURING the formative period (1891–1921) the African Church Movement developed into five major denominations which claimed the adherence of one-third of the Christian Yoruba, and one-fifth of the total Christian population of Southern Nigeria. Each of the Protestant mission societies—the C.M.S., Wesleyan Methodist, and Southern Baptist—experienced a revolt within their membership which resulted in the establishment of an African Church essentially similar to its parent society.

The African churches were a revolt against changing mission practice in the twentieth century, but lightly veiled under proclamations of adherence to policy laid down in the nineteenth century. Broad and liberal theories aiming to create churches culturally identified with Africa were replaced by policies of stifling conformity which sought to produce in Africa an exact replica of the parent denomination.

Policies of conformity pursued after 1891 were not entirely new. They originated in the controversy over English missionary bishops (1853–62), which the C.M.S. opposed because they made an indigenous episcopate 'forever unattainable'. Once foreign control was established, it would not be easily given up. The C.M.S. attempted to circumvent the obvious goal of English control by the appointment of Crowther as a missionary bishop to inaugurate the

Native episcopate. On the issue of polygamy it was the C.M.S. who became the conformists in Venn's Memorandum of 1857, which was labelled intolerant by High Church opinion.[1]

By 1891 the policy of conformity had triumphed in dogma and the episcopate. The Lambeth ruling against polygamy in 1888, a pronouncement against the entire social system of Africa, placed the authority of the church behind Venn's Memorandum. By the succession of a European to Crowther, the C.M.S. rejected Native leadership, realizing the advantages of an English episcopate to ensure the Society's control. Control became a paramount consideration. If a foreign code was to be imposed upon Africa it required foreigners to impose it.

No compromise with the new policy was possible. The choice was either submit or revolt. The African churches who chose revolt found few champions on the international missionary stage. They became not merely rebels, but outlaws. They remained on the defensive against the overwhelming tide of foreign money, foreign personnel, foreign government, foreign education, and foreign thought which swept the mission societies along to statistical success.

The policy of conformity and the revolt which it induced were the result of the evangelical revival associated with the Keswick convention in England and West Africa. Between 1883 and 1890 the Evangelicals in England were involved in a purist movement emphasizing 'sin', 'holiness', 'perfection', and 'submission to the will of God'. Although opposed by the High and Broad Church parties, the movement remained within the Church of England.

Many felt that total submission and the greatest sacrifice of self-will to God's work lay in accepting work in the 'submerged half of the world' outside Christendom. As a result, in the year 1890 there was an unprecedented exodus of missionaries overseas. Upon offering for the mission fields, their submission to the will of God became self-assertion against the restraints of the missionary societies which contained older elements of nineteenth-century tolerance. Four groups of youths, Brooke's Niger party being one, refused to work within the framework of the C.M.S. but on a basis of association with it—a useful device to avoid the responsibilities while enjoying the benefits of the Society.

The young recruits, products of a movement to revive the traditional moral code of England, preached against the sins of the flesh

[1] Stock, *History*, ii, pp. 13–14, 111, 646.

while failing to recognize their own sins of the spirit. They lacked tolerance, the feeling for another society, or appreciation for different social mores and moral codes. They brought a strong contrary influence to bear upon the mission field from the earlier nineteenth-century missionaries, some of whom had become cognizant of the virtues of African morality.

As a result of the Keswick excitement, travelling 'Missioners' visited Lagos and Freetown in 1886, followed by others in 1888 and 1889. The missioners were surprised that they were not confronted with the 'lapsed masses' as in England but with churches crowded to capacity. Unable to comprehend a moral system different from but not necessarily as bad as that in England, they dwelt at length upon the sins of the flesh. African congregations accepted this in the relative privacy of their own churches. When the missioners returned to England and spoke as if 'sin' was the exclusive habit of the Africans it aroused a flood of bitterness in Lagos.[1]

Only James Johnson's parish, St. Pauls Breadfruit, escaped condemnation. There the missioners were struck 'by evidence of real spiritual life'. Johnson was ascetic by nature, and the spirit of Keswick found a quick response in his nature.

Prior to the special missioners, Johnson had held conversion meetings in St. Pauls, and a number of young men, who later became the founders of the African Church, received a personal experience of salvation. Inspired by Johnson's sermons, they developed a burning desire to carry the gospel to the Yoruba people, and in their lifetime to see Christianity become the national religion of the Yorubas.[2] This desire was partly religious and partly patriotic, just as many of the newly recruited English were activated by mixed religious and imperial interests. The Keswick upsurge of missionary enthusiasm coincided with a new wave of imperial expansion.

The Keswick revival produced a generation of missionaries willing to use moral reasons to deny black leadership, and supporting imperial expansion as a means to the evangelization of Africa. Keswick hastened the missionary impulse in Lagos among a group of men who interpreted the moral slurs against black leadership and

[1] Stock, *History*, iii, pp. 30, 285–8, 364, 369, 378–9, 382; *Lagos Weekly Record*, 12 and 19 July 1890.
[2] J. K. Coker, 'The History of the African Church', 1941, *Coker Papers*. J. K. Coker, 'The African Church', *The African Hope*, Feb. 1922, pp. 12–13.

the support for imperialism as designed to exclude them from leading the expansion of Christianity.

The settlement of 1894, which rejected an African successor to Crowther and created assistant bishops, was a clear victory for the spirit of Keswick. Lagos Christians believed that by rejecting African leadership the evangelization of Africa was indefinitely delayed. The missionaries were able to crack the hard shell of paganism, but they lacked the ability to gather a Christian church, usually producing converts to Islam, where a black agency was waiting to organize them.

Following the settlement of 1894, one measure after another was taken to retain supreme control of the church in English hands. The promise of territorial jurisdiction for assistant bishops was dropped except in the case of one white assistant bishop. The Archbishop of Canterbury's promise of a Delta diocesan bishop was forgotten. The educational qualifications of the clergy were lowered so that the next generation would be at a more decided disadvantage to their English counterparts. Constitutions subordinated the clergy to the bishop in the same way the missionary was subordinated to the Society. The synod, its constitution prepared in England, was dominated by laity of the 'right kind', and aroused little interest. An ecclesiastical province was urged upon the bishops at a number of Lambeth conferences. The urging was ignored.

Similar policies were pursued by the Methodists. They reduced the status of their black clergy by removing them from the common roll. The European missionary meeting became more powerful at the expense of the synod. African district superintendents were gradually eliminated.

Meanwhile in both societies self-support was pushed until church and fund raising became synonymous. While the English-raised budget remained static between 1895 and 1920, the Anglicans were noting in 1920 that African funds would soon cover the total expenses of black and white workers.[1] This was a reversal of 1890, when English supervision was introduced to look after English money.

Among the Baptists the financial trend was reversed. Their budget increased elevenfold between 1895 and 1920, dwarfing African contributions, which as late as 1914 had exceeded those of the Society. If the trend was different the results were the same. The expanded

[1] C. W. Wakeman to G. T. Manley, 14 May 1920, *C.M.S.* (*Ibadan*), Y, 1/2, 4.

funds were used as patronage to favour the submissive and pressure the rebels to conform.[1]

Increasing white control required turning a congregationally governed church into a hierarchy. The policy of conformity fell short of transferring the governmental structure of the parent denomination to Africa. Excuses were found for adaptations which prevented African control. The Anglicans invented assistant bishops. The Baptists reversed their tradition of congregational dominance to elevate the missionary above the congregation. Ordinations were recommended by an ordaining council, which in the United States was elected by the congregation but which in Africa became the standing committee of the missionaries.[2] By favouring the submissive, the Baptists prevented the growth of a leadership class among the clergy.

The reaction of the clergy to this progression of events was complete submission. Only four of the two hundred mission clergy voluntarily joined the African Church Movement before 1920. Thoroughly indoctrinated by European teachers, chosen for their submissiveness to European control, the butt of criticism by their parishioners, without the courage of their convictions, but praised for their loyalty to the mission, the clergy of the twentieth century never attained the pre-eminence of their forerunners in the nineteenth.

The laity who refused to follow their clergy in this submission formed a continual stream out of the missions into the African churches. The missions never appeared more quiescent. This no doubt contributed to the dullness of the synods, where the 'right kind' of public opinion prevailed.

Under competitive conditions Societies would have had incentive to modify the rules of discipline in the interest of more freedom of behaviour. The church might have become integrated into African society, and a new attitude evolved towards polygamy. But competition was eliminated through gentlemen's agreements, whereby in towns and rural areas the first society to enter the district was given a monopoly.

The Society could be dictatorial in its demand for money, reserving the right to decree where the church should be built and how

---

[1] Baptist Mission Meeting Minutes, 10 July 1916; 'The Mission Policy Regarding Polygamy', *The Nigerian Baptist*, Apr. 1932, pp. 51–52.

[2] S. G. Pinnock to Drs. Love and Ray, 16 Oct. 1920. Baptist Mission Meeting Minutes, 12 Jan. 1921, *Roberson Collection*.

much education should be provided. In larger cities such as Lagos members disconnected by one Society were not accepted by another.[1] Disconnexions became excommunication affecting vital aspects of life—the education of children and in some cases the successful pursuit of a profession,[2] to say nothing of the welfare of the soul.

Africans became impatient with Societies which put so many obstacles in the way of heathen converts. As late as 1900, Christianity was almost exclusively confined to a small coterie of western educated, living in separate quarters of pagan cities which were slowly turning to Islam. The popularity of Islam was due to the same causes which sustained the growth of the African churches. Missionary teaching and other alien influences were creating a people who were losing faith in their pagan gods. They were denied membership in the missions until they possessed an intellectual grasp of Christianity and had divested themselves of wives and children. African churchmen believed this denied the workings of a divine power. The lost pagans were left in a spiritual vacuum. Intellectual attainment left a rather cold impression upon men seeking a new faith.[3]

Yoruba society sought within Islam a bulwark against the moral laxness introduced by Christians. Many believed that the pagan morals of the Yoruba were superior to those offered by Christianity. The church's duty lay in re-enforcing this code. The pagan convert was not only expected to accept a new faith but develop a new set of values, or rather, a different conscience. It was the time it took to develop this different conscience which caused the delay in acceptance into the mission. Into this spiritual vacuum Islam stepped, ready to uphold the known moral code and offering a spiritual exercise—the daily prayers—in contrast to the mission catechumen class. Upon these arguments the African Church based its evangelistic method of preach, baptize, teach, which reversed the mission's preach, teach, baptize.[4]

The African intellectual was stifled in the atmosphere created by

[1] Annual Letter from the Society to the Lagos District Synod, 20 Dec. 1917. O. Griffin to Bishop Tugwell, 28 Feb. 1917, *W.M.M.S.* (*Ibadan*), 1/1/1 and 1/3/2.
[2] James Johnson to Wigram, 25 Sept. 1891, *C.M.S.*, G3 A2/O, no. 156; A. O. Ijaoye, 'Loss of Originality . . . in the Anglican Church of Nigeria', 1918? Unpublished manuscript, *Oke Collection*.
[3] Mojola Agbebi, 'The West African Problem', in G. Spiller, *Papers on Inter-Racial Relations*, London, 1911, p. 348.
[4] J. K. Coker, 'The Defence of the Order of Catechism', in Coker's sermon notebook, n.d.; Coker to N. A. Onatolu, n.d., *Coker Papers*.

E

the mission societies. The C.M.S. controlled the major printing press of Lagos. It had ample funds arising from its bookshop profits[1] to provide an outlet for African writers. But the Press was white-controlled, and through indifference or censorship or unfair royalty practices it did not encourage creative writing. Thus the African churches took a lively interest in the printing press. Eighty per cent. of all the creative literature produced before 1920 was written by African churchmen, who comprised 30 per cent. of the Christian population. Periodically the mission executive or synod became alarmed at the dearth of vernacular and English literature. Theological discussion relevant to the Yoruba situation was non-existent. Mission clergy or laity holding contrary views to the bishop dared not express them, while white missionaries interested in African views turned surreptitiously to African church publications.[2]

These publications occasionally stirred the bishop or a missionary to a reply. One of the best examples of the paucity of mission thinking was the synod's rebuttal to the mounting arguments of the African Church for a new policy towards polygamy. The synod of 1914 re-stated word for word Henry Venn's memorandum on polygamy.[3] Venn's arguments may have been satisfactory in 1857 when they were published, but they were inadequate defence in the more sophisticated debate of 1914.

Polygamy was only one of the issues which ought to have been widely debated in the Christian community. Chieftaincy and societies such as the Ogboni fraternity were as easily disposed of as polygamy by a snap pronouncement of an uninformed bishop without public debate.

Neither the missions nor the African churches, as organizations, took an active part in politics. It was not difficult to discover where their support lay—usually in opposing positions. The missions applauded the extension of British sovereignty. They hesitated to challenge the abuses of imperial rule or to acknowledge the justice of

[1] 1904–10 = £4,958; 1915 = £2,000; 1920 = £2,500, various sources see Ex. Co. Minutes May 1915, C.M.S., G3 A2/O, no. 61; Wakeman to Manley, 14 May 1920, C.M.S. (Ibadan), Y 1/2/4.
[2] J. G. Campbell, 'Something We Ought to Take Note Of', Times of Nigeria, 21 Nov. 1921; E. M. Lijadu, The Effects of Foreign Literature and Science Upon the Natives of the Yoruba Country, Lagos, 1887, p. 5; Campbell, Lagos Awake, Lagos, 1923, pp. 11–13; E. E. Williams to J. K. Coker, 8 Oct. 1914, Coker Papers.
[3] For the Memorandum and the African Church rebuttal, see J. K. Coker, Polygamy Defended, Lagos, 1915.

protest movements. They actively opposed the early nationalist movements in 1919.[1] African churchmen were engaged in all the early protest movements of Lagos—the land tenure question, the seditious ordinance bill, the extension of the franchise, and the National Congress of British West Africa.[2]

The first of the African churches of Lagos came into existence in 1888 out of the mission organization of the Southern Baptist Convention with headquarters in Richmond, Virginia. The Native Baptist organization which emerged did not claim to be an African church, but Native Baptist, as its name implied. The aim of the schismatics was to create a truly Baptist organization governed by the congregation as in the United States. After a schism in 1903 over the issue Baptist versus African, one wing of the Native Baptists—Araromi—aligned itself with the African churches, and its pastor became a leading exponent of the aims of the movement.

The causes of the founding of the Native Baptist were partly those which contributed to the rise of the African Church Movement in general. Others were unique, arising out of the connexions with a mission society in the United States rather than in Britain. Of the latter, the influence of American coloured people and the war between the states were the most powerful.

Early Baptist missionary activity centred around the cities of Ogbomoso and Ijaiye. The destruction of Ijaiye during the Yoruba civil war in 1862 forced the missionaries to withdraw. Prior to the fall of the city, the White Americans R. H. Stone and A. D. Phillips, and the Coloured American J. C. Vaughan, taking with them a number of war orphans, fled to the safety of Abeokuta. During the 'Ifole' (expulsion of the Christians from Abeokuta) of 1867 they fled to Lagos, where they were dependent upon the slender resources of the Baptist membership.[3]

[1] *Address by Rt. Revd. Bishop Oluwole to the Third Session of the Second Synod*, May 1911; *African Messenger*, 15 Sept. 1921 and 18 May 1922; Cust, *Evangelization*, p. 190; J. T. F. Halligey, 'Africa and Opportunities in the West', *Missionary Notices*, 1898, pp. 182–5; Griffin to Brown, 9 May 1910, *W.M.M.S.*, Lagos O.P.; M. T. Euler-Ajayi, 'Annual Sermon 1907', Lagos, 1907, p. 18. A.C. (Bethel), *Conference Proceedings 1901–1908*.

[2] *The African Messenger*, 17 Mar. 1921; J. G. Campbell, *Lagos Awake*, Lagos, 1923, pp. 11–13; *The African Hope*, editorial, July 1920, p. 9.

[3] Semi-Official Missionary historians, S. G. Pinnock, *The Romance of Missions in Nigeria*, Richmond, 1917; L. M. Duval, *Baptist Missions in Nigeria*, Richmond, 1928; C. E. Maddry, *Day Dawn in Yorubaland*, Nashville, 1936; G. W. Saddler, *A Century in Nigeria*, Nashville, 1950.

The missionaries returned to the United States because remittance of funds had ceased in the financial confusion following the American Civil War. Between 1863 and 1875 the Baptists of Lagos were thrown on their own resources. They survived great hardship, and without outside finance they maintained the cohesion of the Baptist community. The period produced a confidence and pride in African achievement and a belief in African ability which was a cause of conflict when white missionaries returned and expected the old deference and dependence. The prominent figures of the Ifole and the hard years in Lagos later became the founders of the Native Baptist Church. One African Baptist traced the roots of the independent church to this period.

It is worthy of observation that they (the Negroes) were liberated on the ground of political expediency by the same civil war which gave self-support to the Liberian churches and subsequently to the Yoruba churches.[1]

Baptist survival, 1867–75, was the result of the efforts of the American Negro J. C. Vaughan, and two Africans, M. L. Stone and Sarah Harden. Vaughan, born in South Carolina in 1828, emigrated to Liberia in 1847, where after six years in agriculture he joined the pioneer Baptist missionary, T. J. Bowen, on a visit to the Yoruba country. From that year forward he was a participant in the main events in Baptist history. Earning his living by carpentry and agriculture, Vaughan preached the gospel in Ogbomoso and Ijaiye. After a narrow escape from Ijaiye he and his wife opened an industrial school for the Ijaiye orphans in Abeokuta. The Ifole of 1867 closed the school, and Vaughan and his students came to Lagos, where he began afresh in the hardware business. A number of his boys continued as apprentices in their trades.[2]

In Lagos Baptist work was under the Coloured American, Rev. J. M. Harden, who landed in Liberia with Bowen in 1853. In the following year he came to Lagos, where he founded the American Baptist Church. In 1863 his support from the Southern Baptist Foreign Mission Board was cut off. He kept the church open and supported his wife and child, Samuel, by making and selling some of

---

[1] 'Address of Mojola Agbebi to the Yoruba Baptist Association', in Pinnock (ed.), *The Yoruba Baptist Association Year Book*, 1915, p. 24. The Anglicans also lost their Christian refugees of the Ifole to an African church.

[2] Duval, *Baptist Missions*, pp. 70, 75, 76, 93; Alistair Macmillan (compiler), *The Red Book of West Africa*, London, 1920, p. 108; Adeoye Deniga, *African Leaders*, Lagos, 1919, pp. 12–13; Robert Campbell, *A Pilgrimage to My Motherland*, London, 1862, p. 113.

the first local building bricks ever used in Lagos. His wife, Sarah, was a Sierra Leonian, her father being one of the first graduates along with S. A. (later Bishop) Crowther from Fourah Bay College. The family came to Lagos in 1857. After her husband's death in 1864 the responsibility for the refugees and Baptist work fell upon her and J. C. Vaughan. Sarah supported her son and a number of refugee children by teaching and selling needlework.[1]

Six Baptist leaders emerged from the care and teaching of Sarah Harden and J. C. Vaughan: M. L. Stone, Lajide Tubi, L. D. Fadipe, the Vaughan brothers, and Samuel Harden. All but one became clergy or prominent laymen of the Native Baptist Church. Gradually M. L. Stone began to show the leadership qualities for which he later became noted. He became a lay preacher in the church, organized regular weekly prayer meetings, and kept the primary school in operation. He maintained fraternal relations with the Methodist missionaries, who provided ministerial functions for the church, including baptism by immersion. The Baptist membership grew steadily but modestly.

Upon the return of the American missionaries to Lagos three events occurred which were common to all missionary organizations of the period and which were contributory causes of the African Church Movement. There arose the seemingly inevitable conflict of leadership between white missionary and black pastor. The missionary neglected the organization of the Native church. There was the influence of a revival with effects similar to those of the Keswick convention.

W. J. David (White American) and W. W. Colley (Coloured American) arrived in Lagos in 1875. David, a southerner, was unlikely to subordinate himself to the established leadership of an African pastor. But the conflict of leadership was delayed. David sent Stone as an interpreter to Abeokuta and then to Ogbomoso. Stone remained for seven years (1876–83) pastor of the Ogbomoso church. During this period he was free to act as he chose, there being no superintending missionary. Stone developed his qualities of leadership and gained the confidence of the congregation, so that in February 1878 they licensed him as their preacher.[2]

---

[1] Duval, *Baptist Missions*, p. 96; Agbebi, 'S. M. Harden', *Roberson Collection, Campos Square Cemetery*, Lagos; *African Times*, 23 Jan. 1863, p. 75, and 22 Aug. 1863, p. 17.
[2] Cecil Roberson, 'The First Baptist Minister of Note in Nigeria', *The Nigerian Baptist*, Aug. 1955, pp. 5–6.

David was a missionary to Lagos for thirteen years, half of which time he was resident in Lagos, the other half in America. When David returned to America in 1878 the Lagos church passed a resolution asking for Stone's ordination to the ministry as recognition for his valuable work 1869–75 in keeping together the Baptist community of Lagos. David ordained Stone in 1880.[1] When David left on furlough to America in 1884 Stone was called to be pastor of Lagos church, where he was again free for nearly two years to manage as he saw fit. In the latter part of 1885 David returned to take charge of Lagos church, and Stone for the first time in his career found himself in a subordinate position. Both David and Stone were thirty-six years of age.

The Baptists of Lagos were obliged to W. J. David for both the spiritual and material progress of the work. The growth in membership was steady. David had conducted successful revival services in Lagos in 1883 which resulted in numerical additions to the church and infused it with new vigour and enthusiasm. The outstanding converts were D. B. Vincent and his wife, who later, reverting to their Yoruba names, Mojola and Adeotan Agbebi, were the most eloquent exponents of the African Church Movement. Mojola Agbebi became a vigorous missionary, encouraged the development of Yoruba forms within his church, and was recognized as the voice of the African churches in Lagos, in Britain, and in the United States. He resembled the Anglican converts of the Keswick revivals in Lagos in his enthusiasm for a national Yoruba Christianity.

By 1884 David had collected £500 in Lagos and had persuaded the Mission Board to advance £1,000 to purchase materials for a church. He chartered a ship from the United States and shipped the material to Lagos. The foundation stone of the church was laid in January 1886 and the completed structure dedicated a year later. David was also responsible for establishing the Baptist Academy, which enrolled 250 when it opened in 1886. Mr. and Mrs. D. B. Vincent and S. A. Allen were on the staff of the primary division. S. M. Harden and J. A. Harrison (English) were in charge of the upper classes. The Academy, due to the qualifications of its staff and its enrolment, became one of the leading educational institutions of Lagos.

David's theory of missions, like Stone's, was in harmony with that prevailing in the nineteenth-century C.M.S. and Methodist missions.

---

[1] In the same year the C.M.S. had fourteen and the Methodist had eight ordained Africans.

He believed that Africa must be evangelized by Africans under the training and supervision of white men.[1] His actions in sending S. M. Harden to America for education and organizing the Academy in Lagos were consistent with the theory of promoting an African missionary agency. Lagos church had passed the phase of white supervision. It was ready for self-support and the accompanying independence which that implied in Baptist polity. David had neglected this aspect of the work. With all the increase in numbers and the large sums raised and spent on the church and Academy, Stone was still paid half of his salary by the mission and the other half by the congregation, as he had been in 1880.

The years 1886–7 were years of excessive activity among Lagos Baptists—the church was built and the Academy established. By the middle of 1887 this activity was over, and a conflict occurred between Stone and David. Both men understandably felt they had made large contributions to the Baptist work. Neither man had been accustomed to a subordinate position. A conflict of leadership seemed almost inevitable.

There may have been a certain jealousy on the part of W. J. David regarding the hold which Stone had over the congregation of the American Baptist Church. David may have resented Stone's extraordinary ability to preach in Yoruba.[2] For some reason inconsistent with his policy of training Africans, David refused to entertain the idea of Stone going to America. He would not use his influence, as he had done in the case of S. M. Harden, to secure finances for Stone's further training. Among the Christian ministers of Lagos, Stone was undoubtedly the most poorly educated. His English was extremely weak at a time and place when command of English and education were considered synonymous. This lack of education created a feeling of inadequacy which Stone never overcame until after 1900 when he became widely known as the most eloquent of Yoruba speakers. In 1887 David's refusal to consider higher education for Stone broke down the confidence which previously existed between them.

As the actual crisis which led to secession approached, David behaved as missionaries often did in such circumstances. He refused

[1] H. A. Tupper, *A Decade of Foreign Missions 1880–1890*, Richmond, 1891, pp. 170–1.

[2] S. G. Pinnock, *Foreign Mission Journal* (hereafter *F.M.J.*), Nov. 1894, p. 111, and T. Lumbley, *F.M.J.*, June 1895, p. 337. Smith to Foreign Mission Board, 30 Jan. 1891; Pinnock to Willingham, 25 Aug. 1901, *Roberson Collection*.

to follow recognized Baptist constitutional procedure (which was not to his advantage) on the excuse that the church was not fully self-supporting, and therefore not independent. Furthermore, in cases of friction which led to secession the parent committee of the missionary society was usually the final court of decision to which both the missionary and the congregation appealed. If the committee waited to hear both sides of the dispute before arbitrating, and gave a verdict which had the appearance of fairness, secession was often avoided. The Lagos Methodist trouble in 1884 and the Niger Delta Anglican dispute of 1891 were examples of the parent committee influence in preventing secession. If, on the other hand, the Board supported the missionary unquestionably in the interests of maintaining his authority and its ultimate control, then the congregation, which has lost respect for the missionary, lost confidence in the Board and the denomination. Schism usually followed.

After 1900 this danger increased, as most parent committees had begun to place more power in 'on the spot' authorities. Appeals over the head of the local committee were not welcomed by the missionary boards, as it was supposed contrary to the policy they were pursuing of delegating power to local authorities. It would have been wiser had the boards set up well-recognized channels of appeal at the time they were decentralizing authority. The closing of these channels ought to have been the last act in the independence of the Native church. Ideally the Board should not have been its own court of appeal, but it would have been better than nothing. Africans customarily had greater faith in the impartiality of the Boards than of their local authorities. The Methodists had this—the English conference being the final arbiter between the missionary society and the African congregation. As a result, the Methodists never experienced a schism over issues of church government. Among the Anglicans, the bishop should have been the arbiter. But his designation as missionary bishop indicated the difficulty. Bishop Tugwell was in fact (not in theory) the local authority for the C.M.S. in Nigeria prior to 1920. When the delegation of power was complete and the C.M.S. had virtually withdrawn from Lagos the bishop became the all-powerful head of the Native church. It was unwise to allow full episcopal power until Africans were appointed as bishops and the independent ecclesiastical province created. The Baptists made no provision for appeal once power came into the hands of the local missionary executive committee. The mitigating factor was the wide scope of self-government which local churches received upon attaining self-support.

In 1888 the Board first supported David, then on second thought recalled him. The result was that the customary bitterness of schism was lessened and left open the path to eventual resumption of fellow-ship between the mission and the Native church. As a result, the Baptists were the only denomination which succeeded in ultimately restoring amity between the estranged organization and the mission society. Had the Board openly expressed disapproval of David's action, schism would have been avoided.

A second disagreement arose when Stone was unable to maintain payments on a piece of land he had purchased. He began to trade to supplement his income of sixty pounds per year.[1] David objected on the grounds that a preacher ought to devote his entire time to the ministry. Stone asked for a raise in pay which David refused. Stone resigned. A deputation of church members waited on David and pointed out that they paid half of Stone's salary. According to Baptist custom, they ought to have been consulted before the resignation had been accepted. David answered that he was mission-ary-in-charge and pastor. Stone was only assistant pastor. He felt as free to dismiss Stone 'as he would any of his servants. . . .'[2]

A congregational meeting of the church was called for 15 March, 1888. David approached the two leaders of the Stone party—S. M. Harden and D. B. Vincent—and sought their support. They refused. He dismissed them from the staff of the Academy. He approached S. A. Allen, also on the staff, and secured his support. With the head teachers of the Academy gone, Allen was promoted in status and given a raise in pay.[3] The deputation reported to a stormy congrega-tional meeting. The members were more disturbed by David's tact-lessness in dealing with the deputation than in the illegality or

[1] There were eleven clergymen in Lagos in 1888. Seven held university degrees. Stone was the only one who did not have secondary education or the experience of a Training Institution. He was also the poorest paid. Had he been an Anglican on the Niger in 1890 or a Methodist in Lagos in 1895, he would have received £100 per annum. *C.M.S.* Correspondence Committee Minutes, 11 Nov. 1889, and *W.M.M.S.*, Lagos Synod Minutes 1895, Appendix A.

[2] E. A. Ojo, 'Historical Sketch of the Native Baptist Church', *Roberson Collection.*

[3] Stone to Tupper, 6 June 1888, and Resolution of the Executive Committee, 30 Apr. 1888, *Roberson Collection*, Missionary secondary sources say they re-signed. Duval, *Baptist Missions*, p. 118. In 1889 Allen was the highest paid agent in the Baptist Mission, Newton to Willingham, 15 June 1894, *Roberson Collection.*

un-Baptist nature of his action. David remained inflexible. The split in the church was unavoidable when one member warned David that 'if the new church just completed was intended for a barracoon the people would leave it. . . .'[1]

Soon after, a resolution of separation was passed by fifty of the members. They began holding services in a temporary shed in Stone's compound. The new church became known as the Native Baptist to distinguish it from the American Baptist Mission. It was the pioneer independent church in Lagos. Of the two hundred Baptist members, only a handful remained with the mission. All of the outstanding members joined the Native Baptists—the Hardens, the Vaughans, and the Vincents. The recently opened Academy was closed for lack of staff.

There was a sympathy secession from the Ogbomoso church due to Stone's influence there. Three-quarters of the congregation of eighty left under the leadership of Daddy Baraka. [2]

Following the secession of almost his total congregation and the collapse of the Academy, David sought endorsement for his actions. He called a meeting of the missionaries (P. A. Eubank, C. E. Smith, and himself). This meeting endorsed David's actions; his refusal to increase Stone's salary, his acceptance of the resignation, and his dismissal of Harden and Vincent. The meeting admitted Stone's right under Baptist custom to set up another church, but they condemned him for the spirit in which he had carried it out. A placard was prepared, signed by the three missionaries, and posted prominently. It proclaimed to Lagos that the Baptist Mission had withdrawn fellowship from Stone because he was unqualified for the ministry, since he had been repeatedly untruthful. The same day the missionaries convened a meeting of the remaining members of the American Baptist Church which passed a resolution excluding Stone from the pulpit.[3] Rather belatedly Baptist constitutional practices were being followed.

[1] Barracoons were depots where slaves were kept prior to shipment to America. E. A. Ojo, loc. cit. Considering these references to slaves and servants, it is relevant to point out that David's attitude towards Africans left much to be desired. There are frequent references to 'flogging' and 'clubbing' not only of mission personnel but also of tradesmen who serviced the mission. See W. J. David's Diary, 1 Nov. 1876; 5 Mar. 1876; 23 Sept. 1876; Smith to the F.M.B., 7 Apr. 1887, *Roberson Collection.*

[2] Duval, *Baptist Missions*, p. 119.

[3] P. A. Eubank, Letter of Resolution to the F.M.B., 30 Apr. 1888; David, Eubank, Smith, Statement concerning Moses L. Stone, 30 Apr. 1888; J. J. Tubi

The Foreign Mission Board of the Southern Baptist Convention, upon hearing from the missionaries of the trouble in Lagos, wrote David expressing their sympathy and support and guaranteed him their unimpaired confidence. Later the Board received a number of documents from the independent church. One was a dignified statement from M. L. Stone. He took for granted in his letter that the setting up of an independent Baptist church was in accord with Baptist practice and that the placard in Lagos was an attempt to stamp out the new church. He pointed out that the charge of untruthfulness had never before been mentioned. He questioned the missionaries' right to withdraw fellowship.

After receiving this letter the Board had second thoughts about Lagos. They questioned David's missionary methods and bluntly asked him if the missionaries would welcome the establishment of an independent church. David replied that the missionaries would welcome an independent church, but there was no prospect of a strong Native church either spiritually or numerically. David asked the Board to abide by its initial decision and leave affairs in Lagos in the hands of the missionaries.[1] David left Lagos the following month, ostensibly because of illness, but more likely because of humiliation and the feeling that he had lost the confidence of the Board. The Lagos papers implied that he was recalled.[2] This was one of the last instances of a mission board siding with an African congregation and humiliating the missionary. In the coming years missionary societies became infected with the imperial slogan that White authority must be built on White prestige. Admitting the mistakes of the individual undermined the infallibility of the race.

It was typical of secessions that the policy of the mission immediately after the crisis was of vital importance. The independents had set up a local church. It remained Baptist. They would proceed to schism (organization of another denomination) if the mission attitude remained inflexible. Had David remained in Lagos, schism

to G. W. Saddler, 25 May 1922; Stone to Tupper, 4 June 1888, *Roberson Collection*.

[1] David to Tupper, 25 July and 18 Oct. 1888; Stone to Tupper, 4 June and 6 June 1888; it is unfortunate in the light of the subsequent fellowship which prevailed between the Baptist Mission and the independent churches that G. W. Saddler's *A Century in Nigeria*, 1950, records the first reaction of the Board (pp. 90–91) but not the second.

[2] Tupper, *A Decade of Foreign Missions 1880–1890*, p. 630. David offered to return to Abeokuta or Oyo, but was not re-engaged. *F.M.J.*, Oct. 1893, p. 85, for newspaper reports see *Lagos Observer*, 10 and 17 Nov. 1888.

was inevitable. With the advent of a new missionary fellowship could have been restored without any loss of face to either side. But the new missionary took a common attitude, considering any reaction of African congregations other than submission as 'sin'. He used the weapon of hinting at gross immorality among the seceders; a technique to become more familiar as the African Church Movement gained momentum. Furthermore, outside influences were working against *rapprochement*, hardening African attitudes and pushing them towards the African churches—the Niger purge and the invasion of Ijebu Ode.

When the Lagos events of 1888 became known in the southern United States there was criticism of African missionary methods. The critics said that the African mission was progressing in reverse. It had lost its ablest African evangelist. Some pointed out that there was only one ordained clergyman after forty years of missionary effort. Others suggested that the missionaries should withdraw, pointing out that the Liberian Baptist churches had prospered when that mission had withdrawn after the war between the states.[1] In the light of these criticisms, David's replacement, C. C. Newton, was under considerable pressure to bring unity to the Baptist community of Lagos. He had two courses open to him, either suggest that the mission extend the hand of fellowship to the Native Baptists or attempt to destroy them. He chose the latter. The independent church was willing to return on agreed conditions: first, that the independent church membership be received back as a body; second, that Stone, Harden, and Vincent be reinstated; third, that the church building be turned over to them, and fourth, that they be constituted a properly independent Baptist church.[2]

Newton insisted that reconciliation would be considered on the basis of individual confession of guilt. He was emphatic that by this act of secession the people had sinned—'a shameful fall of prominent members and teachers' he called it. The principle involved was membership submission to the missionary. He warned that if this principle was 'run over rough shod' it would 'give trouble in all the future of African missions'. Newton insisted that the setting up of the independent church—'the shameful fall'—had to be confessed

[1] T. P. Bell, *F.M.J.* (editorial), June 1891, p. 32; C. E. Smith, 'Small Results in Africa', *F.M.J.*, Aug. 1891, p. 9.

[2] Newton to F.M.B., 1889, quoted in *Proceedings of the Southern Baptist Convention*, 1890, p. 35; David to Tupper, 18 Oct. 1888; S. M. Cook to Tupper, 29 Dec. 1890, *Roberson Collection*.

by the individual members. He hinted that the Lagos church was full of sinners and he was taking this means of purging it. In case this condition of the church should reflect on W. J. David, its former pastor, Newton stated that the missionaries were not to blame.[1] He did not say who was.

The year 1890 was particularly unpropitious for a settlement on the basis of African submission to white missionaries. The C.M.S. purge of their Niger Mission, with its subordination of the entire African agency to English supervision, was announced. The nine disconnected Niger clergymen arrived in Lagos, and 'filled the air with the tale of wrongs which they had endured at the hands of the white missionaries'. A wave of bitter race feeling swept over Lagos and aroused great hostility against all white missionaries.[2]

At the close of 1890 Newton, consistent with his policy of individual confession, sent a letter to each member of the independent church asking them to return to the mission. On 10 January 1891 (less than two weeks after Blyden's speech on church independence in Lagos) the Church Council of the Native Baptists met. Consistent with their policy of collective action, they replied to Newton's letter expressing feelings of brotherly love to the mission church, 'but that it is not their desire, neither do they see their way clear to an effectual union of the two organizations'.[3] The reply indicated a hardening attitude. They were no longer stating conditions on which they would return, but simply refusing to consider union on any terms.

After this blunt refusal Newton made no further direct overtures to the independent church. There were, however, indications that bitterness was lessening. In the next year Newton was occasionally invited to occupy the pulpit in the Native Baptist Church. But as in 1890, when events in the Niger Mission made peace making impossible, so in early 1892 rumours spread that the British were preparing to invade Ijebu-Ode and Abeokuta. On top of the bitterness arising out of the treatment of educated Africans on the Niger was this attempt to destroy the independence of two interior kingdoms.

Newton's attitude to the Niger and Ijebu-Ode invasion was opposed to that prevailing among African Baptists. On the Niger question the members of the independent church had long held up

---

[1] *Baptist Proceedings*, 1890, p. 35 and 1891, p. 16.
[2] Newton to Tupper, 2 Mar. 1891, *Roberson Collection*.
[3] . . . 'Historical Sketch of the First Baptist Church, Lagos', *Ogbomoso Library*.

the C.M.S. Niger Mission as an example of how a mission in Africa should be operated. They had urged American Baptists to emulate the C.M.S. After the purge of the Niger Mission Newton warned the Foreign Mission Board of entrusting the evangelization of Africa to Africans. He used the Niger as an example of the results of this policy. David had believed in the Niger system of Africa evangelized by Africans, even though in the end he may have been disillusioned. Newton had very little hope of saving Africa with 'employed natives'. He claimed that this policy was in error, 'however good the men who are engaged in the employment system'. Baptist mission agents he referred to as 'workers of low grade on very high salaries'. Newton carried out a Brooke-like purge of the mission staff, cutting by half the salaries of the few who remained. He extended his purge to the Yoruba interior while the missionaries of Abeokuta and Oyo were on furlough.[1] His early death prevented an explosion among the interior missionaries who maintained the old-fashioned idea that '. . . the Natives must do the greater part of the work of spreading the gospel'.[2]

When preparations were going forward in Lagos to invade Ijebu-Ode Newton was strongly in favour of British action. He felt that nothing permanent could be accomplished by missionaries in the interior until this was done. 'A sword of steel often goes before the sword of the spirit.' The Native Baptists opposed Newton on both his views of an African agency and the interior kingdoms. On one occasion while occupying the independent church pulpit he was 'hissed, scoffed at, and almost sworn at' when he expressed his views.[3]

When in July 1894 Newton and his wife died in the yellow-fever epidemic which had caused the death of six C.M.S. missionaries, including Bishop and Mrs. Hill, the Foreign Mission Board was unable to find a replacement. Thereafter no Baptist missionary was located in Lagos until 1920. While the Anglicans, by their settlement of 1894, entrenched white control over their Lagos churches, the Baptists surrendered to African leadership in the same year. The Anglicans reaped a major schism in 1901; the Baptists enjoyed a reunion in 1914.

After 1894 the Baptist Mission church of Lagos, dealing directly

---

[1] Newton to Willingham, 15 June 1894, *Roberson Collection*.
[2] Smith to Lumbley in *F.M.J.*, Mar. 1893, p. 242, and Mar. 1895, p. 240.
[3] *F.M.J.*, July 1892, p. 369.

with the Foreign Mission Board, purchased its building from the mission society and secured its independence. Amiable relations developed between the rival Baptist organizations in Lagos. In 1914 the independent Lagos churches returned to fellowship with the mission, being then able to negotiate from a position of strength, since they had larger membership rolls and financial strength than the mission organization.[1] By 1914 the missionaries saw that they had gained immeasurably by having pulled out of Lagos in 1894. It was the pity of it that the mission society did not grasp the implication of this for future policy elsewhere in the Yoruba country. But by 1920 the missionaries who had learned the lessons of 1894 were no longer in the field. A new and youthful crowd of missionaries emerged in Western Nigeria on the crest of a wave of foreign mission enthusiasm in the United States. They had money and new plans, which turned out in the end to be plans as old as the missionary movement itself—the evangelization of Africa under white leadership.

Without being aware of it, the Native Baptists in 1888 ushered in a new era of Christianity among the Yoruba. A spell had been broken, a door had been opened for Christians of every mission affiliation to find a dignified means of escape from the tyranny of the rule of the societies. It was significant that the revolt first developed among Baptists. In the first place, Baptist members enjoyed more freedom than members of other societies, and a little freedom invariably creates the desire for more. Secondly, the missionaries in 1888 turned their backs upon their own preaching. The glory of Baptist polity was the freedom which a local congregation exercised. The local congregation is *the* church in Baptist belief. Thus the pastor or the missionary is the servant, never the master. Considering the feelings of racial superiority with which the Southern white missionary was imbued, he invariably fell farther short of his denominational ideal than missionaries of other persuasions. Thus David in 1888 behaved exactly as Bishop Tugwell of the C.M.S. a decade later. But while Tugwell acted within his right as provided by custom, David had no such authority. When Baptist practice strayed so far from Baptist

[1]

1914	Members	Contributions	Day School Scholars
Independents	4,552	£1,796	837
Mission	2,001	£454	651

From *Yoruba Baptist Association Year Book*, 1916, p. 160.

preaching the honourable course for Baptist members was to withdraw and form a truly Baptist church.

The Baptists, the smallest Christian group in Lagos, successfully
defied the Society. What shame and reproach this heaped on discontented Anglicans and Methodists. The manly course was obvious,
cease to grumble and establish a new organization. Thus the precedent set in 1888 was repeated in 1891, 1901, and 1917 until every
mission society had been chastized. It is for this precedent and the
pattern it set that the African churches, and ultimately the Yoruba
people, have to thank the Native Baptist Church. Almost immediately manœuvres began among Anglicans and Methodists which
culminated in the United Native African Church (U.N.A.). But these
men thought first in terms of West Africa rather than Lagos.

The foundation meeting of the U.N.A. on 14 August 1891 was the
anti-climax to a scheme designed to sink foreign denominationalism
in a West African church embracing Anglicans, Methodists, and
Baptists, first in Lagos, followed by a call to Africans from Sierra
Leone to the Cameroons to break their mission ties and affiliate. A
firm and convincing lead from Lagos might well have produced such
a church. Crowther's clergy on the Niger were related to influential
people in all the large cities on the coast. These relationships crossed
denominational lines. For example, three principal sufferers on the
Niger were related to the Crowther family, who in turn were relatives
of the Macaulays. One wing of the Macaulay family was Anglican,
the other Methodist. The Macaulays were related to the Lawsons,
one of the royal families of Little Popo. The Lawson family was
partly Methodist and partly Anglican.

All the main cities of the West Coast from Sierra Leone to the
Cameroons were in a state of upheaval. Europeans were on the
imperial move; politically, penetrating the African continent,
religiously, securing absolute control over the Christian congregations. In the wave of imperialism Germany, France, and Britain
all began their penetration of the interior—Germany in Little Popo
and the Cameroons; France in Dahomey; Britain in Egba and Ijebu.
The Christian communities resented this European advance upon
African kingdoms. Even more serious was the effect which it had
upon the mission churches in the areas of penetration.

After German occupation of the Cameroons the British Baptists
withdrew, handing over the churches to the Basle Missionary
Society without the consent of African Baptists. The Baptist churches

of the Cameroons resented this barter arrangement between two foreign societies and declared their independence. They then found themselves in long disputes with their new mentors over ownership of property. Ultimately, much reduced in strength, they appealed to Lagos Native Baptists for assistance.[1] In Little Popo (Togoland)— a circuit of the Lagos Methodist district—the new German administration expelled the English superintendent for political reasons, charged the congregation with treasonous activities, and demanded the teaching of German in the schools. The Methodist parent society in England recruited a German, J. F. Muhleder, as superintendent. No African clergyman could be found to work under him, and Muhleder was alone at Little Popo.[2]

At Porto Novo (Dahomey)—another circuit of the Lagos district —the Methodists opposed French occupation, preferring the British as the lesser of two evils. Persecution of the English-speaking Yoruba community followed. Many left for Lagos or cities in the Yoruba states. As long as the African old-timer, Rev. T. J. Marshall, who had opened the mission in 1862, remained, the worst crisis was averted. Upon his death in 1899 a French Methodist was recruited. Again no African would work under him, and a large secession followed.[3]

In 1891 the British seized Ilaro, part of the Egba kingdom. The Egba chiefs, fearing the divided loyalty of the Christians, accused them of sympathizing with the Lagos government and threatened them with expulsion.[4] In 1892 the British defeated the Yoruba kingdom of Ijebu-Ode. The missionaries professed to see this defeat as a prelude to Christian penetration. African Christians accused the missionaries of hypocrisy.

On the narrower religious field the arrogance which accompanied imperial expansion was reflected in growing missionary intolerance of African customs and leadership. The Lambeth Conference of the bishops of the Anglican church resolved against tolerance of

[1] W. Hughes, *Dark Africa and the Way Out*, London, 1892, pp. 31, 71–2; *Lagos Weekly Record*, 16 Aug. 1902.

[2] S.M., Reports of Little Popo Circuit for 1889 and 1892, Roe to Hartley, 31 July and 18 Oct. 1893, *W.M.M.S.*, Lagos, O.P.

[3] Joseph Rhodes, 'Porto Novo: The Church and its Founder', *Work and Workers*, 1895, pp. 406–12; S.M., Report of Porto Novo Circuit for 1890; Martin to Findlay, 2 Apr. 1901, Sutcliffe to Findlay, 28 Nov. 1901, *W.M.M.S.*, Lagos, O.P.

[4] Wood to Lang, 19 Jan. 1891 and Wood to Fenn, 17 July 1891, *C.M.S.*, G3 A2/O, nos. 36, 133; S.M., Abeokuta Report of 1891, *W.M.M.S.*, Lagos, O.P.

F

polygamy in any form. This set the church firmly on the path to introducing western modes of life before Christianity. The Lambeth pronouncement hardened missionaries against African customs. The result was discontent among those Africans who had hoped that Lambeth would restrain the westernizing tendencies of the missions.

The enforcement of the polygamy rule and the economic depression of the 'eighties caused a rift between the clergy and laity. The clergy accused the laity of laxity in supporting the church. The laity accused the clergy of insincerity in their support of monogamy. Among the Anglicans in Lagos no congregation was satisfied with its clergy. In Abeokuta there was talk of getting rid of the European and Sierra Leonian clergy and replacing them by Native Egbas less impressed with the sanctity of Lambeth. Among the Methodists small secessions took place in both Lagos and Abeokuta of those who refused to accept the goals towards which Lambeth was pointing the way.[1]

In Lagos, the Gold Coast, and Sierra Leone English heads of the church were attempting to strengthen their hold over African organizations which appeared to be taking too much under their authority. In Lagos a schism in the American Baptist mission left the missionary in charge of the property but minus a congregation. In the Gold Coast the Methodist church was in turmoil. The district synod was suspended. In Sierra Leone the Anglican bishop, determined to gain wider powers over his clergy, found himself in long, drawn-out litigation. Five of his pastors were defying him. Anglicans and Methodists combined to belittle and humiliate him. His support for Brooke's purge and refusal to employ those clergy expelled from the Niger added to his unpopularity.[2]

The Christians of the West Coast saw all the elements of their local situation in the great drama being played out on the Niger. It appeared as multiple prongs of one large European intrigue to sub-

[1] 'Report of the Committee on Polygamy', *The Six Lambeth Conferences 1867–1920*, S.P.C.K., 1929, p. 133; J. H. Willington, 'A Bible Class for Polygamists', *Wesleyan Notices*, 1890, p. 14; S.M. Report of the Lagos Circuit for 1892 and 'Religious State of the Churches 1893', *W.M.M.S.*, Lagos, O.P.; *Lagos Observer*, 14 June 1890; *C.M.S. Proceedings 1894–6*, p. 64; Harding to Lang, 11 Oct. 1889 and Wood to Baylis, 20 Sept. 1895, *C.M.S.*, G3 A2/O, nos. 148 and 161.

[2] Roe to Hartley, 16 Mar. 1895, *W.M.M.S.*, Lagos, O.P.; Bishop Ingham to the Archbishop, 15 Aug. 1893, *Lambeth*, Benson, I, 12d, 1893, For.; Harding to Baylis, 21 Aug. 1896, *C.M.S.*, G3 A2/O, no. 150; C. Fyfe, *A History of Sierra Leone*, 1962, pp. 509–12.

due them. The issues were the same from Sierra Leone to the Cameroons. Only on the Niger was the situation so dramatized and so publicized. The depression was pushing European merchants to dislodge their African competitors and forcing stringent economic measures upon the Niger churches. The Lambeth ruling on polygamy was the signal to unleash a wave of intolerance for African customs and a purge of mission churches. European supervision was being tightened over African congregations; by the Basle Society, by Brooke, by Muhleder, and by the Bishop of Sierra Leone. Crowther was the symbolic victim. But everywhere Africans found themselves the victims of a new hardening attitude, an uninformed intolerance, a pushing and grasping for absolute authority. Seldom were Christians so prepared for a convincing lead towards a magnificent assertion of religious independence.

Lagos was the key because of its wealthy Christian class and leaders of interdenominational West Coast renown. Christianity in Lagos had stagnated among the few having some connexions with Sierra Leone. Missionaries were unmoved by the spread of Islam and continued their intransigent attitude to African society. They were intolerant of divergent views. They held a monopoly on higher education. Most annoying of all was their ruthless use of excommunication. Upon all this the damning reports of Brooke, Eden, and Robinson from the Niger were eroding English confidence in Bishop Crowther and educated Africans. There was evidence that this challenge to African leadership begun on the Niger was spreading to other societies. The year 1891 was the end of one era and the beginning of another more hostile to African advancement. Seldom were great changes so loudly proclaimed.

On 23 December 1890 Blyden arrived in Lagos welcomed by an interdenominational committee. He addressed the people of Lagos at St. Pauls schoolroom on 2 January 1891 on 'The Return of the Exiles and the West African Church'. He declared that as long as the evangelization of Africa was left in foreign hands and imposed through foreign forms it would never be accomplished. He warned that even the alien church structure evident at present would collapse the moment it was not supported by foreign funds.[1] This stirred those

---

[1] E. W. Blyden, *The Return of the Exiles and the West African Church*, London, 1891; *Lagos Times*, 3 Jan. and 21 Feb. and 21 Mar. 1891; Vernal to Hamilton, 14 Mar. 1891, *C.M.S.*, G3 A2/O, no. 101; Newton to Tupper, 2 Mar. 1891, *Roberson Collection;* Deniga, *African Leaders*, pp. 3–4.

nurtured on James Johnson's plans for eventual independence within the existing denominational structures. The Niger purge rendered Johnson's ideas impractical. Blyden's proposals would wipe away foreign denominationalism and unite Africans for the salvation of the continent and against the policies pursued by the missions.

As a result of Blyden's lecture, interdenominational discussions were arranged among the clergy and laity of all the mission societies. The meetings were convened at St. Pauls parsonage under the chairmanship of Johnson. A resolution was carried instructing Johnson to draw up a constitution and doctrinal statement to be circulated among the clergy and laity for their comments and approval. The Basis of Union was drawn up by James Johnson and Archdeacon Henry Johnson (disconnected and now unemployed as a result of the Niger purge). It was circulated and apparently approved by 1 March. Accordingly, upon a signal from James Johnson all the ministers of Lagos agreed to switch pulpits and declare the inauguration of the West African Church, thereafter reading the Basis of Union. The *Lagos Times* reported that all Lagos was eagerly awaiting the proclamation. Johnson never gave the signal.

It is impossible to say why Johnson came to the brink and refused to jump. The West African Church was the best kept secret in Lagos history. For an issue of such importance to the missionaries it was remarkable that no hint of it appeared in mission correspondence. The missionaries were more than usually isolated from their parishioners. Tugwell wrote to the C.M.S. two weeks after Blyden's public lecture on the West African Church that Blyden had not yet spoken on church matters. Something did leak out to the friends of African leadership in England. R. N. Cust implored Johnson not to approach the Methodist, Baptist, or Roman Catholics in the interest of an independent church.[1] Peculiarly enough this was a year after the issue had been shelved in Lagos.

Why did the West African Church scheme collapse? Some said the wealthy laity were unwilling to finance it. This was unlikely, since the Lagos churches of all missions were self-supporting. Others said that dogma, rites, and ceremonies prevented its acceptance, that some clergy could not forgo Anglican recognition. Its doctrinal programme was too broad. The evidence suggests it had already

---

[1] Tugwell to Lang, 13 Jan. 1891, *C.M.S.*, G3 A2/O, no. 13. Cust to the Archbishop, 27 Sept. 1892, and James Johnson to Cust, 19 July 1892, *Lambeth*, Benson, I, 11g, 1892, For.

been accepted. It was unlikely that Johnson would become unorthodox in doctrine. Another writer blamed Johnson for holding back.[1] Other possibilities appear more plausible. To win universal support Bishop Crowther must give the new church his blessing and its apostolic succession if it was to be acceptable to many Anglicans. English sources hint that Crowther contemplated schism before his death. African sources—Johnson being one—indignantly deny this.[2] The supporters of African leadership in the C.M.S. parent committee may have promised more than they were able to deliver. The struggle over Crowther's successor had not begun. Cust and Whiting may have over-estimated their influence in the C.M.S. Reliance on their English friends might have persuaded Johnson and even Crowther to delay independent action. Furthermore, for all the show of unanimity among the clergy, it was unlikely that Isaac Oluwole and Nathaniel Johnson would willingly co-operate.

Possibly most important of all was the basically unChristian inspiration behind the West African Church. For all its other noble motives, it was an effort to spite the English missionaries. It could be a success only if black racism was called to its support. This was contrary to the spirit of African Christianity deeply permeated with the concept of brotherhood in Christ. If Africans denied this brotherhood, had not the foundation been removed from Christianity itself? Nobler feelings prevented Africans from believing that the crisis was entirely caused by English prejudice. They would have been shocked by the almost unanimous racist tone of missionary letters to London. The planners of the West African Church were, like Venn, the product of the nineteenth century who had watched the mission societies struggle against the detractors of the Negro race. Was it possible that these same societies were joining the detractors? Regardless of much of the evidence, most could not believe it. Had they comprehended the momentous change in attitude with which they were dealing, the plans for the West African Church would have been carried through.

[1] Newton to Tupper, 2 Mar. 1891, *Roberson Collection*; J. K. Coker, *The African Church*, p. 13, 'Life of Bishop Johnson, Part II', *Nigerian Pioneer*, 6 July 1917; D. A. Hughes, *African Hope*, Feb. 1921; *African Hope*, Oct. 1919; Hughes, *Nigerian Spectator*, 23 Aug. 1924; N. A. Winfunke, *The Cause of the Establishment of African Churches*, Lagos, 1957, p. 4.

[2] D. C. Crowther to J. B. Whiting, 11 July 1891, *C.M.S.*, G3 A3/O, no. 160; Bishop Crowther to R. Lang, 1 Dec. 1891, and Allen to Wigram, 22 Dec. 1891, *C.M.S.*, G3 A3/O, 1891, *C.M.S.*, G3 A2/O, no. 156.

When it was certain that the West African Church had been abandoned one of its eager advocates, W. E. Cole, convened a meeting on 14 August 1891 of nine laymen, who resolved to establish an African church—the United Native African Church. The founders represented the laity who had lost faith in clerical leadership. Lay leadership became a pattern to the African Church Movement, in 1891, repeated in 1901–2 and again in 1917.

The U.N.A. was not created as the result of a fight or schism from a particular denomination. It was founded by men of several denominations as a purely African missionary effort. The founders justified their actions around three main arguments; the evangelization of the continent, the cleansing of foreign forms, and the amelioration of the race. In order to carry out its purpose, the new church must remould Christianity to suit African conditions rather than uproot African society to conform to Christianity. Claiming that no Native church properly so-called had as yet been created, the founders wished to design a church where everything was purely Native. The machinery of working must be Native, the idea of the organization African, a Native ministry trained on the spot, a Native literature and architecture, with the full cleansing of foreign forms and the incidental features of western Christianity. The success of the missionary effort would ultimately command the respect and admiration of the foreign missionary agencies. It would wipe away the disgrace and calumny heaped upon the Africans in the missions —an answer to the detractors and contemners of the black Christians.[1] The result was the foundation resolution:

. . . that Africa is to be evangelized and that the foreign agencies at work at the present moment taking into consideration climatic and other influences cannot grasp the situation; resolved that a purely Native African church be founded for the evangelization and amelioration of our race, to be governed by Africans.[2]

The U.N.A. was a modest effort contrasted with the ambitious scheme just laid to rest. It was not a clarion call to the Christians of Lagos to desert the missions, but a goal set to evangelize the race and command the respect of the foreigners. In two definite ways the U.N.A. rejected the philosophy of building themselves on the ruins

[1] Hughes, *African Hope*, Feb. 1921; *Nigerian Spectator*, 23 Aug. 1924; U.N.A. Minutes, 20 Aug. 1894 and 24 Aug. 1891, vol. i, pp. 145–6 and 9–13. J. K. Coker, *The African Church*, 1913, p. 13; G. A. Oke, *A Short History of the U.N.A.*, Part I, 1891–1903, Lagos, 1918, chapter 1.

[2] U.N.A. Minutes, 14 Aug. 1891, p. 4.

of the missions. They refused to accept excommunicated members from other churches. They refused to make their school a race issue, even though promised financial support to do so.[1] They chose the noble course. It was also the weaker. Extending the hand of fellowship did not stem the wave of persecution from the Societies which fiercely resented an indigenous intruder. Without the racial appeal they were unable to muster the strength which would provide the finances necessary for the large task they had set themselves.

By not realizing that the African church would be built upon the discontent in the missions, the U.N.A. slipped into becoming another denomination in Lagos rather than an alternative to mission Christianity. The Niger purge, African leadership, Blyden, and foreign forms loomed so large in U.N.A. thinking that it failed to realize that other issues were at stake. Later it dropped the matter of comity, but only reluctantly. The whole approach of the U.N.A. was too moderate, lacking fire and dynamism. The Native Baptists could never provide a real alternative for Anglicans and Methodists, because for fifteen years (until 1903) they remained far too Baptist and not sufficiently African. The U.N.A. could have provided the alternative had it promoted itself vigorously among Lagos Christians. It could have drawn the majority of the discontented out of the Anglican mission. It might have thus prevented the major schism of 1901–2 and the consequent splintering and denominationalism within the African Church Movement. The U.N.A. chose the path of moderation. Ten years later it was completely overshadowed by the foundation of the militant African Church Organization which set out to provide an alternative church to the missions in every city and town in the Yoruba country.

Although the U.N.A. was the result of the Niger purge and the shabby treatment of Bishop Crowther, in fact, the mission churches came through the crisis without a schism to disturb them. It would be a mistake (and one which Bishop Tugwell made) to think that since the Lagos churches apparently accepted the settlement of 1894, the crisis was over. The major schism which resulted in the foundation of the African Church Organization in 1901 had its roots in the settlement of 1894, whereby an African diocesan bishop was rejected and assistant bishops created to mask the obviously retrogressive step. Lagos hostility to the settlement of 1894 was

[1] U.N.A. Minutes, 21 Aug. 1891, 18 Nov. 1892, 25 Nov. 1892; 22 Mar. 1895, 23 Aug. 1895, pp. 7–8, 82–6, 168–9, 178–80.

specifically directed towards the two men who had deserted the cause of African advancement and accepted positions under the new scheme—the assistant bishops, Isaac Oluwole and Charles Phillips. Outside of a mass 'stay at home' Lagos had little opportunity to show its resentment, since it did not come under the jurisdiction of the 'settlement'. Lagos was still part of the diocese of Sierra Leone rather than of Western Equatorial Africa.

The interior, Abeokuta and Ibadan, heartily welcomed the new assistant bishops. Tugwell therefore placed Bishop Phillips over Ondo, a pagan area where no English missionaries had ever worked. Phillips led a team of black clergy to evangelize Ondo in a similar arrangement to Crowther's in 1864. Bishop Oluwole was to take over Abeokuta, an area of long-established Christian congregations. At this point the theory and practice of the C.M.S. broke down. In theory, the C.M.S. proposed to place assistant bishops over the larger Christian communities, such as Lagos, Freetown, and Bonny, which were self-supporting, possessed some diocesan organization and well-established schools. After a few years of successful operation the area would be created a diocese and the assistant bishop raised to a full and independent bishop. This theory in the circumstances was impractical, since in the larger Christian communities the English missionary had firmly entrenched himself and refused to work under a black bishop. Furthermore, a large section of Africans opposed this scheme as being designed to postpone independent bishops. Even those willing to try the C.M.S. theory were unwilling to submit to assistant bishops who were appointed, not because they were natural leaders or gifted men, but because they were willing to be pliable instruments in white hands. The Abeokuta English missionaries refused to work under Bishop Oluwole. Since Bonny would not have him and Lagos was in another diocese, Oluwole resided in Lagos and ran errands for Bishop Tugwell.

In 1898 Lagos was transferred to the diocese of Western Equatorial Africa. Oluwole was placed in charge, entrusted with full powers in Tugwell's absence. This put Oluwole in a position where he was sure to fail. He, too, could be used as another Crowther to prove the inability of Africans to lead and the unwillingness of Africans to follow men of their own colour.

Tugwell failed as a bishop in two ways. In the first place he was first a missionary, then a bishop. He desired to place his assistants in charge of the episcopal work, while he was free to push missionary plans on the Christian frontiers. Granted, his diocese was immense. No one man could handle properly the established Christian communities on the coast, as well as organize the advance into the Ibo country and Northern Nigeria. The missionaries of the interior complained that he was always in Lagos, while every crisis in Lagos found him in the far interior. The C.M.S. were prepared to remedy the situation if Tugwell gave them leadership. But he wished to keep all of Nigeria and the Gold Coast under his personal control, multiplying assistant bishops as his emissaries. His second failing arose partly out of the first and partly out of his own view of Africans. He never grasped that religious politics were as much a part of African society as of English. In passing through a serious church crisis he never understood the most simple and fundamental facts of local politics. The cavalier manner in which he placed full power in Oluwole's hands in the explosive situation in Lagos and promptly left on a fourteen-month tour of the north proved this. Upon returning to Lagos he seemed not to grasp that a bishop's power lay in moral suasion and respect, and not in the colour of his skin.[1]

He was not unaware of the subtleties of power in an English context. He adroitly quelled doubts in England over his policies. He refused to force the English Abeokuta missionaries to submit to Oluwole's supervision, or move them, upon their threats of 'pulling strings' in London.[2] He appeared super-sensitive to issues involving the parent committee of the C.M.S. His skilful manipulation vetoed all its plans for West Africa without an explosion. But in West Africa he seldom remained long enough in one place to grasp the fundamentals of church life.

Tugwell recognized three problems—the desire for African supervision in Lagos and the Delta, his own belief that African diocesans would leave the Anglican church, and an old element now returned to the C.M.S. Committee who were determined to create African bishops. In the C.M.S. Wigram and Lang, the architects of the settlement of 1894 to which Tugwell was committed, had been replaced. The rebels, Cust and Whiting, who resigned in protest against that settlement were back and determined to press on with promoting African leadership.

[1] Tugwell to the Church Wardens, 12 Mar. 1901, and 16 Mar. 1901, *Standard Collection*, nos. 12 and 18.
[2] H. Duncan and Mrs. Wood to Harding, 20 Feb. 1899, *C.M.S.*, G3 A2/O, no. 54.

In 1899 the committee persuaded James Johnson to accept the position of assistant bishop over the Niger Delta. Tugwell swung behind this proposal, since it would bring the Delta under C.M.S. influence. It would quieten those hostile to the settlement of 1894 and provide Oluwole with solid support in Lagos. It would appease the C.M.S. parent committee.

The price he had to pay was high. Johnson accepted on condition he be allowed to begin a £10,000 endowment fund to support an independent African bishop. The liberals in the C.M.S. Committee favoured the idea. It would destroy the financial argument against a diocesan bishop and provide him with real independence. In their view it was Crowther's financial dependence on the C.M.S. which contributed to his downfall. The endowment scheme was an advance over Crowther's day because the bishop would be free of the C.M.S. and only amenable to his oath of allegiance to Canterbury. The C.M.S. further strengthened Johnson's position by warning Tugwell that it would not continue indefinitely to finance assistant bishops. That was not in the direction they wished to go.[1]

Tugwell was surprised at the energy the endowment scheme let loose on the West Coast. Before Johnson arrived back in Lagos from his consecration he had collected £6,000 from members of all denominations in Freetown and the Gold Coast. Panicky letters poured in to Tugwell and the C.M.S. Committee from English missionaries on the coast. It was obvious that the £10,000 would be subscribed by the time Johnson had passed through Lagos and reached the Delta. The fact that Methodists had subscribed equally with Anglicans revived fears that Johnson was planning to resuscitate the West African Church scheme.[2]

Lagos again, as in 1891, was the crisis city. There was, however, a difference between 1891 and 1900. Lagos was no longer united. In the interval Tugwell and Temple Hamlyn (English minister at Christ Church) had worked to popularize the settlement of 1894 with Oluwole as its symbol. Their efforts were directed towards the *élite* of Lagos—the wealthy merchants, the higher professionals, and civil servants. The majority of the *élite* remained exterior to the Native

[1] Correspondence Committee Minutes, 26 Sept. and 24 Oct. 1899, *C.M.S.*, G3/M, no. 64, pp. 109 and 192.
[2] Tugwell to Baylis, 25 May 1900; Johnson to Baylis, 18 Feb. 1903; Hamlyn to Baylis, 21 Apr. 1902, *C.M.S.*, G3 A2/O, nos. 106, 57, 71; Winfunke, *Causes of African Churches*, p. 6; 'Life of James Johnson', Part iv, *Nigerian Pioneer*, 20 July 1917.

church, worshipping in the white man's church—Christ Church, which did not come under the pastorate—the super organization which embraced all the other Anglican churches of Lagos. It had been Hamlyn's policy at Christ Church to emphasize denominationalism, to inculcate a love of Anglicanism, which had appeared to the missionaries as sadly lacking in 1891. Hamlyn changed procedures towards high Anglican forms in order to differentiate Anglicanism from other denominations, which since they all used the Anglican Book of Common Prayer, were organized on the Methodist class system, and carried out Baptist-type street meetings and revivals, had a surprising similarity. Hamlyn also stopped the interdenominational week of prayer.[1] It was easy at Christ Church to arouse hostility against James Johnson's doctrine of an indigenized Christianity which would leave the Anglo-Yorubas as uneasy in the church as their English counterparts. They preferred the sophistication of Bishop Oluwole and his society-conscious wife.

In the other churches of Lagos the attitude of the congregation depended upon that adopted by their respective pastors. Nathaniel Johnson, the only minister who openly welcomed the settlement of 1894, became a solid supporter of Bishop Oluwole. St. Johns Aroloya, under his direction, was almost as loyal to the establishment as Christ Church. Ebute Ero and St. Peters Faji had less vigorous leadership, inclined to sympathy for Johnson. They would fall to the successful party in the final showdown.

St. Judes Ebute Metta, composed of the Christian refugees of 1867 from Abeokuta and their descendants, were of an independent spirit. Under the leadership of J. S. Williams, a Johnson supporter, they harboured a dislike of the pastorate not only because Oluwole headed it but also because it was Lagos dominated. St. Judes on the mainland did not fancy themselves Lagosians.

The most solid hostility to the settlement of 1894 came from Breadfruit parish. St. Pauls was the heart of Lagos Christianity. It was the largest church, the most wealthy, and the most dynamic. It encompassed the entire class system of Lagos from the snobbish Anglo-Yoruba to the illiterate pagan inquirer. Its school, the best in the city, turned out a younger generation inspired by the revivals of the

---

[1] Harding to C.M.S., 16 July 1902; Harding's Memorandum to the Executive Committee, Minutes, 28 Jan.–3 Feb. 1902, *C.M.S.*, G3 A2/O, nos. 104 and 48; *Lagos Standard*, 11 Jan. 1911; J. G. Campbell, 'This, That, and Another', *Times of Nigeria*, 27 June 1921.

'eighties, who were now old enough to command respect. St. Pauls had for forty years been under the tutelage of the best African pastors—Henry and James Johnson. In no other church was the settlement of 1894 so fiercely disliked. Johnson's compromise with that settlement by his acceptance of position under it was resented and caricatured as the Anglican Church selling bishoprics at £10,000 apiece.[1]

Six months before Johnson's return Lagos was aflame. Tugwell, as usual, was hundreds of miles in the interior, having made no provision for Johnson's residence. The C.M.S. asked the Lagos church governing body—the Church Committee—if they would allow Bishop Johnson to remain as pastor of St. Pauls until Tugwell could arrange permanent accommodation for him. Bishop Oluwole influenced the Church Committee to refuse this request.[2] If Oluwole was to secure his position it was important that the immensely popular Johnson, returning as a bishop, should not long remain in Lagos. Furthermore, the key church of St. Pauls must be provided with a pastor unswervingly loyal to Oluwole who would uproot the core of hostility to the settlement of 1894.[3]

The news of the Church Committee's refusal leaked out to the public. It was surmised that Johnson was again being victimized by church authorities as he had been so often in the past. As English concern grew with the success of the endowment scheme, some in Lagos believed that the English were trying to prevent Johnson from making his appeal for funds. Oluwole was frightened at the prospect of African diocesan bishops. He had not the support or respect to hold an independent position. His power rested upon C.M.S. authority.

The Lagos churches formed a People's Committee which petitioned the Church Committee to reconsider its decision. In an interview Bishop Oluwole showed his hand. He was determined to keep Johnson from returning to St. Pauls. The disaffection began to

[1] Mojola Agbebi, 'Inaugural Sermon', 21 Dec. 1902, A.C. (Bethel), *Conference Proceedings 1901–1908*, p. 92; *Lagos Standard*, 1 Jan. 1902.
[2] Baylis to Lagos Church Committee, 10 Apr. 1900, and Lagos Church Committee to C.M.S., 29 May 1900, *Standard Collection*, nos. 2 and 3.
[3] Lagos Church Committee interview with Breadfruit delegates, 13 Sept. 1900; Phelan to Tugwell, 23 Sept. 1901. Breadfruit petition to Bishop Tugwell, 27 Sept. 1901, *Standard Collection*, nos. 7, 31, 31A; Harding to Baylis, 27 Dec. 1900. *C.M.S.*, G3 A2/O, no. 7; Baylis to Tugwell, 13 Dec. 1901, *C.M.S.*, G3 A2/L8. pp. 39–40.

crystallize around Oluwole. Though warned of possible confusion, he came to St. Pauls on Sunday, 30 September 1900, to conduct the service. As he mounted the pulpit during the singing of a hymn, half of the congregation left their seats and walked out of the church. Word flashed through Lagos. During the sermon a number of youths vigorously rang the church bell, which, being the firebell signal for Lagos, brought crowds milling around the church door. The incident embittered the two factions. Oluwole was for the first time since 1894 publicly marked as the object of dislike.

A petition of appeal was sent to Tugwell in the North. Six months after the 'bell incident' Tugwell returned to Lagos to answer the petition. During the six months both parties remained hostile. Just prior to Tugwell's arrival Bishop Johnson arrived in Lagos and returned to St. Pauls parsonage, where his family and belongings were located.

Tugwell demanded an apology from St. Pauls' parishioners for the 'bell incident' of 30 September. Johnson, as pastor, secured it for him. Tugwell rejected it. Johnson secured another which cleared the way for negotiations.[1] This first act of submission led Tugwell to underestimate the opposition and overestimate Johnson's influence in St. Pauls. Tugwell entered into correspondence with the People's Committee, in which he outlined his theory of church government. He said that Bishop Oluwole had been in charge with full powers. If the people refused to accept his authority they were indicating that the assistant bishops could never evolve into diocesans—an evolution which Tugwell assured them was his greatest desire. The People's Committee emphasized that they desired a voice in church government whether the bishop was black or white. Only in blatant autocracies was there no right of appeal. In England, even in endowed benefices, the parishioners had a right to protest. How much more was this necessary in Lagos, where pastors were wholly supported by their parishioners! The People's Committee were asking for the substance of a resolution passed by the C.M.S. in London while this correspondence was in progress that unwanted pastors should not be foisted on unwilling congregations.[2]

---

[1] Johnson to Breadfruit Parishioners, 17 Oct. 1900; S. E. Savage to Tugwell, 31 Mar. 1901, *Standard Collection*, nos. 10 and 21; Jones to Baylis, 27 Oct. 1900, Tugwell to Baylis, 20 Mar. 1901, *C.M.S.*, G3 A2/O, nos. 149 and 58. J. K. Coker to Tugwell, 15 Mar. 1901, *Coker Papers; Lagos Standard*, 11 Dec. 1901; J. O. Lucas, *The History of St. Pauls 1852–1945*, Lagos, 1945, p. 37.

[2] For the correspondence between Tugwell and the People's Committee culminating in an interview, 12 Mar.–4 Apr. 1901, see *Standard Collection*, nos. 11–

Tugwell did not concede this right, but he worked out a compromise satisfactory to both sides. He upheld the Church Committee and Bishop Oluwole by asking Johnson to resign, and then requested the Committee to allow him to decide when the resignation should take effect. He extracted a promise from Johnson that he would not make his appeal for the Endowment Fund in the tense atmosphere then prevailing in Lagos.

Tugwell had won a breathing space through a compromise which kept everything in balance. The missionaries were pacified by stopping the Endowment. Oluwole's authority had been upheld and Johnson was pastor of Breadfruit. But the arrangement, which left all the problems unsolved, was temporary. One would have expected that in the few months of respite given him Tugwell would not only have been fair but also have taken great pains to appear so. In his clumsy handling of the transition which still had to be made he showed that he had never understood the problem he had temporarily solved. He relied on his own prestige and white skin.

In July 1901 Johnson went to the Delta on an episcopal visit. While he was away Tugwell announced that his resignation had taken effect. Johnson returned and found his family and belongings in the street. He had neither a place of residence nor taken formal leave of his congregation. Immediately the Patronage Board (Bishop Oluwole being one of its three members) nominated Nathaniel Johnson, a close friend of Oluwole, to the vacant incumbency. It was difficult for the parishioners to believe that Tugwell was not a party to the whole affair.

Breadfruit parishioners were infuriated. The shabby treatment of Johnson was overshadowed by his successor. They petitioned for Rev. S. A. Coker, curate of St. Pauls, and the foremost pastor in the Johnson tradition. Treating the petition with silence, the Patronage Board announced six days later that Nathaniel Johnson had accepted the nomination.

Nathaniel Johnson and Simeon Coker were leading protagonists of opposing views in Lagos. Johnson, the elder and conservative, and a loyal friend of the missionaries and Oluwole, supported the settlement of 1894 as the safest path to an orderly and responsible church. Coker, at thirty-nine, was discontented with the premium placed upon age in the pastorate and eloquent in defence of African leadership.

22; Memorandum on the Constitution of Churches in the Mission Field, revised Mar. 1901, *C.M.S.*, G3/M, no. 65, p. 679.

Instead of compromising with a clergyman less committed to either viewpoint, Tugwell confirmed the nomination 'with pleasure'. The People's Committee persisted in continuing correspondence over the rights of laity to have a voice in the choice of their pastor. Tugwell refused to reply.[1]

The first crisis had been a threat to the authority of Oluwole. In Tugwell's mind it was caused by the contempt in which Blacks held Black leadership. The second crisis was a threat to his own authority. No compromise was possible. He called in S. A. Coker and accused him of encouraging the petition to secure the pastorship of St. Pauls. Coker resigned. He called on the officers of St. Pauls demanding a written pledge of loyalty to N. Johnson, the new pastor. The officers asked permission to consult the parishioners. Tugwell refused and accepted their collective resignations. He turned down offers of mediation from Bishop Johnson, Christ Church parishioners, and the uncommitted clergy of Lagos. He accused Bishop Johnson of fomenting the whole affair for his own selfish ends and ordered him to leave immediately for the Niger Delta.[2]

Bishop Johnson preached his farewell on 13 October 1901, the anniversary of the expulsion of the Christians from Abeokuta in 1867. At the same hour eight hundred of the parishioners were holding their first separate service nearby on the Marina.[3] D. J. A. Oguntolu was laying the foundation of the African Church Organization with a sermon from the text:

Look not upon me, because I am black . . . they made me the keeper of the vineyards; but mine own vineyard have I not kept.[4]

Four days later Tugwell instituted N. Johnson as the new pastor of St. Pauls Breadfruit Church.

Bishop Johnson made one last effort at conciliation. After long hours of bargaining he persuaded J. K. Coker, who was now leading the secession, to change his stand. Coker asked for a week's

---

[1] *Standard Collection*, 3 Aug.–27 Sept. 1901, nos. 23, 31A; Tugwell to Baylis, 12 July and 9 Aug. 1901, *C.M.S.*, G3 A2/O, nos. 103, 108; *Lagos Standard*, 4 Dec. 1901. *Revised Constitution of the African Church*, Lagos, 1951, p. 2.

[2] *Standard Collection*, nos. 31B–31D; Yoruba Executive Committee Minutes, 14 Oct. 1901; Tugwell's interview with Johnson, 15 Oct. 1901 (Private);Tugwell to Baylis, 11 Nov. 1901, *C.M.S.*, G3 A2/O, no. 137 and enclosure, 136; J. K. Coker in *Lagos Standard*, 4 Dec. 1901; J. K. Coker, History, 1941, *Coker Papers*: A.C. (Bethel) *Conference Proceedings 1901–1908*, pp. 28–29.

[3] Tugwell to Baylis, 11 Nov. 1901 and Tugwell interview with Johnson, 15 Oct. 1901 (Private), *C.M.S.*, G3 A2/O, nos. 136, 137: J. K. Coker, History, 1941, *Coker Papers*.   [4] Song of Sol. i. 6, quoted in Coker's History.

postponement of the installation of N. Johnson to give him time to effect a reconciliation. Johnson confidently approached Tugwell, who refused a postponement.

The second service of secession was held the following Sunday. At the close of the service a messenger arrived calling, 'Come back, come back, Bishop Johnson is weeping'. After a brief pause a woman remarked that if Christ had turned back at his mother's tears the salvation of the world would have been lost, and taking up 'Onward Christian Soldiers', the secession hardened into schism.[1] Johnson had lost his magic leadership over those whose ideas he had moulded. He now appeared conservative and committed to the established order. The secession left Johnson inside the Anglican Church without a following, and the secessionists embarking on a historic adventure, leaderless.

The *Lagos Standard*, owned and edited by a foundation member of the U.N.A., published a special issue devoted to the correspondence and history of the secession.[2] Contributions poured in from all over Lagos. Labour and materials were donated by the community. Within a month a building had been erected. On 22 December 1901 the new building was dedicated and named 'Bethel' by J. S. Williams, the Anglican pastor of St. Judes with the words, 'this day we lay the foundation of the church for the black race. . . .'[3]

After the institution of N. Johnson while Tugwell left for the interior the seceders continued to agitate until every church of the pastorate was 'honeycombed' with them. Conciliators, J. S. Williams acting as one, hoped Bethel would settle down as another Anglican church in Lagos. Conciliation was unwelcome, and Oluwole condemned Williams' service to Bethel as traitorous, ordering him to confine his activities to St. Judes.

Under Williams' leadership the congregation of St. Judes severed their connexion with the pastorate (not the Church of England). They claimed that the church land had been given to the Christian refugees from Abeokuta in 1867. The C.M.S. had no claim to it.[4] With Tugwell away, and Oluwole powerless, the Church Committee made no effort to replace Williams at St. Judes.

[1] Coker's History: A.C. (Bethel) *Conference Proceedings 1901–1908*, p. 29.
[2] *Lagos Standard*, Special Issue, vol. viii, no. 8, 8 Nov. 1901, referred to as the *Standard Collection*.
[3] Coker's History: A.C. (Bethel) *Conference Proceedings 1901–1908*, pp. 30–31.
[4] Harding to Baylis, 10 Jan. 1902; Resolution of St. Judes Church, 29 Dec. 1901; St. Judes to Tugwell, 31 Dec. 1901; Oluwole to J. S. Williams, 26 Dec. 1901: Williams to Oluwole, 28 Dec. 1901: St. Judes to C.M.S., G3 A2/O, nos. 24, 39

The C.M.S. delayed a year before deciding to test their rights to the property. They had just emerged the loser from long litigation in Sierra Leone upon a similar issue of removing an unwilling clergyman, which outside of the expense had damaged the image of the church in that colony.

The C.M.S. was ill informed of the crisis for which the pastorate was requesting permission to go to court. Tugwell was in the interior, and the missionaries in Lagos wrote conflicting reports. Hamlyn at Christ Church blamed the whole affair on Bishop Johnson, criticizing any attempt at conciliation, claiming that firmness was all that Africans understood. Hamlyn took over the organization of resistance to the 'Bethelites'. Under police protection he went to St. Judes to occupy the church and parsonage for the C.M.S. On his command the police broke up the service and arrested J. S. Williams in the pulpit for disturbing the peace. In the fray Hamlyn got 'roughed up' and the police arrested his assailants. Hamlyn occupied the parsonage for two weeks, but after another disturbance the Government sealed the buildings and put a police guard on the property, forbidding its use to either party. Williams won his case with damages awarded, and the other cases were thrown out of court. Hamlyn continued to write the parent committee of the C.M.S. in hysterical tones claiming the whole Anglican work would collapse if St. Judes property fell to the 'Bethelites'.[1]

The man to whom the C.M.S. officially looked for advice was their field secretary, Tom Harding. Harding was unsure that the seceders had committed any sin for which forgiveness was impossible. He warned the C.M.S. against legal action, believing that when tempers cooled both Bethel and St. Judes would return to communion. Although he warned the C.M.S. that it had heard only one side of the dispute, he refrained from saying any more, possibly fearing Tugwell's wrath. He hinted that episcopacy was the cause of it all and condemned the policy of placing the top stone (bishop) into the foundation of the Native church.[2] Whether these veiled gibes were

---

(plus four enclosures), 40; Hamlyn to Fox, 25 Sept. 1902, *C.M.S.*, G3 A2/O, no. 146; *Lagos Standard*, 19 Feb. 1902; J. K. Coker, 'The First Five Years of the African Church 1901–1906', typescript, *Coker Papers*.

[1] Hamlyn to Baylis, 21 Apr., 29 Aug., 31 Aug. 1902, *C.M.S.*, G3 A2/O, nos. 71, 139, 140.

[2] Harding to Baylis, 30 Oct. 1901, 25 Apr. and 16 July 1902, Harding to Gladstone, 15 Nov. 1902, *C.M.S.*, G3 A2/O, nos. 129, 79, 104, 156; Hamlyn to Baylis, 29 Aug. 1902, Oluwole to Tugwell, 21 Apr. 1902, *C.M.S.*, G3 A2/O, nos. 139, 77.

G

levelled at Tugwell, Oluwole, or Johnson, or episcopacy in general, was unclear.

In this confusion the C.M.S. sent Melville Jones, missionary at Oyo, to Lagos to report. At first he inclined to take Harding's view, but swung around to Hamlyn's and recommended action in the courts. Hamlyn was rewarded by Tugwell first with an Archdeaconship in Lagos, then an assistant bishopric in the Gold Coast, converted into full diocesan bishop in 1909. Harding was rapped for his view on episcopacy and relieved of his secretaryship. At his death in 1912 after thirty-two years of active service he warranted one line in Stock's four-volume history of the C.M.S.[1]

Melville Jones took charge of the court case. Neither of the contending parties held a deed. The decision rested upon oral evidence as to the exact wording of the chiefs (now deceased) when the land was given. The C.M.S. position deteriorated when the Government discovered that the police seals were illegal, hastily removed them, and the seceders recommenced services undisturbed.

After numerous meetings between the governor (a relation of Melville Jones), the attorney general, and Jones, it was agreed that the Government would enlarge its proposed expropriation of land at Ebute Metta to include St. Judes property, after which it would be returned to the C.M.S. with a proper title. The Chief Justice privately objected to the Government expropriating land it did not require for public purposes. This objection was circumvented by promising to lease St. Judes to the C.M.S. for 999 years at a peppercorn rent.[2]

The seceders contested the title before the Chief Justice, who ruled in favour of the C.M.S. They appealed before two judges from Lagos and one from the Gold Coast. The Lagos judges ruled in favour of the C.M.S., but the Gold Coast Justice had reservations. The Colonial Secretary had said in testimony that the Government had not originally intended to expropriate St. Judes property, and decided to do so only after the trouble there. Later recalled to the

---

[1] None of Hamlyn's promotions found favour with the C.M.S. Baylis to Tugwell, 25 Mar. 1904, *C.M.S.*, G3 A2/L8, p. 204; Baylis to Harding, 10 June 1902 (Personal), *C.M.S.*, Yoruba Letter Book, vol. 8, p. 62; Stock, *History*, iv, p. 65.

[2] Jones to Gladstone, 28 Nov. 1902, 7 Feb. 1903; Jones to Baylis, 26 Feb. and 9 June 1903, 20 Apr. and 10 May 1904; Hamlyn to Fox, 25 Feb. 1902; Tugwell to Baylis, 2 June 1903; Governor Macgregor to Jones, 9 June 1903; Government Notice of Expropriation, 16 June 1903; *C.M.S.*, G3 A2/O, nos. 166, 38, 55, 99, 76, 81, 100, 110.

witness stand, the Colonial Secretary claimed that he was mistaken in his earlier evidence. The Gold Coast Justice said he would have liked the court to have cleared up what appeared to him to be a serious discrepancy in the Colonial Secretary's evidence.[1] The Bethelites were granted an appeal, but the strain on funds was too great and the case failed to come before the Privy Council.

As Hamlyn had predicted, the verdict stopped the defection of Anglicans. The 'Bethelites' on their first anniversary turned themselves into a denomination under the name African Church Organization. By 1905 the new church and the Anglican mission had settled down to mutual hostility.

The crisis, the most severe ever experienced by a mission among the Yorubas, lasted two and a half years. It coloured the thinking of Anglican authorities in Nigeria, the C.M.S., and the newly formed African Church. To Tugwell and Archdeacon Hamlyn (later Bishop of the Gold Coast), followed by Archdeacon Melville Jones, who succeeded Tugwell as bishop in 1920, the schism of 1900–3 was the total failure of the policy of advancing Africans to positions of leadership.

This conviction was gradually translated into policy. When Bishop Phillips died in 1906, although there had been nothing but praise for his work in Ondo, he was not replaced. After the death of Bishop Johnson in 1917 the terms of the trust of his endowment were altered. The money was used for the support of assistant bishops—a rank perversion of the purpose for which it had been subscribed.[2] When Tugwell retired in 1920 the diocese was three times as large as in 1900. Yet he had only one assistant, Oluwole, and two English Archdeacons.

After the death of Johnson, Oluwole secured his position in the mission church. To the end he remained the White man's friend,[3] blocking all schemes for African advancement. Occasionally the bishops passed pious resolutions about provincial organization or the synod urged action towards African leadership, but there is not a shred of evidence to show that they had any intention of going beyond recording the resolution. By 1920 the settlement of 1894 had become the divine order of things accepted by all alike, English as well as African.

---

[1] F. M. Jones *vs.* J. S. Williams, 25 Jan. 1904, *High Court Records*, Chief Justice's Record Book, Oct. 1903–Jan. 1904, vol. 31, p. 38.

[2] Rt. Rev. T. S. Johnson, *The Story of a Mission*, London, 1953, pp. 123–4.

[3] Melville Jones, *The Life and Death of Bishop Isaac Oluwole*, Lagos, 1932, p. 12.

The reformers left the Anglican mission in the schism of 1900–3. In the following years Anglicans who disliked the mission policy could, and did, leave for the African Church, whose forms varied ever so slightly from its parent mission. The African Church was a safety valve for the Anglican mission, providing a home for thwarted clergy and frustrated laymen. Never before had the Anglican mission appeared so quiet and orderly—or so dead. It did not produce creative thinkers or new ideas on indigenization, organization, or evangelization. New ideas came from the English, who never before enjoyed such unchecked authority and who consequently became more indispensable than they had ever been.

The crisis of 1900–3 spurred the parent committee of the C.M.S. to action along the lines of Native Church organization. They recommended turning Johnson, Phillips, and Oluwole into diocesan bishops and united West Africa in an ecclesiastical province. They tried to persuade Tugwell to give his assistants territorial jurisdiction with salaries drawn from African sources.[1] They paid for a conference of West African bishops to discuss these issues.

The conference was held (1906). A resolution was passed to please the C.M.S.[2] Nothing was done. At the Lambeth Conference (1908) it was Tugwell and Jones who talked of going slow and the dangers of a non-White episcopate.[3] With the diocese of Western Equatorial Africa getting larger, Tugwell could only recommend its division if English bishops headed the new dioceses. Since Oluwole feared the multiplication of English bishops would cause another explosion in Nigeria, the plan was dropped.[4] Nevertheless, this was the direction in which the diocese was moving. Finally, the C.M.S. realized that it did not have the power to create diocesan organization. It could not force Tugwell to move. Since there was no agitation on the part of Africans for these changes, the C.M.S. would provoke dissension by forcing them on an unwilling bishop and an apathetic laity.

The crisis of 1900–3 left a deep division within the church to which

[1] Baylis to Tugwell, 9 Oct., 30 Oct., and 20 Nov. 1903, *C.M.S.*, G3 A2/L8, pp. 146, 147, 149–50, 168–78, Memorandum, Interview Tugwell and Group III Committee, 28 Sept. 1908, *C.M.S.*, G3 A2/O, nos. 30, 149.

[2] *Resolution Adopted by a Conference of Bishops of the Anglican Communion held in Lagos, Mar. 1906*, London, 1906.

[3] Melville Jones, 'Local Churches: Steps Towards Permanent Organization', and Herbert Tugwell, 'The Anglican Communion: Its Place in the Christian World', *Pan Anglican Congress Proceedings*, London, 1908, pp. 195–6, 251.

[4] Tugwell to Baylis, 8 Feb. 1906; 9 Apr. 1908, and 1 Oct. 1908, *C.M.S.*, G3 A2/O, nos. 35, 86, 151.

it had given birth. The majority of the seceders had been fighting the settlement of 1894, which was derogatory to the African race. The new organization wholly governed by Africans must be a witness to the promoters of 1894 of the quality of African leadership. It must wipe away the shame of 1894. Ultimately they had to champion the rights of the laity because the Government of the pastorate was manipulated in the cause of autocracy. A minority had always been irked by the way the laity had been ignored in the Anglican mission. To them this was the basic cause of the secession. They carried into the African Church an intense dislike of the historic episcopate. To be reform at all, the new organization must renounce government by bishops and enshrine lay rights in its constitution.[1] The diversion in aims plagued the African Church, causing division and strife until 1922 and an uneasy compromise thereafter.

The crisis provoked unprecedented denominational bitterness. The Anglicans had ignored the comity-minded U.N.A., but became aware of the threat of the African Church Movement to mission hegemony by the establishment of the new militant organization. The Anglicans lost no opportunity to degrade their unwelcome off-spring. The African Church retaliated by dogging the missionaries into every town in the Yoruba country and building a church across the street from each Anglican mission to proclaim freedom from 'the thraldom of the priesthood' and 'spiritual policemen'.

Even before the crisis had subsided, the African Church was confronted with the problem of polygamy, when delegates from an interior Anglican mission offered to join the new organization if they were allowed to keep their wives and children. Two factors influenced the church. During the crisis 'foreign forms' and indigenous Christianity had not been prominent factors as in 1891 when the U.N.A. was established. The new organization was content with Anglican forms, resenting any efforts by their new leaders to tamper with them.[2] On the other hand, the founding fathers realized that the African Church required support if it was to carry its heavy financial obligations in Lagos as well as push a vigorous missionary programme in the interior. The crisis had unleashed a wave of enthusiasm, but enthusiasm in competition with mission education would not win support in the interior.

[1] *Conference Proceedings of the African Church, Ebute Metta, April 28–May 5, 1907*, pp. 32–46.
[2] N. A. Onatolu to J. K. Coker, 3 June 1919, *Coker Papers*.

The admittance of polygamists to membership and the communion table had two attractions. There was much literature written by both black and white questioning the morality of preventing converts from partaking of communion because they refused the questionable step of expelling their wives and children from the home.[1] There was the belief that polygamy was a question of social and economic rather than moral issues. Furthermore, the Bible seemed non-committal. Secondly, by admitting polygamists, the African Church would have the powerful lever it needed to break into the interior. For although Anglican membership in the interior was meagre, their catechumen classes were filled with eager inquirers who were denied the sacraments year after year. In no other mission were the sacraments so stressed and valued. The African Church could capitalize on the desire of Anglican catechumens for the sacraments and entice them away from the mission.

When the decision was taken the majority supported admission of polygamists to membership from necessity, the minority from conviction. The majority called it 'toleration', the minority, 'acceptance'. A substantial number called it 'a lowering of moral standards' and returned to the Anglican Church.

The ruling provided an escape for Tugwell and Hamlyn. They explained the schism, in England and Nigeria, as a case of impurity and unwillingness to accept the moral teachings of the Bible. It saved Tugwell from having to answer searching questions at Salisbury Square in London. The explanation that the African Church was set up as a refuge for fornicators and adulterers implied a moral code in the missions which could not be upheld.[2] The African Church retaliated by some rather startling exposures of mission members which forced Tugwell to privately admit that:

As far as the church [Anglican] as a whole is concerned I am more and more satisfied that its condition is deplorably corrupt. It is a question

[1] The Bishops of India (notably Bishop Milman of Calcutta) were careful to take a broad position on baptism of polygamists. African bishops (with the exception of Colenso) opposed any concessions. Prior to the Lambeth decision of 1888, Bishop Bickersteth of Exeter led liberal opinion in the Church of England. Among others, T. J. Bowen, 'Should Missionaries Baptize Polygamists', *The Christian Index* (1858); E. W. Blyden, *Christianity, Islam and the Negro Race* (1887); T. J. Sawyer, *The Sierra Leone Native Church: Two Papers Read at the Freetown Church Conference* (1888); H. A. Caulcrick, *Views of Some Native Christians . . . on . . . Polygamy* (1894).

[2] S. A. Coker, *Three Sermons on the Christian Ministry*, London 1904, p. 29; Hamlyn to Baylis, 21 Apr. 1902, *C.M.S.*, G3 A2/O, no. 71.

whether those who remained are any better than those who seceded. The latter declare that all are guilty of the same offence and that monogamy does not exist in the church . . . I am quite satisfied that the number of those who are living pure lives is very small.[1]

The Anglicans were caught in a web of their own spinning. Should they undertake membership purges and drive out the secretly polygamous in their midst, they would simply swell the membership of the African Church. The African Church policy forced a softening of discipline in the Anglican mission. The result was a tacit acceptance of the polygamous member as long as he did not enrol both his wives for church membership or attempt to baptize the second wife's children. Consequently, a family of the same father would be brought up part Anglican, part Methodist, and part African Church.

The African Church insisted that the clergy be monogamous and that they uphold monogamy in the pulpit as the ideal marriage, particularly for those in modern urban economic circumstances. They refused to put bars before the communion table which God had not put there. They insisted that it was the duty of polygamous men to present all their wives to the church and bring all their children forward for baptism and Christian instruction. They were quite unwilling to lose the second and third wives and their children to other denominations as the missions continued to do.

Regardless of creeping mission tolerance of polygamy, the façade was kept well up. The ever-widening gulf of hatred and recrimination which separated the missions from their African offspring was a direct result of their but slightly diverging policies towards polygamy. The result was three great divisions in Yoruba Christendom—Roman Catholic, Protestant, and African.

The question of polygamy led to the last great schism. The Wesleyan Methodists, the third of the Protestant societies at work among the Yoruba, nearly survived the period without schism. Methodist government gave considerable scope for the laity. A Methodist circuit called its ministers. It was impossible for a situation such as St. Pauls to develop. There had been occasional friction as the laity pushed towards the adoption of certain Anglican forms, but the missionary accepted the argument that the circuit had expressed a clear desire for these changes.

An African Methodist claimed in 1911 that the mission had

[1] Tugwell to Fox, 9 Jan. 1903, *C.M.S.*, G3 A2/O, no. 28.

escaped schism because it believed in reformation after a fall. Members and ministers found guilty of misdemeanours were not expelled in disgrace, but accepted back upon repentance. Ministers were sometimes retired on half salary or no salary for a year, then re-engaged.[1] Licences were seldom revoked, since this required action by the English conference. Insubordination of an African clergyman to a European missionary might appear a serious offence in Lugard's Nigeria, but was unlikely to move an English conference to action.

The Wesleyan Methodist Missionary Society early in its history had organized the mission circuits as in England. No other mission organization had the long experience of self-government which the Methodists passed down to the African. There was little record of complaint in the mission over governmental institutions. The Methodist schismatics took over the structure they inherited with no modifications. In no other African church was the transition as smooth or the history of the new church so free from constitutional struggles. The African Methodists found it unnecessary to draft a written constitution until thirty-five years after their formation.

In 1908 G. O. Griffin became chairman of the Lagos district comprising eight circuits—two in Lagos, two in Dahomey and Togoland, and four in the Yoruba interior. He undertook a purge which either arose from the unabashed corruption under the former chairman or from Griffin's tendency towards autocracy. Griffin justified it on the basis of the former, his enemies the latter. Unlike the purges carried out on the Niger and in the American Baptist Church, Griffin let the axe fall on members of both races indiscriminately. In 'cleaning up the old régime' he charged the English with dipping into mission funds and sent them packing home. He reversed the usual procedure, and placed the financial accounts in African hands. Tagging the English as 'holiday missionaries', he accused them of being second rate. He informed the Society that if it had nothing better to send it was best to send no one. He began with a staff of seven. By 1911 he was alone for most of the year. He claimed that the Methodist work had never gone forward so rapidly. He made fluency in Yoruba a prerequisite of promotion for those who stayed with him. He doubled the number of African circuit superintendents and supervised the remaining ones himself.[2]

[1] 'Religious Denominations in Lagos', *Lagos Standard*, 6 Sept. 1911.
[2] Griffin to Brown, 21 Feb. 1910; Griffin to Perkins, 1 Mar. 1911; Griffin to Perkins, 3 Apr. 1912; *W.M.M.S.*, Lagos O.P.

He was equally thorough with the African clergy. By various means, not always orthodox Methodism, he dropped eight African clergy (half of the 1908 total) before 1917. This was a real blessing to the African churches, who inherited well-trained men. At the same time Griffin rapidly brought forward new men loyal to himself. By 1917 thirteen of the total staff of eighteen Methodist clergy had been ordained under Griffin. By 1917 the English were again in favour, with six of the circuits and the Boys High School under their control. However, it appears only fair to comment that Griffin appeared more colour blind than many missionaries, and ruthlessly dealt with either race without favour. His blinding fault was his desire to rule. He placed everything under his personal control. This gained him an ever-widening circle of African enemies within the Lagos circuit. His friends, in contrast, were devotedly loyal. Methodist work went forward. Domineered by his Anglican wife, who was older than himself and of higher social class, he drove himself on an average of sixteen hours a day. Under her influence, he freely borrowed Anglican forms and techniques.

The Lagos synod finally erupted in revolt. One African clergyman was charged before a minor synod for insubordination to an English missionary. The synod recommended leniency. Griffin appealed over its head to England. Two English missionaries, after they had left on leave, were charged, one for gross immorality, the other for habitual drunkenness and expropriation of mission funds. They were tried before the conference in England. Without witnesses they escaped the charge, one sent 'on to full connexion', and the other to 'Didsbury College for further training'.[1] A storm arose in Lagos, since the African woman accomplice of the missionary was up for disconnexion for immorality. In six months an African clergyman was accused of immorality and confessed. The Lagos synod, smarting from the earlier snub to its recommendations, stubbornly refused to vote his disconnexion.[2] One of the disconnected clergy belonged to a family which controlled one of the Lagos newspapers which took up the anti-missionary line and joined the Lagos Press in praise of the African churches. This induced Griffin to support the seditious

[1] Griffin to Brown, 10 May and 27 June 1910; Griffin to Perkins, 1 Mar. 1911; E. T. Johnson to Brown, 11 July 1910; *W.M.M.S.*, Lagos O.P.; *Nigerian Chronicle*, 18 Mar. 1910.
[2] Griffin to Perkins, 1 Mar. 1911, *W.M.M.S.*, Lagos O.P.

ordinance,[1] which was directed against the Lagos Press. His circle of enemies widened.

It was remarkable that under such provocation the Methodist clergy did not lead a schism. But in line with all other secessions from the mission churches, it was the laity who took the lead. In the Baptists in 1888 M. L. Stone went with the secession, but it was obvious when he returned to the mission that the real leadership lay with the laity. In 1891 not one of the half-dozen unemployed clergy joined the newly formed U.N.A.

In 1901 St. Pauls went into schism against the wishes of their leader, Bishop Johnson. S. A. Coker joined after the break was complete. The exception was St. Judes, where the parishioners followed their minister into the African Church. This was in marked contrast to the African churches, where invariably secessions were led by the clergy.

The missions were hierarchical organizations where the clergy enjoyed positions of power and influence. Yet they were seldom leaders, having gained ordination through willingness to render respect and obedience. Moreover, it was difficult to attain to leadership through becoming adviser in the parishioners' domestic affairs since these were primarily of a polygamous nature. The parishioner could not approach the pastor without revealing his hypocrisy. The minister mindful of mission rules was reluctant to have the domestic arrangements of the parishioner brought to his official attention. The façade of hypocrisy was a barrier between pastor and people. Disaffections arose among, and were led by, the laity.

In the African churches governed by the laity the clergy were more apt to be leaders and given opportunity to develop leadership. Since the congregation requested ordination, natural leaders were chosen. There was no façade of hypocrisy as a barrier to the clergyman becoming adviser, counsellor, and judge in his parish. The clergy submitted to only so much pressure from the hierarchy before turning to the ultimate weapon—secession.

Many English missionaries were as knowledgeable about the operation of the façade of hypocrisy as their African clergy. At an Anglican conference on marriage customs in 1902 a layman discussed its operation before the clergy, laity, missionaries, and Bishop Tugwell. At one point he turned to the audience and asked, 'Are we not all guilty of this practice?' He received a thunderous affirmative

[1] Griffin to Brown, 9 May 1910, *W.M.M.S.*, Lagos O.P.

from the audience. He then turned to the bishop and pleaded with him to 'make us all honest men'.[1] This was not a display of African race solidarity, but a striking example of African honesty. While the mission insisted upon monogamy for those seeking membership, it maintained the façade over those who went into polygamy once they were members. Occasionally examples were made of men who too openly made polygamous arrangements and by so doing endangered the hypocritical system.

Griffin (sometimes called an Anglo-Yoruba) after twenty years in Western Nigeria certainly knew the situation. Whether he undertook to extend his purge to the laity in 1917 in the interest of a 'pure church' or whether the eager new minister, D. H. Loko, was currying favours with his chairman was unclear. Possibly Methodist laymen were becoming less careful to conceal something which they had never been convinced was immoral. The year 1917 was not 1880, when the mission could expect those expelled to return repentant. Now at least four African churches were competing for mission exiles.

The break was short, clean, and without recrimination. At the Faji circuit leaders' meeting on 25 November Rev. D. H. Loko raised the issue of marriage custom and named the ten top men and leaders of Ereko Church. Two days later a crowded meeting of the members of Lagos Methodist churches listened to the indictment read by Loko. The ten admitted their 'guilt'. Griffin ordered their names removed from membership. Another member from the audience stood and asked why these ten were singled out for censure when many were guilty. On being told that evidence was available only against these ten, fifty-five stood and provided the evidence, whereby their names were removed from the rolls.

The sixty-five began to hold separate class meetings resolving to found a church 'ungoverned and uncontrolled by any foreign missionary body', in which we may 'serve God as Africans in spirit and in truth and without hypocrisy'. The first regular service was held 29 December, the leading layman preaching from the text 'What have I done now? Is there not a cause?' The new organization set a modest aim—'to give autonomy in matters of Methodist policy to a section of its adherents in Nigeria'.[2] There were few recriminations

[1] J. K. Coker, 'The First Five Years of the African Church 1901–1908', *Coker Papers*.

[2] U.A.M. (Eleja), *The Twenty Fifth Annual Report*, Lagos 1942, pp. 2–3; *The New Constitution of the U.A.M. (Eleja) Organization*, Lagos, 1951, preamble; Winfunke, *Causes of African Churches*, p. 11.

from either side. The seceders did not set out to break the parent mission. The mission set forth simply the uncoloured facts.

There are many polygamists in this organization [African Methodists] who are genuine supporters of the church and apart from their marriage complications are leading upright and God-fearing lives.[1]

Officially the new organization took the name United African Methodist Church. The populace derogatively nicknamed it *Eleja* (fish mongers), since the first services were held near the fish market. The U.A.M. cheerfully added *Eleja* after its name. It provided them with an emblem linked with early Christianity and a motto from the Bible, 'Fishers of Men'.

By 1920 the U.A.M. (Eleja) was the smallest of the African churches, and proportionately the wealthiest. It had 500 members, expenses of £300, and an income of £1,000.[2] Since it had no clergy, the laity ran the classes. The other African churches co-operated to supply a clergyman for the Sunday services. The congregation received communion from the hands of the African Church one Sunday and the U.N.A. the next without any apparent friction or confusion.

The U.A.M. (Eleja) was the only African church founded as a revolt against mission insistence upon monogamy. It made no apology for its attitude, believing that polygamy was a matter of a social framework interwoven with a certain type of economic organization. If the economic arrangement changed from one generation to another (as it had for many families in Lagos) the social framework would change, altering the marriage custom with it. It was not a moral problem. European missionaries appeared to base their hostility to polygamy not on the Bible nor on reason, but on the belief that it implied more sexual activity, and was therefore immoral. To the African it did not imply this. But the problems raised by monogamy appeared as highly immoral, bastardy and illegitimacy, with their attendant shame and fear of fathers to acknowledge their sons, brothels which flourished best in the most Christian quarters of the city, and the narrow selfishness displayed by monogamous family units.

The mission societies circulated the myth that the cause of the

[1] Griffin, *Methodist Recorder*, 1922, quoted in *The Twenty Fifth Annual Report*, 1942.
[2] *Lagos Weekly Record*, 30 Oct. 1920.

African Church Movement was the desire to practise polygamy, the unwillingness, as they put it, to accept the moral standards laid down in the Bible, and a retrogressive reversion to neo-paganism. The vehemence and persistence of mission propaganda was in itself an indication of the unwillingness of the missionaries to face the real causes, which they had largely fashioned with their own hands. If polygamy played any part at all it was in the manner in which missions used it. They tolerated concealed polygamy to prevent their demise as a denomination, but exposed it at any moment as a weapon to further their aims, to cover their mistakes, to block African leadership, and even to raise funds overseas.

The African churches protested at this misrepresentation of the facts. Yet at the same time they were convinced that their policy towards polygamy had created something of a reformation in Christianity in Nigeria. It brought the church into touch with the society in a way in which all the mission schemes of indigenization failed to do. It broke the weapon of excommunication and forced church practice to conform to that prevailing in England. It freed its converts from that alternating 'guilt-protest' mentality of mission adherents. It presented Islam with its first real challenge. It fostered the growth of a body of critical writing which the missions with all their resources had not the enthusiasm to match.

PART III

Patterns, Procedures, and Policies of Evangelization

It is the African hope that one day the African Church shall be the national church in Africa.

G. A. OKE, June 1919

BY 1922 the African Church Movement had ended its formative period, split, and divided. New denominations (or organizations as they preferred to call themselves) had been established after 1888 at the rate of one every second year, until by 1922 seventeen distinct African churches were competing for adherents. Twelve had their origin and headquarters in Lagos. Four resulted from schisms from the foreign missions; six from schism in the African churches; three were the result of the Garrick Braid movement in the Delta; another three were founded in the Yoruba interior.

The main cause of division centred around the government best suited to an African church, whether hierarchical and controlled by the clergy, or governed by a lay bureaucracy or whether congregational. If congregational, how was local church autonomy to be reconciled with organizational unity? A threefold division in the African Church Organization (1907–9) produced one of each. The A.C. (Bethel) chose a lay bureaucracy, the A.C. (Salem), a clerical hierarchy, and the A.C. (Zion), congregational democracy. In 1903 the W.A.E. established a clerically autocratic organization after a schism from the congregationally controlled U.N.A.[1]

Another cause of disunity was the degree of Africanization desirable. Was the European denomination of its origin to predominate in the new church—in its hymns, litany, dogmas, and ceremonies, or were African airs, prayer patterns, and customs to be introduced?

[1] A.C. (Salem), Conference Report, 1907; A.C. (Bethel), *Conference Proceedings 1901–8*; The Origin of St. Stephens, Lagos, 1903, W.A.E. Minute Book, pp. 1–3; Campbell, *Origin of the Thirty-six Articles of Faith and the Constitution*, Lagos, 1945, p. 2; U.N.A. Minutes, 25 Apr. and 1 May 1902, vol. i, pp. 394–8.

Was African leadership enough to create an African church, or was it merely the first step? In 1903 the Native Baptists divided over the issue African versus Baptist, Ebenezer emphasizing the Baptist and Araromi the African nature of the church. In 1921 the Ethiopian church was born out of the discontent engendered by a rigid adherence to foreign forms within many of the African churches.[1]

The divergent attitude to polygamy divided the African churches into two hostile groups. On the one side were those who, like the U.N.A. and W.A.E., claimed marriage customs were non-essentials of Christianity and permitted polygamy to the clergy and laity. On the other side were the African Church (Bethel and Salem) and U.A.M. (Eleja), which tolerated polygamy among the laity, enjoining strict monogamy upon their clergy.

The African Church Movement unleashed the pent-up energy of African leadership, which found little outlet in colonial civil life. The African churches suffered from too much leadership, while the missions complained of too little. Excess of leadership increased division.

There was an awareness of the weakness produced by disunity. As early as 1898 the Native Baptists organized a fellowship which embraced the independent Baptist churches from Sierra Leone to the Cameroons. A similar organization of the W.A.E. linked churches in the Gold Coast, Lagos, and the Niger Delta.[2] The Baptist fellowship and W.A.E. communion, like the political organization, the National Congress of British West Africa, linked the inter-colonial coastal cities with common characteristics and problems, rather than the cities with their hinterlands. The African Communion was founded in 1913 to provide fellowship among the four major organizations in Lagos. By fostering inter-communion it assisted in promoting organic unions in the following decades.

After 1922 eleven of the organizations carried out eight organic unions. By the 1940s there remained only the four major organizations: the U.N.A., the African Church, the U.A.M. (Eleja), and the W.A.E. Communion. Consolidation was influenced by the unexpected tenacity of the missions in holding their adherents and the

---

[1] *Native Baptist Church vs. Mojola Agbebi*, Suit No. 59 of 1903 in the Supreme Court of the Colony of Lagos; Adeniran, *The African Religion*, Ibadan, 1927.

[2] S. M. Harden, 'Mojola Agbebi', *Roberson Collection; An Account of Mojola Agbebi's Work in West Africa*, Lagos, 1903; Minutes of the Twelfth Annual Conference, Jan. 1924; W.A.E. Minute Book.

TABLE I

Major Divisions and Unions, 1888–1947

Organization	Date	Organizer	Unions
Ebenezer Baptist	1888	The Laity	
Araromi Baptist	1903	M. Agbebi	1914 Yoruba Baptist Convention
African Church (Bethel)	1907	The Laity	
(Salem)	1907	The Clergy	1923–1932–1936—African Church
(Evangelist)	1927	J. K. Coker	
(Penuel)	1917	A. O. Ijaoye	
United African Methodist	1917	The Laity	1936 1947 U.A.M.
Ind. African Methodist	1922	H. T. Scott	
Ind. Native African	1927	G. M. Fisher	U.N.A.
United Native African	1891	The Laity	
African Congregational	1909	S. A. Coker	
Christ Army–Niger Delta Native	1916	S. A. Coker	1917 Niger Delta Native
Garrick Braid	1919	Moses Hart	Garrick Braid
Christ Army (G.B.C.)	1917	J. G. Campbell	
West African Episcopal	1903	J. G. Campbell	1919 W.A.E. Communion
Evangelist Band	1920	E. M. Lijadu	Evangelist Band
Church of Christ	1899	T. Adebiyi	Died out
The Ethiopian Communion	1921	S. A. Oke	
The Christian Brotherhood	1918	A. Ishola	

rise of the 'Aladura' (Prayer) movement, which threatened to overwhelm orthodox Christianity.

The first association took place in 1914, when the two Native
Baptist organizations—Ebenezer and Araromi—returned to fellowship with the Baptist Mission. Araromi remained a member of the
African Communion for another ten years, but after the death of its
founder in 1917 this bridge position became more and more untenable. In 1924 Araromi fell completely under the domination of the
mission society and severed its communion connexion.[1]

The African Church, which had suffered severely from splintering,
gradually regathered its scattered branches. The major division between Bethel and Salem was healed by a union in 1922. The Evangelist and Penuel branches rejoined in the 1930s. Two of the organizations which grew out of the Garrick Braid revival in the Niger
Delta sought affiliation with organizations in Lagos.

TABLE II

Christian Adherents Southern Nigeria, 1921[2]

Organizations	West	East	Total
African or Independent Churches	32,583	57,650	90,233
Baptist (Mission and Independent)	9,204		9,204
Wesleyan Methodist Mission	13,656		13,656
Anglican Mission	86,084	197,541	283,625
Roman Catholic	26,000	125,000	151,000

The African churches as a group in 1921 controlled the second
largest following in Western Nigeria, with 33,000 adherents, 26,000
of whom belonged to the four major organizations. Added to this
were the 29,000 adherents which they held in Eastern Nigeria, plus
another 28,000 adherents of Independent Eastern churches. These

[1] Yoruba Baptist Association, *Constitution and Bye Laws*, 1914; *Baptist Proceedings*, 1916; J. K. Coker, *The African Communion 1918–1925*: A.C. (Salem)
Minutes v, p. 240.

[2] The statistics used in this chapter are the result of correlation between those
given in P. A. Talbot, *The Peoples of Southern Nigeria*, vol. iv, London, 1926,
pp. 120–4, and the statistics of the missions and African churches. For the
African Church 1907 in A.C. (Bethel), *Conference Proceedings 1901–1908*, and
for 1915, 1921, and 1927, *A.C. Papers*. For the U.N.A. see *Lagos Standard*, 25
Jan. 1911, and *Report of the Twenty Ninth Anniversary*, 1920. For the U.A.M.
'Second Annual Report', *Lagos Weekly Record*, 30 Oct. 1920 and Preacher's
Books 1921–30. For the W.A.E., *Report of the Third Anniversary*, 1906, and
Campbell to Pratt and Wulff, 13 Mar. 1920, in W.A.E. Minute Book and
African Hope, Aug. 1919. For the Native Baptist see S. G. Pinnock, *The Romance
of Missions in Nigeria*, Richmond, 1917, p. 160.

H

90,000 independent churchmen in South Nigeria formed the third
largest Christian group. The Anglicans had 284,000 and the Roman
Catholics, 151,000.

The numerous independent adherents in the Eastern Region were
due to the explosion of Christianity which occurred in the Niger Delta

TABLE III

African and Independent Church Adherents Southern Nigeria

Western Nigeria	1911–16	1919–21
United Native African (1891)	2,916	10,770
Araromi Baptist (1903)	640	1,422
West African Episcopal (1903)	352 (1906)	5,000
African Church (Bethel) 1907	2,555	9,549
(Salem) 1907	1,843	
African Church (Penuel) 1917		2,100
United African Methodist 1917		1,055
Evangelist Band 1920		2,687
Total (Western Nigeria)	8,306	32,583
Eastern Nigeria		
Affiliates of African churches of Lagos		29,225
Indigenous Eastern churches		28,435
Total (Eastern Nigeria)		57,650
Total (Southern Nigeria)		90,233

under the inspiration of the evangelist, Garrick Braid, and the
severity in the application of the comity agreements. Calabar was an
example. Under the comity arrangements, Calabar was the exclusive
preserve of the Presbyterians. Sizeable colonies of Methodists and
Anglicans were faced with Presbyterian worship or nothing. Unrest
as a result of the dislike of the dictatorial methods of the mission
was greater in Calabar than anywhere else in Nigeria. It was an ideal
setting and opportunity for the African churches, who, protected in
a sense by the mission comity agreements, had the field to themselves
and exploited the unrest with good results.[1]

Among the Yoruba, Christianity spread at different rates and in a
variety of directions, being rejected in Oyo, grudgingly and partially
accepted in Abeokuta, welcomed in Ijebu and eagerly sought after in
Ilesha and parts of Ondo. How much of the response was due to the
mission policy or to African Church activity? What part did Islam

[1] Griffin to Goudie, 1 Aug. 1918, *W.M.M.S.* (*Ibadan*), 1/4/6.

play? How much was due to the nature of the society and the political and economic changes taking place in the various Yoruba kingdoms?

The railway line running from Lagos to the Northern Region divided the Yoruba country into two unequal parts. Located on and to the west of the railway, the missionaries had been at work in the cities of Lagos, Abeokuta, Ibadan, Oyo, and Ogbomoso since the early 1850s. Conversion had been slow and results meagre—90,000 Christians by 1921. To the east of the railway, where work began fifty years later, a succession of spiritual movements had produced a conversion rate four times greater than in the west and a Christian population by 1921 of 105,000.

Table IV attempts to correlate the concentration of mission personnel,[1] both European and African, with the Christian and Muslim adherents of the two areas. It shows that the mission agents were west of the line and the spiritual movements east. Disregarding the slow rate of conversion, all the societies continued to concentrate their staff in the west. Where the Europeans were, the largest amount of money was spent, and the largest African staff employed. By 1919 there were seventy-five qualified agents in the west to thirty-five in the east. The full-staffed west was supervised by Europeans, while the neglected east developed under African leadership.

This disparity had developed because of the missionaries' unwillingness to move from the comforts provided by the railway and the financial inability of the societies to provide European amenities outside of the earlier developed centres. In addition, missionaries were disinclined to work under African leadership. The societies lacked a policy for handling spiritual movements at unexpected times and in inconvenient places. They depended upon the theory that spiritual forces could be organized and even induced. Their theories were built on the premiss that if sufficient agents were employed, money expended, and schools opened, paganism would finally yield. This was how the converts in the west had been gained. But it was a slow process, depending on the youths graduated from the schools. The tragedy of immobility was exposed at its worst by a spiritual movement in the Ekiti highlands which passed its climax in the absence of mission agents.[2] Islam reaped a fine reward.

[1] *The Proceedings* of the Mission Societies give the location each year of all missionaries.
[2] Working Plan of the Yoruba Mission, July 1910; Jones to Luggard, 14 Feb. 1913, *C.M.S.*, G3 A2/O, nos. 118, 80; Griffin to Perkins, 23 Oct. 1911, *W.M.M.S.*, Lagos O.P. Delay was caused by a comity debate on mission rights to exploit Ekiti.

TABLE IV

Concentration of Mission Personnel in the Yoruba Country, 1900–20

	1901–3		1909–11		1917–19		Protestant	R.C.	Muslim	Ratio Christian : Muslim
West of railway										
Ibadan–Oyo–Ogbomoso	15	5	17	9	17	13	23,000	1,000	106,000	1 : 4
Lagos and Colony	6	12	7	17	10	15	43,000	9,000	90,000	1 : 2
Egba Kingdom	7	9	6	15	4	15	24,000	2,000	67,000	1 : 3
Totals	28	26	30	41	31	43	90,000	12,000	263,000	1 : 3
East of railway										
Ilesha–Ife–Oshogbo	2	2	2	3	2	5	23,000	2,000	30,000	1 : 1
Ondo Central		4	2	2	3	6 }				
Ondo South (Ikale)							43,000	1,000	16,000	3 : 1
Ekiti Highlands		1		3	2	3 }				
Ijebu Kingdom	1	5	1	10	2	13	39,000	4,000	54,000	1 : 1
Totals	3	12	5	18	9	27	105,000	7,000	100,000	1 : 1

Islam spread in an inverse ratio to Christianity. Missionaries regarded Muslims as worse than pagans, since they were seldom potential Christians. Refusing to explore the advantages of Islam, they believed its success was due to the low moral standard (with specific reference to polygamy) which it tolerated. Secular writers such as E. D. Morel and clergy such as J. F. Schon, T. J. Bowen, and Canon Isaac Taylor, along with Blyden, were prepared to admit its potency—especially its commendable adaptation to African life. A few admitted its moral system was different but equal to that offered by Christianity. Others patronizingly felt it was lower, but the highest to which Africans could aspire.[1] Within the missions the voices of scorn remained preponderant.

The African Church attitude was a synthesis bolstered by a unique contribution. Mojola Agbebi and J. K. Coker believed, like the missionaries, that Yoruba conversion to Islam was a tragedy, but like Blyden, they were impressed with its adaptability. They sought to emulate its methods.[2] They believed that the Yorubas could be as effective in proselytizing for Christ as for Mohammed if the apostolic method used by Muslims replaced the society method.

The African Church was disturbed by the lowering of moral standards among converts to Islam and Christianity. One of the attractions, especially for the youth who fretted under the multiple restraints of paganism, was the greater moral freedom which the new religions offered. The older and more conservative turned to Islam as the less disruptive and the most likely to uphold the familiar moral structure. The African Church sought to replace Islam as the

[1] Stock, II, pp. 103, 449; III, pp. 118, 345–8; IV, pp. 41–3; *Lagos Weekly Record*, 3 Dec. 1892; *African Times*, 22 Oct. 1864; W. T. Balmer, 'The Position of the Negro in the Methodist Church', and W. J. Platt, 'Islam in Dahomey', in the *Foreign Field*, 1911–12, pp. 287–92, and 1917–18, p. 124; G. W. Carpenter, 'The Role of Christianity and Islam in Contemporary Africa', in C. Grove Haines (ed.), *Africa Today*, Baltimore, 1955, pp. 94–7.

[2] Agbebi? 'Our Islamic Prospects', *Lagos Weekly Record*, 26 Aug. 1893; Agbebi, 'The West African Problem', in G. Spiller (compiler), *Papers on Inter-Race Relations*, pp. 347–8; Agbebi in *Lagos Standard*, 16 Apr. 1902; J. K. Coker, *The African Church*, pp. 7–9; J. Sorinolu to J. K. Coker, 16 Aug. 1905, and Ijaiye Young Men (abroad) to J. K. Coker, 4 June 1919, *Coker Papers*; S. A. Coker, *Yoruba News*, 22 and 29 June 1924. For the spread of Islam, see *Southern Nigeria Civil Service List*, London, 1909, pp. 38, 57, 73–74, 106, 109. For a modern attitude resembling that of the African churches, see J. S. Trimingham, *The Christian Church and Islam in West Africa*, London, 1955, pp. 10–11, 17, 22–23, 31–33, and *Islam in West Africa*, London, 1953 (Confidential–not for general circulation), pp. 21–23.

preserver of the traditional structure, of which polygamy formed the core. Agbebi and Coker believed that where missionary work had been intense and European supervision effective, there Islam developed the fastest. West of the railway, where Europeans had been hardest at work for the longest period, Islam had advanced four times as fast as Christianity in Ibadan–Oyo, and three times as fast in Egba. Even in Lagos, where the Sierra Leonians gave Christianity an initial advantage, Islam had twice as many followers. European supervision meant strict discipline, which kept the majority outside the church, prolonged the spiritual vacuum, and created Muslims. African supervision even in the missions was more lax, brought more people into the church, and forestalled Islam. This laxness, which discredited African supervision in European eyes, was its justification in the minds of African churchmen. It was being in touch with reality.

TABLE V

African Churches in Relation to the Railway, 1920

Organizations	West of railway	East of railway
African Church	4,660 (400 in Ilaro)	4,893
United Native African	2,330	7,950
West African Episcopal	1,000	4,000
Araromi Baptist	600	800
Evangelist Band		2,687
African Church (Penuel)	2,000 (Ilaro)	
United African Methodist (Eleja)	1,055	
Totals	11,645 (2,500 in Ilaro)	20,320

The statistics in Table V show that the African churches were even less successful than the missions west of the railroad. The African churches turned away from the ideas of Agbebi and Coker. In the west they concentrated upon the three generations of apprentices, as Coker called them, the overtaught, and exiles of the missions.

In the east the African churches played a full part. New converts from the moment of their disillusionment with paganism (the critical stage) were offered a choice of organizations competing for their adherence. The enthusiasm and fervour of the converts carried Christianity in all directions. Groups were brought into the church. The traditional authorities were swept along and involved in Christian politics in a way those in the west had never been. The fervour and excitement produced unfortunate denominational quarrels. Christianity spread, possibly stronger in quantity than in quality, but Coker queried whether Christ judged in terms of literacy, organization, and financial support. He concluded it was unlikely.[1]

The rapid spread of Christianity east of the railway line intensified the ideological struggle within the African churches. Denominational loyalties were undeveloped. Converts shifted easily from one to the other—as easily out of the African churches into the missions as the reverse, which had become standard procedure in the west. The lapses into the missions shook to their foundations many of the dearly held theories of evangelization of African churchmen. The utility of Anglican forms in the African churches, supposed to smooth the path for the mission exiles to transfer their loyalty, was now working in reverse. It was easy for the African Church converts to go over to the C.M.S. There arose the complaints that the attractiveness of foreign marriage customs was causing serious defections to the missions—a stunning revelation to those who had pinned the hopes of the African Church to polygamy.[2]

African leadership of both the mission and African Church variety proved extraordinarily effective. The Anglican Mission to the Ijebu Kingdom was one of the most brilliantly organized. Begun in 1892 immediately after the British conquest, the Ijebu mission was entirely the work of Anglican Africans. Financed by the Lagos churches, organized by an African superintendent leading an all-Black staff, and under an assistant African bishop, himself an Ijebu, the spiritual movement which began around 1898 had by 1910 numerically and financially surpassed all the other Anglican Yoruba churches. None of the other mission societies or African churches shared this achievement. The White Methodist staff gained small results, the African Church was rendered impotent by internal dissension, and the U.N.A. was occupied elsewhere. In addition to the African staff, Anglican success was due to its emphasis upon education, which suited the materialistic ambitions of Ijebu society. Furthermore, Anglicanism was considered the true religion of the conquerors, and as such, more desirable than Methodism. Initially the African Church had gained a following, but the disputes and divisions which distressed that organization disgusted the Ijebus, who accused the

---

[1] J. K. Coker to O. Taylor, 30 June 1927, *Coker Papers*.
[2] D. A. Hughes, Ijo Report, U.N.A. Minutes, 29 Mar. 1912, II, pp. 20–22; A.C. (Salem) Minutes, 8 Apr. and 13 May 1918, IV, pp. 118–22.

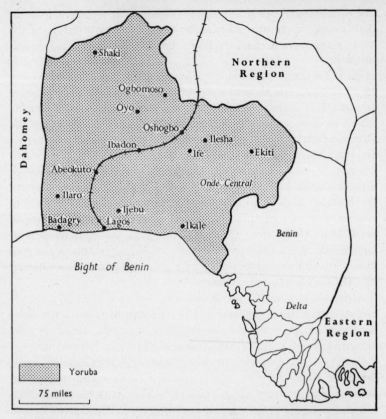

Lagosians of impotence except under White leadership.[1] The Ijebu
mission in addition escaped the depressing influence of the denigrat-
ing reports which missionaries were prone to publish in their periodicals. The reports often became the convert's first contact upon becoming literate with missionary thinking. The following was hardly
calculated to inspire confidence in the White messengers of Christ.

> For dense darkness, stupid ignorance, deep-seated hypocrisy, un-
> hesitating falsehood, shallow courtesy, double-mindedness, adept duplicity,
> to say nothing of the grosser vices, the Ijebu cannot be surpassed.[2]

[1] Reports of the W.M.M.S., 1892, 1894, 1895, 1900, 1901; *C.M.S. Proceedings,*
1900–1, 1904–9. For the A.C., see J. J. S. Nicol to J. K. Coker, 7 Mar. 1907,
Coker Papers; Lagos Standard, 2 Sept. 1903. The Anglicans were agreeably surprised at the African Church failure. Tugwell to Baylis, 14 May 1902, and
Oluwole to Tugwell, 21 Apr. 1902, *C.M.S.,* G3 A2/O, nos. 75, 77.
[2] J. B. Lowther, Ijebu Report for 1900, *W.M.M.S.,* Synod Minutes.

A similar spiritual movement occurred at the same time in the Ikale district of Southern Ondo. Ignored by the mission societies, it became the responsibility of three African churches—the U.N.A., the W.A.E., and the Evangelist Band (an African church of Ondo origin). Through the fortunate conversion of S. Ogunmukomi in Lagos in 1892, the U.N.A. was the pioneer organization in Ikale. A remarkable leader and devout Christian, Ogunmukomi, upon returning to his home, organized the spiritual movement, bringing 8,000 adherents into the U.N.A. He was deaconed by the church in 1904. His full licence was delayed for fifteen years because of the U.N.A. timidity to break with tradition and priest a man not literate in English. The mass of converts were dependent upon a hundred and fifty lay readers. With no resident priest the sacrament had to wait for the visits of the superintendent from Lagos. The pitiful condition caused by the influenza epidemic following the war, when converts were dying without the sacraments or Christian burial, forced the U.N.A. to take drastic action by giving special licence to lay readers. In 1921 Ogunmukomi was priested and made superintendent of the district.[1]

The U.N.A. Ikale mission observed in isolation was a remarkable achievement, and it may be unfair to compare it to Ijebu, one of the most successful mission enterprises. But since they occurred simultaneously and were organized by Africans dealing with a similar spiritual movement, the comparison is hard to avoid. Differences may lie in the nature of the two peoples, the Ikale and the Ijebu, and certainly the Lagos Anglicans were financially and otherwise better equipped than the few U.N.A. members of Lagos for a missionary programme of such gigantic proportions. The U.N.A. was weakened by the decentralization of its government, whereby each local church from its inception became self-governing and self-supporting. This prevented direction from the top and the channeling of the organization's finances behind the Ikale mission. Even a little money would have gone a long way, as the Ijebu mission showed.

When all this had been recorded, judged by their own criteria, and certainly in comparison with Ijebu, the U.N.A. failed in Ikale. Mention has been made of the U.N.A. fear to embark on a bold policy of

[1] G. A. Oke, Life Sketch of Solomon Ogunmukomi, 1930, Oke Collection; Lagos Standard, 11 Mar. 1903; Oke, History of U.N.A. 1904–24, p. 58; among numerous reports on Ikale the following of particular note. U.N.A. Minutes, 26 Aug. 1907, 9 Apr. 1909, 2 July 1910, 29 Mar. 1912, 3 Mar. 1919, i, pp. 444–6, 498–9, 524–6; ii, pp. 20–22, 234–7; Report of the Twenty Ninth Anniversary, 1920.

ordination. Youthful recruits from the secondary schools of Lagos were preferred for the ministry to the unlettered elders of Ikale. Denial of the sacraments could not have been greater under a mission society. Six priests ministered to 2,000 adherents west of the railway, while one attended to 8,000 in Ikale. The alternative to ordination of the unlettered was education, but it was not provided. The method employed by some other African churches of billeting youths with members to be trained in the educational institutions of Lagos was not attempted. The U.N.A. discovered that when the mission societies entered Ikale the attraction of foreign marriage and mission education were twin allurements capable of depleting their membership.[1]

The Evangelist Band was begun in Ondo in 1901 by E. M. Lijadu, a priest in Anglican orders. Until 1920 it operated in association with the Anglican Church, the C.M.S. training its agents. Entirely self-supporting from the beginning, the Band developed some rather remarkable indigenization in organizations and methods under its able promoter. Important men in the C.M.S. supported Lijadu, believing he was developing a unique and worthy missionary method. Upon the death of Lijadu's most ardent missionary supporter, pressure was brought to bear upon the Band by those who had always resented its independence, to bring it under more direct C.M.S. control. In 1920 the Anglican bishop refused to ordain candidates graduated from the C.M.S. training institutions unless the Band placed all its property under C.M.S. trusteeship. Suspicion developed on both sides until Lijadu broke his affiliation with the Anglican Church.[2] The Band claimed its main support from Ode Ondo, south to the Ikale country. Protracted litigation with the C.M.S. retarded and hindered its growth and prevented it from devoting its energy to the work in Ikale.

In Ondo Central Bishop Phillips and an African staff opened work for the C.M.S. in 1894. Like Crowther, Phillips worked in association with the traditional authorities. Even after Phillips' death, African churches were discouraged from promoting in Ondo. The secular authorities continued to show preference for 'those of Bishop Phillips' persuasion'.[3] After Phillips' death in 1906 the leadership of the mission passed to one of the senior pastors. Rapid conversion

---

[1] Hughes, Ijo Report, U.N.A. Minutes, 29 Mar. 1919, ii, pp. 20–22.
[2] Ondo and Ilesha District Papers relating to Development of churches and schools 1907–23, *C.M.S.* (*Ibadan*), Y 2/2/11.
[3] G. M. Fisher to J. K. Coker, 19 Feb. 1914, *Coker Papers*.

began in 1911, and though slower to react than Ijebu, Ondo moved rapidly and steadily to become the most Christian of all the Yoruba areas. Conversion to Islam was negligible.

In the Ilesha–Ife–Oshogbo area the three societies, C.M.S., Methodist, and Baptist, were at work by 1900. Rapid conversions began around 1910. The African Church came to the area through the influence of the labourers from the Agege plantations who had returned to their homes bringing cocoa culture and Christianity. They persuaded their chiefs to invite the African Church. The towns of Oyan and Ikirun became African Church strongholds. Taking advantage of local secessions from the C.M.S., the church spread to Ilesha and Oshogbo.

As in Oyan, the traditional rulers were from the first involved with the Christians. In 1891 a Christian king was installed in Ilesha. He invited the Methodist and his court actively supported their work. In 1904 the Oni invited the African Church to build a church in Ife in order to chastise the C.M.S., who had become intractable. The secular authorities assisted in the building of the new church and lent their official patronage by attending the dedication of the first edifice in 1906.[1]

The secessions were not all towards the African Church. In 1918–19 there were lapses back into the missions in both Oshogbo and Ilesha. The healthy competition pushed all denominations to their utmost efforts. When the heavy flow of converts began after 1920 the stiff competition relaxed discipline and swept many into Christianity who in the circumstances prevailing in areas west of the railway would have turned to Islam. Success in this area was a major victory for Christianity, since all the towns lie on the main north–south trade routes under circumstances in which Islam was believed to have particular advantages.

The African churches preferred to refer to their methods of expansion as evangelism rather than missionary. Mission societies and their employees—the missionaries—represented the professional and indicated a lack of spontaneous enthusiasm for the conversion of the non-Christian. They created missions (or half-churches) in which the secondary motives of conversion—education, position, ambition—appeared more predominant than spiritual forces. The societies

[1] *Work and Workers*, 1903, p. 338; Coker's History, Coker, 'The First Five Years of the African Church 1901–1906', *Coker Papers; C.M.S. Proceedings*, 1904–5, 1905–6.

assumed the pose of being more preoccupied with keeping the converts out when they threatened to overwhelm established order by their numerical strength than they were in sweeping them in. Fear—the fear of losing control and the fear of the church changing its character from the image in which it was conceived by the missionaries—was a deterrent to methods not proven safe by long usage.

In 1925 a group of laymen within the African Church were convinced that the organization was not sufficiently alive to its evangelistic responsibilities. They organized an African Church Evangelistic Society as a branch of the organization patterned upon the example of the C.M.S.—the missionary arm of the Anglican Church. Evangelism took precedence over church order (again like the C.M.S.) and the Society came into conflict with the hierarchy of the church. A period of estrangement followed, when many bishops refused to ordain candidates to holy orders recommended by the Society. For a short while the Society operated as a separate organization.

This copying of foreign forms—a reversion to missionary methods —did not work well. In 1932 the Evangelistic Society was reabsorbed into the main body of the church.[1] Evangelism was too urgent, too vital and central to the life of the church for it to be delegated to a society. It was based on a presumption difficult to maintain that the hierarchy was unconcerned with evangelism.

Evangelism was the main preoccupation of the African churches. Every individual member, lay or clergy, was an evangelist. He was unpaid. There were no missions. From the moment a few individuals came together to worship a church emerged self-governing and self-supporting. Other churches or the organization might assist, but this implied no obligation on the part of the receivers nor conferred any privilege upon the donors. Evangelistic methods were rarely discussed, since this implied an organization of spiritual forces. They were not the concern of the corporate body of the church. The problem was how to keep up to the expansion and how to meet the demands for the sacraments and teachers.

In most cities an African church was established by a core of seceders from one of the missions. The seceders approached the African church resembling the mission from which they had come. Methodists called upon the U.N.A. or U.A.M. (Eleja). C.M.S.

---

[1] A quantity of material on the A.C.E.S. in the *Coker Papers*.

seceders wrote or sent delegations to the African Church (Bethel or Salem).

Requests from far away were turned down—from Liberia 1901, from C.M.S. members in Opobo 1898, and Afikpo 1913, and from Methodists in Klein Popo and Sekondi 1909. Those closer to Lagos were accepted. The U.N.A. established in Abeokuta in 1893, in Porto Novo 1901, and in Kano 1920 by organizing seceders from the missions. The African Church similarly began in Odopotu 1902, Ife 1904, and Warri 1912. More rarely the secessions were from one African church to another. In 1903 Ikorodu U.N.A. joined the W.A.E. and then in 1916 returned to the U.N.A. In Buguma the Araromi Baptists called upon the A.C. (Bethel) when they refused to follow Araromi organization back into fellowship with the Baptist Mission Society in 1914.[1]

The lack of agents and the working of mission gentlemen's agreements worked to the advantage of the African churches. Under the gentlemen's arrangements the mission society which began operation first held a monopoly. A priest living in a centrally located city claimed (on the strength of a shed for worship and an annual visit) a monopoly of a number of surrounding villages.

The villages resented this neglect. The minimum conditions they demanded was a resident teacher-catechist, a church building with iron roof and bell, and monthly sacraments by a visiting priest. They were not met. Many villages remained unvisited for years. The sacraments were highly valued, yet most Christians were denied them. When this was pointed out to the C.M.S. the bishop questioned the value of too frequent communion for primitive peoples.[2]

The African churches eagerly accepted invitations from the villages. Once they began services, the mission defended its prior claim. Colonial officers, in the interest of tranquillity, preferred to uphold the gentlemen's agreements. A typical case arose in Idoanni, a town

[1] Oke, 'Important Events in History of U.N.A. 1891–1915', *Oke Collection*; U.N.A. Minutes, 28 Aug. 1901 and 30 July 1921, *i*, p. 384, and *ii*, pp. 320–3; A.C. (Bethel), *Conference Proceedings 1901–1908*, pp. 67–70; A.C. (Salem) Minutes, 3 Sept. 1912, *ii*, pp. 125–8; W.A.E. Minutes, 2 Jan. 1904; U.N.A. Minutes, 14 Jan. 1916, *ii*, pp. 121–7; Delta Baptist Mission (Buguma) to Agbebi, 3 Dec. 1913, and Agbebi to J. K. Coker, 19 Jan. 1914, *Coker Papers*; W. A. Amakiri, 'The Spread of the Gospel Message to Okaki and Other Places' and Amakiri to Roberson, June 1955, *Roberson Collection*.

[2] Bengt Sundkler, *The Christian Ministry in Africa*, Uppsala, 1960, p. 70. For similar Methodist attitudes see W. Goudie, 'Progress in West Africa', *Foreign Fields*, 1915–16, p. 46.

near Owo. The C.M.S. arrived first. After a period of neglect the African Church (Salem) took up work, and by the time the C.M.S. asked the government officer to uphold the gentlemen's agreements the African Church was the larger. The Resident asked the African Church to withdraw, since the town was too small for two denominations. The African Church pointed out that it was neither bound by mission agreements nor could be, since it would exist where Africans existed. African Church land was not vested in an authority outside the village like mission property, but in the local Christian community. Since the agreements were enforced through the denial of land to a second mission society, the African Church could not be compelled to abandon Idoanni.[1] The Resident respected the logic of the argument.

Occasionally, as at Ode Ondo, where the chiefs held a strong preference for Bishop Phillips' church, the District officer requested the African Church to delay its entrance temporarily to prevent open strife.[2] The African Church (although built on private property) complied with the Government's request. This compliance was possible because generally the government officers remained impartial and the African Church came to rely on them as judicious arbiters.

Gentlemen's agreements had been designed by the missions with the best intentions, to prevent hostility and strife between denominations which weaken the unity of Christianity in pagan eyes. It seems unlikely that interdenominational strife did have this effect.[3] It was more plausible that these agreements were partly at least caused by the sensitivity of the missions to their European critics, who enjoyed poking fun at the quarrels of new converts over denominational issues, which in their patronizing frame of mind they felt were far too sophisticated for the African to comprehend.[4]

Another powerful advantage of the agreements to the missions was that it gave them freedom of choice in the employment of their money and agents. Schools and churches were built and agents located where they best suited the missionary. Influence which the people might bring to bear by threatening to 'go over' to another society was reduced. In matters of discipline the societies feared inter-

---

[1] A.C. Members of Idoanni to J. K. Coker, 1 Sept. 1918; Coker to A.D.O. (Pategi), 1 Apr. 1921; Coker to ——, n.d., *Coker Papers*. Another example 'Report of a Missionary Tour to Idimu', June 1907, W.A.E. Minute Book.

[2] D.O. (Ondo) to Coker and Lakeru, 22 Feb. 1915, *Coker Papers*.

[3] Trimingham, *Islam in West Africa*, p. 32.

[4] H. Johnston, *The Gay-Dombeys*, London, 1924, pp. 214–15.

denominational competition which might tempt missionaries to 'lower' the standard for admission of members.[1] In the long run the agreements were popular because they assisted the missions to maintain control. As the African churches said, the major consideration was to keep the barriers up rather than tear them down.

It became a severe disappointment to the African churches that although Lagos was their point of origin, they had been unable to break the hold of the missions over their adherents. The African churches never achieved respectable status in Lagos. Upper-class society (wealthy merchants, the professionals, the civil servants) remained within the missions. African church youths, educated for the professions overseas, upon return to Lagos sought membership in the missions not, as they privately admitted, because of conviction but because of social and economic benefits.

In search of this illusive respectability the cathedrals or mother churches of the organizations, especially Bethel and Jehovah Shalom, developed, along the lines of Christ Church, St. Pauls Anglican, and Tinubu Wesley, towards greater formality and ceremony. With the expansion of Lagos, many left the crowded island and built residences on the mainland in Ebute Metta. The missionaries were slow to follow this movement—the African churches quicker. They built large and respectable churches—Salem and Bethlehem (African Church) and Christ Church (U.N.A.), which by 1914 surpassed the cathedrals on Lagos island in numerical and financial strength. The social strictures of Lagos were never completely transferred to Ebute Metta, which engendered a kind of suburban social freedom conducive to the growth of the African churches.

Lagos was a city of comings and goings. New arrivals entered the city in search of economic or educational opportunities and returned a few years later to the interior for retirement or another kind of economic benefit. Many arrived pagan; it was up to the church to see they returned Christian. In the new and strange environment of Lagos the pagan youth was particularly receptive to a new religion, and he presented the church with an opportunity for evangelism which reached far beyond the confines of the city itself. The more sophisticated the churches remained, like the cathedrals with English service and foreign music, the less they attracted the pagan immigrant. Those like St. Stephens (W.A.E.) and Araromi Baptist used

[1] Annual Letter to Lagos District Synod, 20 Dec. 1917, *W.M.M.S.* (*Ibadan*), 1/1/1.

African music to attract and the Yoruba language to instruct. The new Christians, with the enthusiasm of the newly converted, returned to the interior eager to propagate the faith and call upon the denomination of their conversion for assistance. To a greater or less extent, all the churches followed their Lagos converts to the interior.[1]

A similar but more effective system operated at Agege. The construction of the railway enabled a number of African Churchmen, J. K. Coker, F. E. Williams, A. A. Obadina, and others, to escape the frustrations of Lagos economic and social conditions by the development of plantations of coffee and cocoa in the Agege district, a few miles north and west of Ebute Metta. By 1920 Agege was one of the richest agricultural areas in Nigeria. The income of the planters was reflected in their churches, which surpassed the combined Lagos and Ebute Metta churches in 1920, just as Ebute Metta had surpassed Lagos island in 1914.

The plantations required unskilled labour, which was recruited in the interior and hired on a year's contract. Churches were built on the plantation, where the labourers were encouraged to become Christians. They returned to their interior homes to propagate the faith and build churches. They appealed for assistance to the planter, who accepted the position of patron, supplying building materials and agents' wages. In return, the planter's generosity ensured a stable supply of labour for the plantation, an important consideration, especially during the post-war inflation, when high wages in Lagos siphoned off labour coming from the interior to Agege.[2] J. K. Coker was the most generous of the Agege patrons. In 1918 he undertook the entire financial responsibility for Ikirun, Oyan, and Idoanni evangelistic work.[3]

It was typical of African evangelistic endeavours to be of an individual rather than a group nature. This was of immense value in the propagation of a religion, where the personal contact of an in-

[1] C.M.S. Proceedings, 1899; W.M.M.S. Reports, 1907, 1912; 'In no place has the missionary been the actual pioneer of Christianity', Work and Workers, 1892, p. 216; Campbell, Origin of the Thirty-six Articles of Faith, p. 3; J. K. Coker to ——, n.d., Coker Papers.

[2] A.C. (Salem) Minutes, July 1912, ii, p. 124; Interview A. O. Coker, 8 Dec. 1961. For a fuller discussion of how cocoa and the African Church spread from Agege, see J. B. Webster, 'Agege: Plantations and the African Church 1901–1920', Conference Proceedings of the Nigerian Institute of Social and Economic Research, 1962.

[3] Opebi to Coker, 24 Oct. 1918, Coker Papers; A.C. (Salem) Minutes, 22 Oct. and 10 Feb. 1918, 16 Feb. 1920, iv, pp. 157, 172–8, and 223–9.

dividual scores numerous advantages over the formal relations of a group. There was very little evangelism financed by societies in churches—women's societies, or men's clubs.[1]

Individual activity blossomed in multiple forms. John O. George, one of the founders of the U.N.A., worked among the neglected and stubbornly pagan aboriginals of Lagos. Through his efforts, Erelu U.N.A. Church was built and an agent employed—the financing and personal labour of evangelizing being carried out by George. Similarly, D. J. A. Oguntolu introduced Christianity to Otta, his native place. A. A. Obadina, who upon his retirement became a planter at Agege, was an employee of the Nigerian Regiment. While stationed in Calabar, he preached to the local people and was the first to open an opposition church to the Presbyterian mission.[2]

Sometimes these early pioneers were ordained and lived long enough to see the church of their conversion firmly established among their own people. S. Ogunmukomi has been mentioned in connexion with the U.N.A. in Ikale. Charles Jemiriyi, a Lagos convert, established Araromi Baptists in his native Ekiti. In 1916 his long services were rewarded and he was ordained to become superintendent of the Baptist Ekiti Mission.[3]

In 1905 G. T. A. Thompson, a retired government pensioner in the Gold Coast, successfully gathered congregations in Accra and Sekondi. He came to Lagos, sought and gained affiliation with Campbell's W.A.E. Church who priested him to carry on his work. In 1924, after Thompson's death, but as a result of his work, the Christianborg Patriarchate of the W.A.E. Communion was organized under a Patriarch leading an ordained staff of five. The patriarchates of Assim, Ashanti, and Cape Coast originated through similar individual activity.[4]

In a few cases the pioneer organizer operated his church or church organization for a fairly long time before considering it wise to affiliate. H. T. Scott organized an independent African Methodist church in Ibadan in 1922. G. M. Fisher, as a result of evangelistic

---

[1] They were attempted, see A.C. (Salem) Minutes, 6 May 1913, *ii*, pp. 143–4.

[2] U.N.A. Minutes, 11 Dec. 1896, *i*, pp. 235–6; Oke, *History of the U.N.A.* 1891–1903, p. 6; *Lagos Standard*, 24 May 1899; Coker, 'The First Five Years of the African Church 1901–1906': *African Church Chronicle*, Jan.–Mar. 1935.

[3] N. F. Fatunla, 'Short History of the Baptist Mission in Ekiti District', *Ogbomoso Library*, *The Dawn*, Oct. 1916.

[4] Campbell, *Report of the W.A.E. Communion*, 1924; Autobiography of G. T. A. Thompson, 1914, W.A.E. Minute Book.

I

work in Badagry, set up an Independent Native African organization. Both ultimately affiliated with the U.A.M. (Eleja), Scott in 1936 and Fisher in 1947.[1]

All the African churches in Ibadan resulted from the work of individuals. Besides Scott's church, which became the U.A.M. (Eleja) in 1936, the Araromi Baptist was started in 1905 by D. A. Obasa, who was solely responsible for keeping the church operating for six years until Araromi could supply a regular clergyman. In 1910 E. H. Oke sponsored the building and running of the U.N.A. Church, which did not receive the services of a regular clergyman till 1918. In 1912 J. N. D. Somuji, who had been operating a church and school, turned them over to the African Church (Salem) and became a minister in that organization.[2] There was much co-operation and inter-communion between these churches in Ibadan. E. H. Oke assisted Obasa in opening the Araromi Baptists in 1905. Then Obasa helped Oke to open the U.N.A. in 1910. H. T. Scott was a founder of the African Church before he opened the African Methodist Church. The co-operative spirit survived in Ibadan, with the churches freely participating in each other's special occasions.

The activities of the Agege Planters, especially J. K. Coker, as patrons of interior churches have been mentioned. Lagos merchants as well as Agege Planters were also patrons. T. D. Shaw was patron to the Ijebu U.N.A. churches, supplying building materials and paying teachers' salaries. The Vaughan brothers, sons of J. C. Vaughan, the American Negro who played such a leading role in pioneer Baptist activity in Nigeria, were generous patrons to interior Baptist churches—especially in Ijebu and Ekiti. Dada Adeshigbin, the Singer Sewing Machine agent in Lagos, acted as patron to the Ijebu and Ikirun churches. At one time he was personally responsible for agents' wages amounting to £200 per year.[3]

The bishop or superintendent was the link which held together the scattered local churches. If the organization was successful in finding

[1] U.A.M. (Eleja), 'Twenty Fifth Annual Report', 1942, p. 15, typescript; Interview Supt. J. O. Okusanya, 12 Mar. 1962.

[2] *The Dawn*, Oct. 1916; *Nigerian Baptist*, Nov. 1927; U.N.A. Minutes, 2 July, 1910, *i*, pp. 444–5; Oke, 'Important Events of U.N.A. History 1891–1915', Manuscript; Oke, *History of the U.N.A. 1904–1924*, p. 10; U.N.A. Minutes, 5 July 1918, *ii*, pp. 202–4; A.C. (Salem) Minutes, 3 Sept. 1912, *ii*, pp. 125–8.

[3] Oke, *History of the U.N.A. 1891–1903*, p. 3; U.N.A. Minutes, 24 Sept. 1900 and 11 July 1908, *i*, pp. 372–4 and 512–13; Roberson, 'The First Baptist Church Lagos', pp. 15–16, *Ogbomoso Library*; A.C. (Bethel) Minutes, 1 July 1919, *iii*, pp. 85–90; Coker, History of the African Church, 1941, *Coker Papers*.

an eager evangelist as superintendent orderly expansion was assured. He must be a powerful orator in the pulpit in Yoruba and a fluent speaker in English, to be able to confront the colonial officers as a spokesman for his people. He needed to be a tireless traveller, constantly on the move across the country, careful not to let the endless activities of Lagos engage his time. African churches expanded in proportion to the amount of time the superintendent–evangelist could spend in the interior. Disputes within the governing body which occupied his time in Lagos were sure to have an adverse effect upon the interior churches. Members drifted off to other societies, church buildings were neglected, and agents unpaid.

An independent source of income which required a minimum of time was a vital necessity for the evangelist–superintendent. The African churches were prepared to pay the superintendent's salary. It was adequate to keep the family in Lagos, but travelling expenses might run to twice the amount of the salary.

Occasionally the prosperous churches provided the superintendent with a thankoffering, but the poorer churches (most of them were poor) actually looked to him for a donation to their funds. Agents and teachers in arrears of salary expected help. Priests engaged in new projects, building schools, purchasing organs, or choir surplices, were pleased with a small donation from the superintendent.

There was little evidence to show that the superintendent resented the reversal of what the missions would consider the normal order of church life. The superintendent was, after all, the biggest man in the organization, who lived in the golden city of Lagos. Compared to the conditions in the remote villages, he was a wealthy man. Faced with these circumstances, the superintendent needed a private source of income, and most who became successful had one.

A few, such as D. A. Hughes of the U.N.A. and J. A. Lakeru of the African Church, owned cocoa plantations at Agege. An overseer or foreman operated the Hughes plantation. J. K. Coker endowed Lakeru with land and managed the plantation, freeing Lakeru for his evangelistic work. Lakeru drew money from Coker throughout the year. When the accounts were made up, and if the plantation had not made profits equal to the amount drawn, Coker wiped the records clean and opened up the following year's account in balance. Both Lakeru and Hughes had homes on the plantation where they spent their vacations. They had an intimate knowledge of cocoa cultivation.[1] This was an advantage in the interior, where they could advise Christian farmers who were making their first experiments with cocoa. In their travels they easily combined administering the sacraments with advice on cocoa seedlings. One superintendent said that he preached the gospel of 'coffee, cocoa, cotton, and work as well as the scriptures'.[2] This practical knowledge gave them a distinct advantage over the bishops and superintendents of the mission societies.

D. A. Jones and J. S. Williams had property on lease in the Lagos area from which they gained a regular income. A few had wealthy backers. J. K. Coker assisted Agbebi and Lakeru as noted above. S. Alfred Coker, a prominent Wesleyan, financed J. G. Campbell of the W.A.E. Church. J. R. Shanu provided Superintendent A. O. Ijaoye of the A.C. (Penuel) with a monthly allowance. I. B. Williams, another wealthy Methodist merchant, paid his brother J. S. Williams, superintendent of A.C. (Bethel), forty-eight pounds a year for sixteen years, besides educating a number of his children.[3]

I. B. Williams, S. Alfred Coker, and J. H. Doherty were representative of the wealthy men of Lagos. They were willing to finance the African churches, but unwilling to attend them—an indication of the African churches' failure to achieve respectability in Lagos.

Superintendents Agbebi and Campbell supplemented their income as columnists for Lagos newspapers.[4] D. A. Jones, S. Ogunmukomi, and J. S. Williams practised as herbalists and Yoruba physicians, a vocation which provided an income and mobility.[5] Only Agbebi received financial assistance from abroad—from England with the assistance of the Colwyn Bay Institute, and from America through the Yonkers Men's Sunday Club in New York. Mark Hayford, superintendent of the Native Baptists of the Gold Coast (in affilia-

[1] Ifako Farmers Meeting Minutes, 20 Sept. 1911, *Coker Papers*; A.C. (Salem) Minutes, 10 Jan. 1912, 18 Aug. 1919, and 17 Dec. 1919, *ii*, pp. 108–10, *iv*, pp. 203–7, 217–18.

[2] *West African Mail*, 28 Aug. 1903, quoting Agbebi, Superintendent of Native Baptists.

[3] U.N.A. Minutes, 23 June 1919, *ii*, pp. 258–64; 'Report of the Sixth Anniversary 1909', W.A.E. Minute Book; A. O. Ijaoye, The Late J. R. Shanu (Yoruba), manuscript, *Oke Collection*; Interview Charles Ijaoye and A. K. Lamilisa, 16 Mar. 1962.

[4] Campbell contributed to the *Lagos Standard* and wrote a regular column in the *Times of Nigeria*. Agbebi contributed to the *Lagos Observer* and *Standard* and edited at various times the *Lagos Times* and *Weekly Record*. In 1916 he published the first Baptist magazine in Nigeria, *The Dawn*.

[5] Memorial Plaque, Christ Church (U.N.A.) Ebute Metta; Obituary J. S. Williams, *Nigerian Daily Times*, 27 July 1933; Oke, Life Sketch of Solomon Ogunmukomi, *Oke Collection*.

tion with Araromi Baptists), received £1,000 in assistance from England, £200 from the United States, and £500 from Nigeria between 1898 and 1913.[1]

An active evangelist wife was an asset to the superintendents. Agbebi, Lakeru, and Campbell had wives who tramped with them over the Yoruba country organizing women's leagues, visiting the homes, and preaching in the streets. Others took over the financial burden of the family by trading or teaching. Mrs. Agbebi operated her husband's printing press.[2]

The superintendent–evangelists left behind them an unpublished record of perseverance, devotion to duty, courage, and suffering equal to anything in missionary records. The very fact that they were not publicized to arouse sympathy or raise funds, but merely accepted as part of the service expected gave them a poignancy the customarily published stories failed to convey.

J. G. Campbell was stripped and beaten, paraded naked through a village by C.M.S. members, and left in the bush unconscious. Discovered by pagans who covered his nakedness, he was carried thirty miles to the government station, where from his stretcher he pleaded his case before the D.O. He had the consolation of receiving damages and hearing the C.M.S. priest sharply rebuked for his silent acquiescence in this display of denominational hostility. E. M. Lijadu records in his journal the weakening of his faith as he tramped day after day through water and mud, sometimes up to his knees, carrying his medical kit and portable communion set to bring the sacraments and relieve the distress of the sick among his people in the small villages of the Delta. D. A. Jones, then an old man, was handcuffed and treated as a common criminal, only to receive an apology from the authorities for mistaken identity.[3]

The superintendents worked under the disadvantage that their

---

[1] *Native Baptist Church* vs. *Mojola Agbebi*, Suit no. 59 of 1903; T. L. Harrison to J. E. Bruce, 9 Apr. 1907, *Schomberg (Bruce Papers)*; Year Book and Report, *The Baptist Church and Mission and the Christian Army of the Gold Coast*, London, 1913, pp. 68–114.

[2] Interview, Primate E. M. Olulode, 13 Mar. 1962; 'Report of a Visit to Pepe Beach, Feb. 1909', 'Missionary Journey to Idimu and Ado, July–August 1909', W.A.E. Minute Book; *Account of Mojola Agbebi's Work in West Africa*; Oke, 'Report of the Third Triennial Conference of the African Communion, 1919–1922', typescript, *Oke Collection*; 'Biography of Adeotan Agbebi', *Roberson Collection*.

[3] Campbell to the *Lagos Standard*, 18 Aug. 1915; W.A.E. Minute Book; U.N.A. Minutes, 27 June 1905, pp. 460–1.

orders had not been conferred by White men.[1] Many of the *élite* of their own society mocked and laughed at their presumption in ordaining to holy orders. Even in pagan villages, where they gained respect as the first officials of Christianity, it eventually became known that the White man disputed their right or authority because they had not the power passed on to them by the laying on of White hands. Struggling to overcome these misconceptions and to show the legitimate right of the Black man to propagate Christianity, they fought the idea that Christianity was the White man's religion. They kept alive the African's claim to leadership in an age when it was being submerged in church and state. In a sense their struggle for individual recognition was the struggle of the entire African Church Movement.

The superintendents were the heart and soul of the African churches. They were the major bond of unity which held the organizations together. They prevented the massive splintering which in other places in Africa seriously weakened the cause of independent churches. Had all the Yoruba cities given birth to independent churches at the rate which Lagos did, the confusion would have been hopeless.

The superintendents channelled the discontent and guided the numerous local secessions in the interior churches into the organizations already established in Lagos. They maintained the hegemony of Lagos over the whole African Church Movement. Only one African church which developed independent existence outside of Lagos survived, and its future is unclear. The success of the superintendents in developing African organizations over the whole of Nigeria which were in their origins Lagos and Yoruba, spoke well for the Christian leadership of Africans. The politicians were not nearly as successful either in developing support for Lagos political protests or in holding the various tribes in partnership.

The Shanu Mission at Oke Odan in the Egbado District was an illustration of the expansion of the African churches. It exemplified the individual nature of much of the enterprise, the devotion of the pioneers, the philanthropy of wealthy patrons, the discontent caused by mission policy, and the part played by the superintendents in guiding an interior church heading for separate existence within the organization of an established African church.

[1] Campbell, 'This, That and Another', *Times of Nigeria*, 11 July 1921.

Andrew Shanu was converted by S. A. (later Bishop) Crowther at Abeokuta in 1846. He went as an agent under a C.M.S. missionary to open Christian work in Oke Odan, his birthplace. In 1864 the missionary abandoned the town, since his efforts had gone unrewarded. Shanu remained on, unpaid and forgotten by the mission society, but diligently preaching Christianity to his neighbours. After fleeing to Lagos before the destruction of Oke Odan by the Dahmomean armies he returned to help rebuild the town and preach until his death in 1902. He left but a handful of Christians as a memorial to his labours. Shanu's death appeared to end Christian work in Oke Odan.

His son, J. R. Shanu, a Lagos merchant, had amassed a small fortune as an agent for an English firm in the Congo and a recruitment officer for contract labour for the construction of the Matadi–Stanley Pool railway. He made large profits out of the short-lived boom in rubber around the turn of the century. With his capital he settled down to a lucrative trade in beads with the Hausa, conducted from a number of retail outlets in Lagos.

He had been especially concerned with evangelistic work in the jails and the rehabilitation of Christian prisoners, an interest which set him apart from the social 'who's who' of Lagos. When his father died, J. R. Shanu was well established financially. He was distressed that his father's years of Christian labour were threatening to come to naught. He approached his cousin, A. I. Ogunbiyi, one of his father's converts who was earning his livelihood as a bricklayer. Ogunbiyi consented to return to Oke Odan and take up his uncle's neglected work, J. R. Shanu promising to finance him. This agreement continued for sixteen years, Shanu providing the money and Ogunbiyi the labour. Between 1902 and Shanu's death in 1918 the resistance of Oke Odan paganism began to give way before Ogunbiyi's preaching. Success followed in the surrounding villages and spread to other large towns—Ilaro and Ajilete. Shanu spent lavishly on buildings and teachers. The largest church 'Shanu Memorial', gave its name to the whole as 'Shanu Memorial Mission'. By 1917 the mission owned seventeen churches and boasted one thousand adherents.

The work had been carried on nominally under the C.M.S.—the Anglican clergy from Abeokuta baptizing and administering the sacraments. In 1910, in order to bring the mission more directly under C.M.S. control, Oke Odan came under the Abeokuta District

Council of the Anglican Church. It maintained control over its own finances and in possession of its property. In 1914 the C.M.S. closed the doors of the church against Ogunbiyi because he refused to re-marry his only wife of sixteen years' standing in European custom. They also raised complaints of polygamy among the members.

This disrespect for Ogunbiyi's work persuaded Shanu to ask Superintendent A. O. Ijaoye of the African Church (Penuel) to over-see the work. For this service Shanu paid Ijaoye a salary and made an allowance in his will for a continuance of the arrangement. Shanu died shortly after the new system began to operate. In 1920 the Shanu Mission voted to join the African Church (Salem). Ogunbiyi was deaconed and priested and later consecrated bishop over the diocese or district of Oke Odan, which unlike other dioceses of the African Church, possessed its own constitution which governed its special position within the larger organization.

During the years Ogunbiyi ordained five men to help him in the Shanu Mission. When he retired in 1952 the district contained thirty-four churches, ten schools, and an estimated ten thousand adherents.[1] After 1952 the mission lost much of its individual character, becom-ing in practice as well as theory an integral part of the African Church. The Shanu Memorial Mission was typical of the process by which local churches proud of their traditions and bound up with provincial patriotism were gradually brought within more nation-wide organizations.

Next to the interest over constitution and forms of organization (discussed in part four), African churchmen were engrossed in a debate over the nature of the church in Africa. The debate was con-ducted between two opposing cores of thought—the one emphasizing the universal nature of the church and the other stressing its particu-lar and national characteristics. The Lagos or 'Church' school of thought emphasized the universality of the church as it was known to them through the mission societies in their midst. The Agege or Evangelical school was more concerned with the national character-istics, which they argued every branch of the universal church (except the African) possessed. They maintained that the slowness of

---

[1] A. O. Ijaoye, 'The Late J. R. Shanu', *Oke Collection; Constitution of the Shanu Mission Church Organization*, Lagos 1924; *Nigerian Chronicle*, 18 Dec. 1914; Bishop Ogunbiyi to the editor, n.d. (after 1924), *Coker Papers*; Interview Bishop Ogunbiyi and his son, 17 Mar. 1962.

Africans to imprint their culture upon the church was the reason why the church had been tardy in making converts. The stimulus to promote change was evangelical enthusiasm.

The 'church' school grew out of the modern urban conditions of Lagos. It developed in a society already heavily committed to European modes of thinking, European goals and aims. It was composed of individuals trained to European thought, living in economic and social conditions in which traditional African ideas appeared peculiarly out of place. The Lagos school looked upon Yoruba society as in a transitional stage—on the move towards something closely approximating that which prevailed in Europe.[1] There was a tendency (but only a tendency, since the leading protagonists of such ideas were in the missions) to label African customs and beliefs unprogressive. There was conversely a willingness to accept European ideas somewhat uncritically. The influence of missionary teaching was strong and had almost substituted that earthly paradise, England, for the heavenly home. 'Because it is done that way in England' became an irrefutable argument for doing it the same way in Lagos.

The Evangelical school grew out of the modern rural conditions of Agege. The plantations were the result of combining European economic technique and African social conditions. The planters, like the merchants and civil servants of Lagos, had been trained to European thought and were as much as they the products of world economic forces. Yet on the plantations the social system remained essentially Yoruba. The planter became the chief. He was arbiter and judge, benefactor and protector, and high priest leading in worship on Sundays. And he was employer. The planters believed they had discovered a system which provided the benefits of Europe without necessarily destroying the social fibre of Africa. They confidently expected the agricultural revolution of Agege would ultimately spread over the whole of Yorubaland.

The planters looked kindly upon traditional Africa and defended the utility of its social system built upon polygamy, community, chieftancy, and secret societies. They attacked the uncritical acceptance of European ideas which prevailed in Lagos by continually pointing out the weaknesses and unChristian nature of European society—its immorality, its callousness, its rampant materialism, and

[1] M. S. Cole to J. K. Coker, 12 July 1913; *Coker Papers*, H. A. Williams, *African Hope*, Apr. 1921.

its self-centred small family units.[1] Only by destroying the glowing image of Europe which so many Africans held could Agege hope for a dispassionate appraisal of the African way of life.

The two schools of thought originated in divergent interpretations of the causes and aims of the African Church Movement. To Lagos the Movement's basic aim had been to prove the ability of African leadership to missionaries who had rejected it as ineffective. Other than this, Churchmen felt there was no reason to reject other mission policies—the conditions of baptism, stress on education, organization, rites, and ceremonies. To deviate from these essentials destroyed the Movement's basic aim. By 'lowering standards' they were merely proving the missions' contention that African leaders were incapable. They were unduly suspicious of dogmas and forms designed especially for Africa, since they believed that this was a tacit admission of African inferiority.

Churchmen agreed that many Christian forms were overlaid with much that was European. They argued, however, that in the fifty to seventy years of Christian missionary labour in Yorubaland, the people had accepted these forms which were no longer foreign. For many, new ceremonies based on African tradition had become foreign introductions. Morning and evening prayer and the old hymns of Christianity were not the exclusive preserve of the English nation. Originally learned from foreigners, they had become a vital part of divine service, loved and revered forms through which Africans now worshipped God. On a purely practical level they argued that if Christians were to be lured out of the missions, and the African churches built on their ruins, then similar forms of worship would make the transition easy from C.M.S. to African Church, or from Wesleyan to U.A.M. (Eleja).[2]

The Evangelicals believed that the African Church Movement had been caused by more than a snub to African leadership and that the result should be a thorough reformation. They revolted against almost the sum total of mission policies. They maintained that the African Church was not created for a few thousand Christians in Lagos. What was familiar to them was foreign to the millions in the interior. Recent events had shown that the African churches need not depend upon mission exiles (as welcomed as they were) for their sup-

[1] J. K. Coker, Polygamy, manuscript, n.d.; Coker to Bishop Onatolu, 12 Dec. 1934; *Coker Papers*; H. S. A. Thomas, *African Hope*, July 1921, p. 10.
[2] Onatolu to Coker, 3 June 1919, *Coker Papers*.

port. The African churches had gained widespread success among pure pagans, who were the hope of the church. C.M.S. forms might well make an easy transition for those going from mission to church, but the process did work in reverse, the transition just as smooth.

The Evangelicals believed Lagos generally omitted the interior in its thinking. If the African Church continued to follow mission policy, concentrating upon a dubious quality at the expense of quantity and supporting a hypocritical standard among its membership which could not stand scrutiny, then both the missions and the African churches would awake to find themselves Christian islands in a Muslim sea. To Agege, Lagos thinking lacked evangelical fire, and like the missions embodied a callousness to the masses who were knocking on the church doors.

Churchmen became preoccupied with recognition, and were restive in their isolation from the catholic world. Spurned by the mission societies in the week of prayer, comity agreements, and educational policy, the African Church especially, with its close affinity to the C.M.S., resented the favours which the Methodists enjoyed from that society. Recognition would bring respectability, that illusive image which always escaped them, and drove their young men, who rose to the professions out of the church into the missions. Bethel Cathedral (at the time of its construction the tallest building in Lagos) was an expression of this desire.

Lagos never lost hope of ultimately reuniting the African with the Anglican Church when the C.M.S. was ready to fully acknowledge African leadership. When the Lambeth conference of 1920 discussed Christian co-operation, some in the African churches felt the time of reunion was approaching.[1] But the Lambeth discussions merely resulted in Anglican–Methodist co-operation, which had ceased for a time from a spate of denominational fever.

Churchmen were particularly sensitive to the charge by the missions that the African churches were the result of African unwillingness to accept the moral teachings of the Bible. This was a polite way of referring to polygamy—that bête noire of the African Church Movement. Lagos tolerated polygamy among the laity from necessity rather than conviction. It was the only card which the African Church possessed and, furthermore, the Bible appeared noncommittal. But they continued to see monogamy as the ideal, the

[1] H. A. Williams in Times of Nigeria, 20 June 1921; Campbell called the desire for reunion hankering after the 'onions of Egypt', Times of Nigeria, 30 June 1921.

present policy being a temporary one considering the circumstances in which most Yoruba found themselves. Frightened of any extension of the policy of polygamy, they fought against membership in the African Communion, which possessed member churches who under the influence of the Evangelicals accepted rather than tolerated it. When churchmen spoke of reform it was in the direction of returning to a policy of monogamy. Tolerating polygamy had not caused a massive inflow to the church. Some claimed it had hindered the growth of the churches.[1] Monogamy, even hypocritical monogamy, might bring respectability and recognition.

Churchmen aimed for respectability and recognition. Evangelicals aimed at a national Christianity which could only be attained by a massive ingathering of pagans into the church. All policies must be tested against this aim. Recognition would come with success. The missions would then have to either change policy or liquidate. To consider reunion before this aim was achieved was defeat. To enter comity agreements was to perpetuate the evil they were seeking to mitigate. The Evangelical policy of supporting and encouraging unrest in the mission churches, and building a church across the street from every mission in Yorubaland to welcome the exiles, scuttled any chance Lagos might have had to gain respect or establish co-operation with the mission societies.

Some men are so intent upon being recognized by the foreign churches in our midst and having their empty smiles that they have no time to devote to the building of a true and genuine African Church.[2]

The African Communion was the creation of the Evangelicals. It was the answer to the mission gentlemen's agreements. It provided for a united week of prayer, comity in evangelistic efforts, and common action in educational policy. It aimed to unite the African churches in their striving for the common goal—Yoruba national Christianity.

The Evangelicals accepted rather than tolerated polygamy. For this reason they favoured no restrictions upon the marriage customs of the clergy. The most extreme frowned upon monogamy and disapproved of the licensing of churches for European-style marriages.[3]

[1] Onatolu to Coker, 3 June 1919; Coker to Onatolu, n.d., *Coker Papers*.

[2] 'Unity in the African Church', *African Church Chronicle*, Oct.–Dec. 1934, pp. 4–5.

[3] The U.N.A. and W.A.E. were not licensed, The A.C. (Bethel and Salem) were. W.A.E. Minutes, 17 Apr. 1914.

Polygamy did not represent a lower standard of morality. Far from it, in some ways it was higher. Its regulation was provided for in the Old Testament, and they claimed it was more suited to the conditions now or ever likely to prevail in Africa. Mission teaching on monogamy had not significantly changed the marriage customs of the Yoruba people, but thrown a veil over them. Acceptance of polygamy was the beginning of a policy aimed at a full indigenization of the church and acceptance of the total fabric of Yoruba social life. Upon full acceptance it was the duty of the church to regularize and purify—not to uproot and destroy.

It was difficult to estimate accurately the strength of the following of the two schools of thought within the African Church Movement or its member organization. Among the clergy those who had been trained and carried on evangelistic work for the missions either as priests or catechist leaned towards the Lagos school. They were under attack by the opposition as being unable to speak except as they had been taught in the missions, having too long contamination with foreign systems and being unable to deviate from Anglicanism.[1]

Clergy educated and trained within the African churches inclined towards the views of the Evangelicals. They were fewer, generally younger and mostly in the lower ranks. The first of their number to achieve position became assistant superintendents in the U.N.A. in 1921. Otherwise, mission-trained clergy monopolized the hierarchy.

TABLE VI

Origin of Clergy in the African Churches, 1915–22[2]

Organization	From C.M.S.	From Meth.	Mission trained	Church trained	Other sources	Totals
A.C. (Bethel)	4	8	12	0	2	14
A.C. (Salem)	6	1	7	11	1	19
U.N.A.	1	3	4	8	0	12
W.A.E.	1		1	8	1	10
Totals			24	27	4	55

The origin and background of the clergy (Table VI) shows that while mission-trained and church-trained personnel were approximately equal over the whole African Church Movement they were

[1] Othniel Taylor, *The African Church: Necessity for a Standard Policy*, Lagos, 1932, p. 4; J. K. Coker, Sermon Notes, n.d. (after 1915); Aboyade-Cole to Coker, 2 Apr. 1927, *Coker Papers*.

[2] Compiled from comparison of mission and African church sources and autobiographies customarily required before ordination.

unequally distributed as between the individual organizations. The African Church (Bethel), the leader of the Lagos school, was controlled by mission-trained personnel, while the W.A.E., an organization of evangelical thought, was led by clergy who had had no contact with the foreign missions. There was evidence that the background of the clergy was a fairly accurate guide to the origin of the laity. The A.C. (Bethel) membership was overwhelmingly 'old Anglican', who felt that 'our feet should be placed exactly in C.M.S. footprints'.[1] Less than two hundred of the four thousand members of the W.A.E. had previous experience under a mission society.[2]

The U.N.A. supported evangelical theories, even though the General Committee (the highest governing body of the church) was controlled by mission-trained laymen. The Churchmen formed an active 'reform' party which periodically sought to bring the organization back to catholic standards. It was responsible for the timid policy, noted above, of failing to provide priests for the rapidly expanding membership in Ikale. Prior to 1921 it fought and lost a determined battle to change U.N.A. policy on polygamy from Evangelical acceptance to Churchmen tolerance.[3] In the W.A.E. only an occasional voice was raised in support of the policies of the Lagos school. The church went so far as to prohibit European marriage custom to its membership.

Any agent of this church whether minister or lay who marries according to European custom be dismissed at once. . . .[4]

In the A.C. (Salem) the balance between mission-trained and church-trained clergy and between dissident mission laymen and pagan converts was evenly balanced. While the church-trained predominated in numbers, the mission-trained held the positions of influence. The forces were so equally balanced that policies were the result of hard-fought compromises. Friction and tension were severe. The result was deep and profound thinking upon the problems of indigenization.

Disputes frequently revolved around the issue of jurisdiction. If the matter was of a spiritual nature it was within the powers reserved for the bishop. If organizational it was within the legislative rights of

[1] Coker, 'The African Church: Past, Present and Future Reviewed', *African Church Chronicle*, Oct.–Dec. 1934, pp. 13–18.

[2] Campbell to St. Arthurs Church, Accra, 13 Mar. 1920, W.A.E. Minute Book.

[3] H. A. Williams in *Times of Nigeria*, 20 June 1921.

[4] W.A.E. Minutes, 17 Apr. 1914.

the General Committee. As an example, the General Committee under Evangelical influence had prescribed an ordination service which was felt reflected the African nature of the church. The bishop, maintaining that his jurisdiction had been infringed, quietly refused it, continuing to use the Anglican form. The bishop was castigated as an Anglican in spirit who failed to appreciate African customs.[1] It was ironic that the Anglican bishop joined the Agege Evangelicals in criticism of the policies of the Lagos school—the great admirers of the missions. In an effort to justify the European outlook of the C.M.S. he pointed to the 'so-called African churches'.

They call themselves 'African', but their services, the robes and titles of their ministers, their surpliced choirs are all borrowed from England . . . how are they distinctly 'African'?[2]

The Evangelicals failed to persuade the bishops and hierarchy to accept a change in the policy of polygamy from toleration to acceptance. But they had profound influence upon other policies of the organization. The evangelistic programme was vigorous. Accessions to the membership came from the missions and paganism. Opposition was overcome to a liberal policy of ordination, and as a consequence, the A.C. (Salem) had a larger number of priests than any other organization. The membership received the sacraments regularly, since the Evangelicals believed that denial of the sacraments contributed to lapses into Islam and the mission.

The rapid growth, especially among those too poor to contribute to the general finances of the organization, put an unbearable strain upon the A.C. (Salem). Its financial base was narrow, depending upon the plantations of Agege. When the prosperity of the plantations fell during the 1921 commodity prices crisis, the A.C. (Salem) almost collapsed.

Severe retrenchment was staved off by the reunion with the twin branch of the church, A.C. (Bethel), in 1922. Under the threat of financial collapse, ideological differences played a small part in the reunion. Otherwise it was unlikely the Evangelicals would have submitted with so little protest to an arrangement in which they were hopelessly overwhelmed. Mission-trained clergy and the philosophy of Lagos dominated the reunited African Church organization. The

[1] Coker, Memorandum, n.d. (1935?), *Coker Papers.*
[2] Bishop M. Jones, Ibadan Synod, May 1936 quoted in the *African Church Chronicle*, July–Sept. 1936.

reunion was a marriage of expediency. It reunited the financial resources of the A.C. (Bethel) with the numerical strength of the A.C.
(Salem).[1]

One of the specific and contentious issues between the two schools
of thought was over the qualifications of the agency—the clergy and
catechists. The break-up of paganism which began after 1910 produced a new problem. The demand for agents and teachers became so
persistent and frantic that the combined resources of mission and
African churches could not meet them. Agents were not being produced fast enough. The Training Institute initiated by the Evangelicals in the A.C. (Salem) began to produce graduates only in 1921.
There was the discouraging fact that the African churches could not
attract the clergy of their own volition out of the missions, and ex-
pulsions, though numerous, were not nearly sufficient to meet
demands.

As an alternative, the Evangelicals pressed for the utilization of
polygamous unordained catechists, honorary or unpaid agents, and
Yoruba speakers. They argued that this would make more use of
men who had been converted in older life when already polygamous,
who were financially established, and who had not had the opportunity of English education.

Churchmen and the bishops, like the C.M.S., who rejected a vernacular clergy in 1910,[2] believed that Yoruba speakers, besides being
cut off from theological reading, which was in English, lowered the
prestige of the clergy. They pointed out that a few local churches had
rejected clergymen not literate in English. Unpaid agents were prone
to bring the clergy into contempt by disputes occasioned by their
secular occupation, especially trade. Supported by private income,
they were less amenable to church control and discipline. Polygamous agents were a step towards a polygamous clergy which the
church had prohibited in the constitution.[3]

By turning against these proposals the Evangelicals believed the
church was placing undue emphasis upon youth, book-learning, and
intellectual attainment. They were rejecting the respect and traditional knowledge which came with age. They were substituting intellectual for spiritual power. Arguments about control were merely

[1] A.C. (Salem) Minutes (rough), 12 Feb. 1923.
[2] Ex. Co. Minutes, 26–30 July 1910, *C.M.S.*, G3 A2/O, no. 126.
[3] Interview Bishop Aboyade-Cole, 27 Feb. 1962; Supt. G. A. Oke, 10 Nov.
1961; A.C. (Bethel) Minutes, 19 Dec. 1919, *iii*, pp. 102–12; Onatolu to Coker,
3 June 1919, *Coker Papers*.

placing obstacles in the way of the spread of the gospel. The city churches might demand intellectual attainment, but in the villages the knowledge of English was of little utility and mainly a prestige symbol. Africa was varied and could accommodate and use priests of varying talents. There was a place for all.[1]

Cautious use was made of vernacular and honorary clergy, but polygamous unordained agents were never employed by the African Church (Bethel and Salem) unless paid by a patron, in which case the church did not interfere. The issue remained an academic one until J. O. Shopekan (a monogamist), ordained by Campbell (a polygamist), applied to work for the A.C. (Salem). Customarily, priests who came to the African churches from the missions were given a public charge, which occasionally resembled a recantation, but their orders were recognized as valid. Priests who transferred from one organization to another within the Communion did so only if they had the acquiescence of the church they were leaving. Shopekan had been a priest in the W.A.E., which was not a member of the Communion. The constitution did not cover such a contingency. The A.C. (Bethel) had re-ordained without hesitation in a similar case. The Evangelicals expected this from an organization such as Bethel which frequently acted as arbitrarily as a mission society.

The bishops prepared to re-ordain Shopekan, believing that ordination by a polygamist was contrary to the constitution and the desire of the church, and was therefore invalid. They feared that if a polygamous ordination was allowed to stand the Evangelicals would use this as a lever to introduce a polygamous clergy. The Evangelicals pressed the point to the brink of division because the whole issue of the qualification of the clerical agency depended on the outcome. Bishops Lakeru and Onatolu refused to discuss the matter in the General Committee, defending the constitution, which prohibited laymen from legislating on spiritual matters. They ignored the repeated resolutions of the Committee and forced the Evangelicals to back down or be responsible for a break and division in the church. Prominent Evangelicals retired into 'passive membership'.

---

[1] Coker to the bishops 1922, Account Book; Coker to Committee of Arbitration, 1920? A.C. (Salem) Minutes (rough), 25 June 1917, *Coker Papers*; A.C. (Salem) Minutes, 24 Oct. 1916, *iv*, pp. 73–6; A.C. (Bethel) Minutes, 18 Dec. 1919; *iii*, pp. 102–12; M. T. Euler-Ajayi, 'Annual Sermon', *Conference Proceedings 1901–1908*, p. 24.

K

A committee of arbitration restored unity by persuading the Evangelicals to resume active membership in view of the financial crisis of 1920, which threatened to overwhelm the church.[1]

A more fundamental dispute took place over the conditions required of converts before they could be baptized and accepted into membership. The missions, believing that the 'uneducated are always a danger to the whole church',[2] demanded a two or three year catechumen period until candidates possessed a knowledge of the creed and the catechism, and were able to read the scriptures in Yoruba. The African churches had revolted against this system. They had laid down early that faith and 'a few questions on faith and salvation at the discretion of the minister'[3] shall be the basis of membership.

After 1910 when Africans were pouring into the church it was no longer necessary for the African Church to contest with the missions for every member. The bishops used the discretionary clause to insist on longer periods of education prior to membership. By 1919 Bishop Lakeru was instructing his clergy to insist upon literacy in Yoruba before membership.[4] Statistics in 1921 confirm that the African Church ratio of members to adherents (1:7) was almost as high as in the missions. The U.N.A., on the other hand (1:4), was much more in line with Evangelical thinking.

The Evangelicals attacked this change as traitorous to the foundation aims of the Movement when the mission methods of 'preach, teach, baptize' had been reversed to 'preach, baptize, teach'. The long catechumen period and emphasis upon intellectual ability discouraged many from considering Christianity. The same spiritual vacuum was created over which the policy towards polygamy had been fought. The bishops, they complained, were always talking of quality, as if a quick intellect was required for planting the faith. There were hordes in the missions who could produce a neat argument for Christianity but had not the slightest intention of translating their beliefs into action, nor had any conception of spirituality. If so,

---

[1] A.C. (Salem) Minutes, 16 July 1918, *iv*, pp. 129–36; Lakeru to Coker, 1 Dec. 1917; Coker to the bishop, 25 Apr. 1918; Coker to Lakeru, 24 May 1918; Gooding to Coker, 5 Aug. 1918; Opebi to Coker, 22 Mar. 1920; Coker to Committee of Arbitration, n.d., 1920, *Coker Papers*.
[2] *W.M.M.S. Report*, 1920, p. 87.
[3] A.C. (Salem) Minutes, 30 Aug. 1907, *ii*, pp. 11–13.
[4] A.C. (Salem) Minutes, 22 Apr. 1919, *iv*, pp. 179–91.

could the hierarchy give a satisfactory definition of quality? Was it intellectual attainment or financial support?[1]

After the reunion in 1922 and Evangelical influence diminished Churchmen sponsored a change of official policy. A resolution was passed by the General Committee that made baptism conditional upon a confession of faith, a knowledge of catechism, and literacy.[2] This gave the superintendents official power to compel the Evangelical clergy, who continued to act upon the earlier resolution of the Committee, to conform.

Another dispute within the African Church Movement concerned foreign forms and ceremonies. Churchmen upheld the rites inherited from the mission, for which they were castigated by the Evangelicals as 'mimic Anglicans' and 'old parrots of the C.M.S.'.[3] The Evangelicals were willing to dispense with foreign forms, but their distaste for ritual inhibited them from encouraging creative talent desirous of experimenting with new African ceremonies. They felt that ritual was an impediment or substitute for spirituality and interfered with contact between the worshipper and Christ.

In the first flush of enthusiasm after the foundation of the African Church the clergy dispensed with the baptismal sign of the cross. The church was thrown into confusion and the exodus back to the C.M.S. provided a salutary warning of the danger of lightly tampering with custom. In the split of 1907 Churchmen of the A.C. (Bethel) re-established 'the sign', while the Evangelicals in A.C. (Salem) voted against it.[4] Churchmen clung to mission forms; Evangelicals made barren services more austere. The sign of the cross was admittedly a minor matter, but the confusion it caused made a strong impression on both parties that forms had best remain untouched in the interests of tranquillity.

An Anglican conference among the Ibo opposed the majority of Ibo customs calling for civil action to prohibit them. One Ibo clergyman who had spoken for toleration pointed out how stupid it was for

[1] Coker's Sermon Note Book; Coker to Onatolu, n.d.; A. Thomas to Coker, 20 Mar. 1922; Coker to Onatolu, n.d.; Coker to Taylor, 30 June 1927, *Coker Papers*.

[2] Notice of General Committee Meeting, 9 Feb. 1922, *Coker Papers*.

[3] *Lagos Standard*, 4 Nov. 1903, Coker, 'Baptism', *African Church Chronicle*, Apr.–June 1935, p. 9.

[4] A.C. (Bethel), *Conference Proceedings 1901–1908*, pp. 39–40, 63; A.C. (Salem) Minutes, 9 Aug. 1907, *ii*, pp. 9–10; Coker, 'The First Five Years of the African Church 1901–1906', *Coker Papers*.

Anglican clergy to vote against the entire range of Ibo custom, since few adherents or members would pay the least bit of heed. A hard line would simply benefit the Roman Catholic mission, which provided a vigorous alternative to the C.M.S. among the Ibo.[1]

African secular customs continued to develop and modify outside the church. The missions, if the Ibo conference was any indication, were determined to maintain a hostile pose. African churches were willing to accept this, but unwilling to use their influence in the moulding process. The doors of the church were closed to debar any of this development being reflected in ceremonies within it. Whether African Church services were patterned after the C.M.S. or stripped as bare as the Baptists, they remained a European creation in an African setting. Neither Evangelicals nor Churchmen perceived the value which might lie in exploiting African talents in music—both song and dance—within the church. The creative impulse, when it came, originated among a younger generation, less committed to either Churchmen or Evangelicals and critical of both.

. . . in practice, form of worship, custom and other paraphernalia we are still serving our time as pawns or liberated slaves who have naturalized in the country of their bondage, and unless all to one man are prepared to change, our existence, our boastings and vauntings as an African Church are a farce . . . [we are] . . . still in the arena dancing to the tune of . . . [our] foreign masters.[2]

One issue was church music in an African idiom. The missions did not forbid it, but neither did they encourage it as a desirable development. It had been first used as a necessity among pagan illiterates by Rev. James White of the C.M.S. at Otta in 1857. Sometimes it was used in open-air services to attract the pagans, but it was not considered 'proper' for formal service. The U.N.A. had begun its use in 1891 and were prosecuted in the courts for profaning a holy edifice.[3] African music was not respectable, associated with the old, rather

[1] C.M.S., *The Church and Native Customs*, Lagos, 1914; M. S. Cole, in a paper delivered to the Anglican synod, said about Yoruba customs, 'Even Christians are not free from the hold of these customs and so their Christianity becomes more a matter of outward deportment than of inward persuasion . . .' 'The Attitude of the Church to Native Customs', *Anglican Synod Reports*, 1912–14, Appendix 6, p. 119.

[2] Ayo Ajala, 'The African Communion: Its Aims and Objects', *African Church Chronicle*, Apr.–June 1936, pp. 1–13.

[3] *C.M.S. Proceedings*, 1895; *W.M.M.S. Report 1900*; Presidential Charge to the U.N.A. Annual Conference, Sept. 1962.

than the new Africa. It was intimately connected with paganism,[1] and was in the process of being adapted by Muslims. Many, especially in Lagos, had lost their ear for it. It was becoming foreign.

Agbebi began its extensive use among Araromi Baptists in Lagos. In the interior, where churches were developed among pagans, Agbebi did not introduce European hymnology, but began from the first with African music. Upon the establishment of the U.A.M. (Eleja) in 1917 that organization quickly rose to prominence in music under the inspiration and creative genius of A. K. Ajisafe, an outstanding African hymnologist. Drums and symbols were taboo until they were introduced by the Ethiopian and Brotherhood churches, two small groups established after 1918.[2]

A long step forward was taken in 1918 by the formation of the African Church Choir Union, which aimed to improve Native airs for divine service and popularize Native music by means of special concerts. Ajisafe moved to Bethel Cathedral, where facilities were available for his talents. Encouraged by an enthusiastic young priest, Aboyade-Cole, they attempted to develop Native music in the cathedral. Ajisafe created a new liturgy which Aboyade-Cole introduced into the services. It did not find favour with the authorities and was withdrawn. Native hymns continued to be used in spite of resistance. In 1936, eighteen years after they had been in use in the cathedral, Native airs were sanctioned for use throughout the organization.[3]

The greatest contribution to Christianity by the African churches was in the field of hymnology. The Native Baptists published the first hymn book in 1906 by means of a loan from the mission society which was repaid from sales. J. W. Vaughan was the most outstanding composer. The W.A.E. general conference of 1910 resolved to publish a hymn book which first appeared in 1913. In 1904 the U.N.A. appointed a committee which printed a hymn book in 1914. It was reprinted in 1919. Revised and enlarged by including the compositions of composers from other churches, it was republished in 1939.[4]

[1] 'Let no step be taken which revives in any form the spirit of worship of the old religion', *Nigerian Pioneer*, 21 May 1926.
[2] *Eko Akete*, 3 Feb. 1923, p. 4, and 28 Apr. 1923, p. 5; W. A. Amakiri, 'History of Buguma Baptist Church', *Ogbomoso Library*: U.A.M. (Eleja), *Twenty Fifth Annual Report*, p. 16.
[3] *African Church Chronicle*, Oct.–Dec. 1936.
[4] Roberson, 'Historical Sketch of First Baptist Church', *Ogbomoso Library*, N.B.H.C., Oke, *History of the U.N.A. 1904–1924*, pp. 2–4; Second Annual Conference, Oct. 1910, W.A.E. Minute Book; Interview Mrs. Grace Campbell, Mar. 1962.

In 1918 the African Communion resolved to publish a hymnal for use in all its member churches. Two delegates from each of the churches formed a committee. Money was collected and lost in the bankruptcy of the Industrial Bank. Collections were taken again, and finally in 1941 a large hymnal was produced.[1] The African Church, through the influence of the Lagos school, did not share her sister organizations' enthusiasm for African music. Ultimately, however, the idea became popular, and most churches used as many as four hymnals: the Anglican, the African Communion, their denominational, and a district hymnal the creation of a particularly talented local organist.

Other than music, the African churches were tardy to 'distinguish the camp'. Blyden in 1891 advised that the chiefs be enrolled, like European monarchs had been brought in, without too great exaction.[2] After the establishment of the African Church overtures were made to the Eleko of Lagos, who co-operated by attending the church and extending an invitation to hold services at his palace, but he could not be persuaded to declare for the African Church.[3]

Better results were secured in Abeokuta through accommodation with the Ogboni Fraternity—a secret society which held wide political power among the Egba. The missions prohibited their members from joining the Ogboni. An Anglican priest in 1914 attempted to organize a purged Ogboni—the Christian Ogboni. The Anglican bishops forbade the use of the term 'Christian', and the African churches supported this decision.[4]

Later the Ogboni Assembly asked that Christian children be allowed to accept their fathers' titles. The General Committee of the African Church agreed upon two conditions—that Christians be not forced to use heathen rites and that they be given Christian burial. The Ogboni granted these concessions with a significant addition—their willingness to learn and use Christian forms of blessing.[5]

In the year of reunion, when the Evangelicals witnessed the defeat of so much of their cherished programme, they had the pleasure of

[1] A.C. (Salem) Minutes, 2 Sept. 1918, *iv*, pp. 147–54; *African Church Chronicle*, April–June 1936.

[2] E. W. Blyden, *The Return of the Exiles*, p. 27.

[3] *Lagos Standard*, 15 July 1903.

[4] A.C. (Salem) Minutes, 12 Jan. 1914, *ii*, pp. 160–2; S. C. Phillips, *The Heathen Cult Called Reformed Ogboni Society*, Ibadan, 1956.

[5] Coker, 'The African Church: Past, Present and Future Reviewed'. *African Church Chronicle*, Oct.–Dec. 1934, pp. 14–15; Coker's History, *Coker Papers*.

seeing the rules of the church changed to permit members to accept Ogboni titles. A number of Ogboni chiefs embraced Christianity and became baptized members of the African Church. In certain Ogboni houses Christian practice replaced pagan rites.[1]

Accommodating the Ogboni Society was in the nature of the organization's external relations and did not require changes within the ceremonies of the church. Ritual in the cathedrals of Lagos copied the high Anglicanism of Christ Church. While more originality would have been commendable, this copying was welcome, since English Evangelical barrenness pervaded all the churches, mission as well as African. The failure to appreciate the value of ritual in worship must be blamed upon the churchmen of the Lagos school.

One outstanding development of ritual was the composition of a liturgy for the dignified and beautiful Yoruba 'naming ceremony' for infants. This pagan rite had much to commend it to Christianity. Bishop A. I. Ogunbiyi's naming ceremony litany[2] (in use unofficially in the African Church) has never received the organization's official blessing. It was a pity that the timidity of Churchmen prevented encouragement and sanction for such creative activity.

If Churchmen, inspired by the C.M.S., were indifferent to ritual, Evangelicals were hostile, mostly because what had been introduced was a copy of English forms—the copying itself being anathema to Agege. Had Churchmen experimented with unique rituals related to Africa, Evangelicals might well have lent their support. It was most deplorable that Churchmen did not utilize the wood and bronze carving art of the Yorubas in the decoration of their cathedrals and that brass eagles for the lecterns continued to be imported from England. The one example of local carving in an African church met a tragic end. In 1908 a carver placed a memorial to J. E. Ricketts (a West Indian Missionary who worked under Agbebi) in the Native Baptist Church in Lagos. After reunion with the mission society in 1914 the missionaries were instrumental in having the memorial removed in the interests of conformity to Baptist practice.[3]

Had the African churches encouraged the carver's art, and abandoned imported stained-glass windows to the missions, their buildings today could have been veritable treasure houses of African art. In addition to the stimulus which this patronage would have given to

---

[1] Notice of General Committee Meeting, 9 Feb. 1922, *Coker Papers.*
[2] Rev. Supt. A. I. Ogunbiyi, *Iwe Iko-Omo-Jade ati Lati Owo*, Lagos, 1926.
[3] 'Dedication of Araromi Chapel', *Lagos Weekly Record*, 16 Oct. 1909.

a school of Christian carvers, it would have improved the image of the church among the rising generation. The Nationalist Movement created an interest in Africa's artistic past. It also created an educated class indifferent to the church. As preservers of the artistic past African churches might have developed the sympathy of this class for the church.

What little was done was again accomplished outside the walls of the church. In the cemeteries of Lagos, statuary with African features is almost entirely confined to the tombstones of African Churchmen. They form pleasing landmarks among the myriads of European angels and foreign features. Although unmistakably of European-borrowed technique, they are a beginning. It is to be hoped that in future they will be followed by efforts to regain some of the vitality of traditional African figures.

In the first twenty or thirty years of African Church history decorated buildings appeared as a luxury easily done without. More urgent problems occupied the thoughts and energies of the leadership. Its greatest challenge was the creation of a satisfactory and stable form of government. Again the two schools of thought diverged in policy, although the line of demarcation was more blurred than in the disputes over evangelism. Rather unexpectedly it was the Evangelicals who supported episcopal authority and superficially at least were prepared to copy the Anglican system. Churchmen advocated strong lay powers.

From what has gone before, especially the bishops' support for the general views of Churchmen, this may appear as a contradiction. Possibly it was, but the reason was well founded. The Evangelicals' main concern was evangelism. This aim was best promoted in their view by a strong episcopate which gave autocratic control which could direct the greatest amount of the organization's energy and finances towards that area of church life which they held most dear—the evangelization of the Yoruba.

Lay control invariably strengthened the local churches and weakened the central organization, making it more difficult to deploy the financial and other resources of the wealthy to the benefit of the infant and weak churches. Thus the A.C. (Bethel), the leader of the Lagos school, with its unhappy combination of lay control, local church autonomy, and refusal to accommodate itself to African society through the operation of 'Church' views almost stopped moving on the missionary frontiers.

Of the three organizations most influenced by the Evangelical tradition, two gave ultimate power to the clergy. In the W.A.E. organization the laity wielded little influence. The A.C. (Salem) had a wiser and better balance, but the clergy held supreme power over spiritual concerns, which covered a wide range of matters vital to the heart of the church. The U.N.A. alone reserved final power to the laity.

In the reunion of 1922 the Evangelicals appeared to lose all. They did gain one immense victory. In the new constitution the governmental structure of the A.C. (Salem) became the form for the united church. For the first time a primate was appointed, which signalized a victory for the authority of the bishops. The Evangelicals hoped that the greater financial resources of the reunited church could be channelled by means of this centralization towards evangelization of the pagan.

PART IV

Church Government

To pull to pieces, to reduce to atoms, to break, to tear, to disorganize is often the inclination of thoughtless childhood. Such a trait of character is to be met with among some Africans . . . Do not tolerate disorder. It is one of the besetting sins of Native organizations that every man desires to be the leader. It is the spirit of slavery, and is more manifest among Europeanized Africans than among Africans purely Native. Recognize leadership.

MOJOLA AGBEBI, 1902

IN the enthusiasm of the early years and the reaction against the missions there was a naïve equation of clerical control with autocracy and oppression, and lay government with democracy and freedom. Experience produced more mature thinking. Clerical control might result in hypocrisy and cringing, but lay control had caused continual disorder and confusion. It was the gradual achievement of a balance which preoccupied the African churches prior to 1920.

There were four factors in the governing authority of an African Church—the elders, the junior leaders, the clergy, and the congregation. Eldership required wealth, a personal following, and a respected position of leadership within the community. It required a reputation for personal generosity, participation in philanthropic enterprise, and unstinted patronage of the church. J. W. Cole, one of the top ten African merchants and vice-president of the Chamber of Commerce, was the wealthiest member of the Lagos *élite* to join the African Church Movement before 1900. He was the chief patron of Jehovah Shalom (U.N.A.) in Lagos as well as the chief elder of the U.N.A. organization. He had been a supporter of Blyden and a member of the Governor's Legislative Council (1895–7), where he successfully pleaded for government assistance to the U.N.A. school—the first indigenous institution to receive treatment equal to that given the mission schools.[1]

[1] Oke, *History of the U.N.A. 1891–1903*, pp. 3, 15–16; *Iwe Irohin Eko*, 1 Nov. 1890; E. W. Blyden, *The Return of the Exiles and the West African Church*, London, 1891, p. 33; Campbell, 'This, That, and Another', *Times of Nigeria*, 27 June 1921; Denton to Chamberlain, 23 Nov. 1896, *C.O.* 147/107.

H. A. Caulcrick and E. H. Oke, elders of the organization, founders and chief patrons of Ebute Metta and Ibadan local churches respectively, held senior posts in the Colonial civil services. Caulcrick received the Imperial Service Order for his work in the Treasury.[1] Oke retired from the Department of Justice, became secretary to the Ibadan Native authority, and a member of the Legislative Council representing Oyo Division between 1924 and 1930. He was patron of the Egba Agba-o-tan, an organization to preserve and publish material on Ibadan custom and culture, and the president of the Ibadan branch of the National Congress of British West Africa.[2]

G. A. Williams, another elder, witnessed the tragedy of the Niger. His story was in essence its history. As an agent for an African merchant, he lost his position when the Niger Company perfected its monopoly. Employed by the company, he later fell victim to its Europeanization policy. The circumstances surrounding the downfall of Crowther left a vivid impression upon him. Upon return to Lagos he acted as editor of the *Lagos Weekly Record*, and in 1893 established his own paper, the *Lagos Standard*, which he edited until his death in 1919. He was interested in all the progressive and radical protest movements of Lagos, president of the Native Literature Publishing Society, executive member of the Aborigines Protection Society, and vice-president to the Anti-Slavery Society Auxiliary. His reputation was enhanced by fines for libel, once for an anti-missionary article, and once for an attack against the establishment at the time of the land question deputation.[3]

The elders were the inspiration behind the establishment of the U.N.A. They donated or purchased its land, contributed to the building and furnishing of the edifices, and provided at least three-quarters of the organization's finances. J. W. Cole purchased and converted Phoenix Hall into a church, kept the school solvent, and cleared deficits. Similarly, H. A. Caulcrick patronized Ebute Metta and E. H. Oke, Ibadan.

[1] Memorial Plaque Christ Church, U.N.A. Ebute Metta; Oke, *History of the U.N.A. 1891–1903*, chapter 11; Deniga, *African Leaders*, pp. 27–28.

[2] 'Funeral of the late Mr. Oke', *Nigerian Daily Times*, 3 Oct. 1930; Interview, G. A. Oke, 10 Sept. 1961; Oke, Important Events in History of U.N.A. 1891–1915, *Oke Collection; Lagos Weekly Record*, 10 June 1920.

[3] D. H. Hughes, 'Memorial Address', *African Hope Supplement*, Sept. 1919; U.N.A. Minutes, 1 June 1906, pp. 447–82; *Lagos Standard*, 1 Mar. 1905; Rt. Rev. Paul Pellet, Vicar Apostolic *vs.* G. A. Williams, 19 Apr. 1899, Chief Justice Record Book, vol. 22; Sapara Williams *vs.* G. A. Williams and J. B. Benjamin, 16 June 1914, Chief Justice Record Book, vol. 72.

The elder formed the apex of a pyramid of followers, the size dependent upon his wealth, influence, and family. His position rested upon his leadership of an extensive family or as leader of the people from the area in which he had been born. He loaned capital to merchants and traders. He stood surety for small traders for credit with the large firms or for young men seeking employment. He was responsible for the education of youths within his following. He was expected to use his influence to procure employment or favours. His followers turned to him in all cases of emergency. A wedding or funeral celebrated in a manner below the standards expected of the participants was as much a disgrace to the elder as to the immediate family. Normally the elder did not expect or demand repayment of the loans which he gave out.[1]

The wealth of the elder held the pyramid together. He could expect obedience and prior attention to his requests from his followers. He performed the function of arbiter and judge in disputes within the pyramid. Failure to obey his ruling could result in a law-suit for return of capital loaned or withholding of further patronage.

The pyramid was not a mass of people with personal loyalty to the elder. It was composed of junior leaders (not necessarily juniors in age, but in the extent of their following), who led family or small groups. The elder dispensed patronage through them. Their leadership, in turn, depended upon the elder's continuing good will. If the junior leaders increased in wealth they could become less attached to the pyramid. Ultimately they borrowed from the elder on a 'repayment plus interest' basis. They were on their way to becoming independent or elders at the apex of their own pyramid. Other individuals —teachers, clergymen, writers—might opt for this kind of relationship with the elder in order to preserve their personal independence.

An elder could not be such without wealth. If he lost it, custom-

---

[1] J. K. Coker provides an excellent example of the elder and his relationship to his pyramid. For standing surety out of numerous examples see J. K. Coker to McIver and Co., 7 June 1906; Thomas and Sons to J. K. Coker, 19 Sept. 1917; Craig to J. K. Coker, 27 Aug. 1917. Between 1919 and 1922 Coker was educating 28 children, 21 in primary (only 9 of which were Cokers), 4 in secondary school, 3 in higher education (2 in England and 1 in America), see school fees slips, Oct.–Nov. 1922; Eko High School Reports, 1919; Adeniga Coker to J. K. Coker, 11 Sept. 1922; Interview, Aboyade–Coker, 12 Sept. 1961; for a funeral occasion see Phillip Coker to J. K. Coker, 12 Dec. 1918; for requests for patronage see A. C. Olopade to J. K. Coker, 12 Oct. 1920; for philanthropy see A. Folarin to J. K. Coker, 22 Jan. 1917; E. A. Allen to J. K. Coker, n.d., 1920, *Coker Papers*.

arily he lost his following.[1] But money alone did not automatically confer the position. The general respect of the community gained through public activities of a political, philanthropic, and religious nature was also necessary. A reputation for parsimony or western-type small family selfishness could easily destroy an elder's public image.

If the elder stood for a set of principles which passionately appealed to his following the mercenary and ideological bonds which held the pyramid together were strong and durable. Such a pyramid often survived economic disaster.[2] The elder could rely upon his followers to assist him financially to recover his economic position.

A small local church might possess one elder, the pyramid and congregation being one and the same. A larger congregation divided its allegiance among three or four elders. A strong elder with decided views on church policy, such as J. W. Cole, used his influence over his followers to force his ideas upon the church. Others might be content to represent their followers, to reflect the views and ideas of the junior leaders within the pyramid.

The prominent positions in the church were held by the elders—lay preachers, class leaders, parish committee and school board members, treasurers, and chief contributor to the funds. Title deeds to the land and buildings were under their personal control. Policy required the unanimous consent of the elders, which in turn guaranteed the approval of the congregation. Where, as in Lagos, economic opportunity created a number of independent junior leaders, unanimity was more difficult to achieve. Often these independents combined to form a faction or co-operative circle within the congregation. The circle leader became an elder, but of a different kind, acutely sensitive to the ideas of the faction. It was difficult for him to bend in the interest of unanimity without losing his leadership to others. The instability of the co-operative circles and the hard postures they were forced to assume occasionally caused confusion and brought decision-making to a grinding halt.[3]

Permanent deadlock in the General Committee of the church

---

[1] Coker lost control of his pyramid during his bankruptcy 1905 (see p. 165); A. W. Thomas lost his in the crisis of 1921 (see p. 185).

[2] Because of the principles of Evangelism which Coker espoused, he held the loyalty of many within his pyramid during economic disaster.

[3] The best example of a co-operative circle was the minority party which formed an opposition to Elder Thomas in the A.C. (Bethel) and was led by Dada Adeshigbin (see p. 185).

could not be resolved by an appeal to the vestry, since the split in the Committee was reflected in the congregation. Vestry votes were occasionally taken to persuade a recalcitrant minority to give way. Often they had an effect upon co-operative circles who professed adherence to the majority principle. The pyramids were less amenable. A majority vote was not accepted as a valid basis for policy.

In these circumstances the chief elder as chairman of the parish committee or the General Committee was a powerful figure in the smooth operation of governmental machinery. Besides his influence as elder of the largest pyramid, he was allowed, as chairman, considerable manipulatory power over business procedure. His success depended upon his ability to compromise, to prevent decisions being taken until assured of unanimity, to lobby, and to see that all pyramids and circles were fairly considered for appointments to office.

In committee the agenda had to have his approval. He delayed contentious motions by requesting prior notice, then used his influence outside committee to see the motion was never raised. If the mover was adamant he might persuade the elders to permit it a place on the agenda. If division persisted after a full and frank exchange of ideas the chairman could suspend discussion. If the motion was put against his wishes he could defer it, a process which might be repeated for months or even years. Sub-committees were other favourite delaying devices.[1]

If the chairman was confident of his control he might allow the motion to be put to the meeting (that is if the mover was tactically so inept as to move). It would be unanimously defeated, voted down by those who moments before had spoken in its favour. The proposal was then refused further place on the agenda, since a decided issue could not be re-raised for six months to a year. An adverse vote signified the elder's pyramid was dissolving. Sometimes an elder stood against the expressed wishes of the majority for years. Upon his death or removal a long list of measures held up by his opposition were suddenly translated into policy.[2]

Customarily the elders stood for conservatism leavened by an astute ability to compromise. The junior leaders, those within the pyramids or co-operative circles, often represented the radical and progressive. The elders of the following generation emerged from their ranks. Generally they began as retail traders or commission agents (R. A. Williams), junior civil servants (T. D. Shaw), small

[1] See pp. 125, 184.   [2] See pp. 147, 186.

planters or farmers (D. A. Hughes), or Yoruba physicians (D. A. Jones).[1]

They held positions as organists, choir masters, teachers, and evangelists within the church. A following was usually attracted by their ideas and beliefs, and their will to change the established order. They held the majority of seats in church committees, and occupied subsidiary positions as secretaries, assistant secretaries, and auditors. Their majority did not give them control even if united against the policy of the elders.

If the power of the elders was weakened by death, economic misfortune, or dissension, the junior leaders might occupy the positions generally held by the former. The result often indicated their political immaturity. They were unable to maintain unity among themselves. They passed impulsive and radical legislation for which the congregation was unprepared. The junior leaders failed to realize that since they did not control a large personal following like the elders, intensive educating of the congregation as to the purpose of their new legislation was necessary.

The clergy were chosen from among the junior leaders. Their chance of success increased in proportion to their independence. Those too closely identified with one or other of the pyramids remained suspect. For this reason the African churches showed a marked aversion to the ordination of elders. Not one became a clergyman prior to 1920, though many aspired to the office.[2] An independent origin was enhanced by ordination. A sincere and able clergyman was able to command respect and gain influence over a congregation in a way which cut across the pyramids, circles, and factions in an unusual manner.

The power of the clergy partly arose from their independence from the sullied and shoddy relations which often held the pyramids together. Partly it grew out of the Yoruba Christian belief in the divine sanction which accompanied ordination. Sometimes the women (excluded from the governing bodies of the church), many of whom were

---

[1] Memorial Plaque Christ Church, U.N.A. Ebute Metta; J. K. Coker vs. J. O'Connor Williams, Chief Justice Record Book, vol. 17, p. 129; Interview G. A. Oke, 10 Nov. 1961; Native Service Record Books, vol. 3, p. 130, Ibadan, CSO2/13; U.N.A. Minutes, 17 Mar. 1919, pp. 239–42; Farmers Meeting Minutes, Ifako, 20 Sept. 1911, Coker Papers.

[2] Elder J. K. Coker actually wore clerical dress. Mrs. C. G. Lumbley to J. K. Coker, 6 Aug. 1920, Coker Papers. For similar aspirations of J. W. Cole see H. A. Williams to the editor, Times of Nigeria, 20 June 1921.

independent leaders in their own rights, were strong clerical supporters.[1] On occasions of friction and deadlock the advice of the
clergy was of convincing impartiality. They spoke as if the entire
congregation was their pyramid.

With few exceptions, the African churches were fortunate in their
choice of clergy. Their integrity and education could have brought
them remunerative positions in government and commerce had they
chosen. They were poor. Their humble circumstances were in marked
contrast to the ostentatious display of clothes and wealth of the leading laity. That they had the moral courage to lecture the elders on
their sins gave the clergy prestige. Those who implicitly obeyed their
elders nevertheless enjoyed their occasional discomfiture.

It was vital that the clergy thoroughly appreciated the role of the
elders and the necessity of unanimity. A wise pastor never sought to
directly challenge the chief elder. If he did so his defeat was almost
certain. His power was strictly that of moral suasion. Applied
over months, many elders saw their duty and did it.

From what has gone before it would appear that the voice of the
congregation expressed through the vestry meeting was merely a
rubber stamp. When the vestry was called upon to pronounce on a
deadlocked issue in the committee the vote at the end formed a minor
part of the proceedings. In the pre-vote discussion the elders and
junior leaders were thoroughly lectured on their inability to take
decisions, on their factiousness, and selfishness. Proposals were put
forward and debated, rejected, others introduced, and possible solu-
tions suggested.

The vestry was jealous of its prerogatives. Normally it voted back
the same members into office year after year. Yet any effort to tamper
with its right of election created a general revolt. It was believed to be
going too far to defeat an elder standing for office. If in the heat of
election it ever happened the winning candidate, with the approval of
all, stepped down for the defeated elder.

The system was effective. The vestry was a last resort after all other
avenues to peace had been explored. It was not a pleasant experience
for an elder to face a vestry exposure of his sins of omission and commission. Many an elder left the vestry in a rage. The bonds of the
pyramid prevented an adverse vote, but they did not muzzle free
speech. Once a dispute had been laid before the vestry it became

[1] For a similar situation in the Ethiopian churches of South Africa see Sundkler,
Bantu Prophets, 1961, p. 142.

public and the wider community exerted pressure. The weekly Press
occasionally joined in cajoling a stubborn elder.

The whole government structure shunned a majority decision. Between 1900 and 1920, in the African Church Movement, policy was
not initiated a dozen times without unanimity. In half of the instances
where it was, the result was confusion, disaffection, stagnation, withheld finances, and retrogression. It was doubtful if the reform—no
matter how urgent—was really worth it.

To the western-trained the frustration appeared unbearable. This
was possibly one reason why the African churches appealed so little
to those educated in England. It helped to explain the conservatism
of the movement. By the time the junior leaders had become elders
and were able to initiate policy the radical ideas of their youth had
become conservative by the standards of the new age. Opportunities
were missed, the young disheartened, and finances disorganized. On
the other hand, once a unanimous decision had been taken, it could
be executed with exceptional vigour.

Many youths supported the majority principle only to abandon it
when they became elders. This was realism. Majority decisions were
incompatible with eldership. A disruptive situation arose when the
number of independents equalled or exceeded those within the
pyramids. The demand for the majority principle challenged eldership. In such situations the criticism that every African aspired to
leadership had some validity. To base consent upon majority votes
would have led to endless division and splintering. Large united
organizations were the result of adherence to the principle of
unanimity suited to the economic and social conditions of the membership. In other fields the African churches have been castigated for
their rigid adherence to foreign forms. In the governing authorities
which they developed they balanced a judicious blend of Africa and
the West to create something unique, something adapted to the
modern Africa in which they lived.

The U.N.A. and the African Church Organization demonstrate
contrasting methods and results in their development. The former
worked through patient compromise to a lay-dominated organization. The latter through ceaseless turmoil to clerical control.

In 1891 the elders and junior leaders who established the U.N.A.
drew up a skeleton constitution which indicated their Methodist and
Anglican background. It signified the desire to enshrine lay control
L

by means of a lay president. In doctrine and usages the new organization would resemble the Methodists. The Sunday-morning service followed the Anglican litany, while the evening provided for extempore prayer as in the Methodist fashion.[1] Six lay founders constituted themselves into the General Committee, the supreme and only governing body.

There was reluctance on the part of the elders to stand for election. During the first five years they did not seek any kind of mandate from the people. Occasionally dissatisfaction was hushed by co-optation of extraordinary members. Both times this method was resorted to, a permanent enlargement of the General Committee followed.[2]

The General Committee employed D. B. Vincent (later Dr. Mojola Agbebi) to minister to the new organization. Vincent, previously a Baptist, had been one of the leaders of the secession from the Baptist Mission in 1888. He had been operating a school for Baptist children which he brought under U.N.A. control. Vincent pushed evangelism, organized a Sunday school and choir, and published a number of tracts, which favourably contributed to the image of the infant U.N.A.[3]

From the beginning Vincent showed leadership qualities and radical ideas for which he later became noted. He favoured Native dress and Yoruba names. The U.N.A. prohibited him from adopting either. Friction arose over his opposition to churching the dead and his Baptist methods of administering the sacraments, especially baptism. The elders disliked the popularity of immersion as opposed to sprinkling. Legally both were acceptable, but the almost unanimous demand for immersion was an indication of Vincent's growing influence.[4]

Vincent sought to democratize the government. He challenged the self-constituted General Committee and agitated for trustees for the church property, which the chief elder, J. W. Cole, kept under his personal control.[5] Vincent's radicalism, his democratic view on church government, and his popularity and influence with the congregation all combined to create a challenge to the elders' control.

[1] Report of the rules and regulations sub-committee, U.N.A. Minutes, 24 Aug. 1891, pp. 9–13.
[2] U.N.A. Minutes, 31 July 1893 and 9 Aug. 1895, pp. 102–3 and 174–5.
[3] U.N.A. Minutes, Jan.–Aug. 1892, pp. 41–77.
[4] U.N.A. Minutes, Oct. 1891–Sept. 1892, pp. 26–82.
[5] U.N.A. Minutes, May 1892–July 1893, pp. 65–103.

DR. MOJOLA AGBEBI

When the question of his ordination arose the chairman began the customary delaying tactics.

Vincent's challenge to lay authority was typical of clergy with marked qualities of leadership. Given his influence over the congregation, and a system whereby major policies were decided by the vestry, his power would have increased at the expense of the General Committee. Similar clerical challenges of eldership were repeated in 1903 and 1920.

In the early years the choice of churches in Lagos was between either lay control with extempore prayer, immersion, and the doctrine of personal 'conversion' or clerical control with formal prayer, sprinkling in baptism, and belief in growth in the habits of Christian living. Vincent's later history exemplified the dilemma of a man who desired the doctrines of the first and government of the second. He returned to the Native Baptists, where doctrine was congenial but lay control equally as frustrating as in the U.N.A. A decade later he led a schism which created an organization of clerical control based upon Baptist doctrine and ceremony.[1]

After the resignation of Vincent in early 1894 three views of the clergy developed within the General Committee. J. W. Cole, fearing a further challenge to lay control, favoured an honorary lay ministry of the elders. D. A. Jones and E. H. Oke preferred an ordained ministry, but like Cole, they wanted it Native, honorary, and of the elders. H. A. Caulcrick and G. A. Williams proposed a paid ministry and suggested inviting a prominent clergyman from Sierra Leone. They feared that a Native, if chosen, would be polygamous.

J. W. Cole won over Jones and Oke to an honorary lay ministry of the elders. To avoid defeat in the General Committee, Caulcrick and Williams proposed the choice be made by the vestry. Cole shunned setting a precedent of congregational consultation. The General Committee nominated Cole, Jones, Oke, and J. O. George as ministering elders.[2] Within a year complaints arose, class attendance

---

[1] The Native Baptist elders signed an agreement with Vincent which guaranteed their authority. For the agreement and causes of the schism see: The Native Baptist Church *vs.* Mojola Agbebi, suit no. 59 of 1903 in the Supreme Court of the Colony of Lagos, in *Coker Papers* or *Roberson Collection*.

[2] U.N.A. Minutes, 30 July 1894, p. 141. The U.N.A. designated these men, 'chief elders'. I prefer 'ministering elders', since I use the term chief elders as it is customarily employed by the African churches to refer to those paramount among the elders but without power of ministerial functions.

dropped, and membership declined. Caulcrick and Williams challenged the validity of lay sacraments and a polygamous agency. Caulcrick read a number of papers in support of a professional ministry. Williams opened a private fund to challenge Cole's monopoly of church finance and overcome his argument that the church could not afford a paid ministry.[1]

The General Committee voted in favour of a paid ministry. Cole took no action. Six months later it reaffirmed its stand. Cole still refused to move. When pushed, he threatened to resign, and since he held the property and paid over half the church expenses, the General Committee was powerless. Six months later, as the situation deteriorated, three of the ministering elders resigned. Cole was isolated.[2]

Meanwhile Caulcrick and Williams had been conducting negotiations through Blyden for the services of J. E. Fredericks, an African Methodist Episcopal clergyman in Sierra Leone. A motion was tabled in the General Committee to extend an official invitation to Fredericks. The vote was three to two in favour. Cole, acting as chairman, cast a tying vote—a desperate device to avert an adverse vote. The deadlock was complete. Cole became passive, withholding his contributions. The church faced financial collapse. An impulsive junior leader nominated Jones as a replacement for Cole. Fortunately the motion was defeated.[3]

Cole was urged by his supporters to appeal to the congregation. Thus followed the first election to the General Committee and the precedent Cole had previously feared. Oke and Jones called on the support of Cole's pyramid, and with an election cry against foreign ministers and their mistletoe rules (a probable reference to monogamy), they and Cole were overwhelmingly elected. Caulcrick, Williams, and their supporters lost their offices. The new General Committee reaffirmed Cole's position as ministering elder. He died shortly afterwards, and the General Committee invited Caulcrick and Williams to resume their seats. Jones was appointed temporary

[1] U.N.A. Minutes, 25 Jan., 22 Mar., 11 Oct., 22 Nov. 1895, and 31 Jan. 1896, pp. 162, 168, 189, 194, and 202; D. A. Hughes, *Charge to the U.N.A. General Conference*, 1922. Since J. W. Cole paid half of the church expenses, he could ensure that funds were not available for a clergyman. Williams' fund was a device to demolish Cole's argument and undermine his support in the congregation. Similar tactics were employed by Dada Adeshigbin after 1917 in undermining the chief elder, A. W. Thomas, of the A.C. (Bethel). See p. 185.

[2] U.N.A. Minutes, 8 Mar., 16 Aug., 29 Nov. 1895, 17 Jan. and 8 Feb. 1896, pp. 166, 176, 197, 200, and 204.

[3] U.N.A. Minutes, 22 May and 11 June 1896, pp. 216, 218.

ministering elder, and the General Committee promised to provide an ordained and professional clergy in the near future.[1]

Since Cole towered over the other elders in every way, his rule had been autocratic. The rush of changes following his death indicated that while his pyramid supported him to the last, he had lost ideological leadership to Williams and Caulcrick. The situation altered upon his death. The five remaining elders shared influence equally. The autocracy became an oligarchy. Meanwhile the precedent of congregational consultation had been set. Vestry power grew as it was called upon more frequently to settle disputes within the oligarchy.

The elders remained divided. Jones and Oke wanted Natives of the church employed as clergy. Caulcrick and Williams desired a monogamous foreigner. Correspondence was opened with Bishop Small of the African Methodists in America. Small demanded monogamy as a condition of membership and affiliation with his denomination. Monogamy had a chance on its own, but loss of U.N.A. independence was intolerable and the negotiations were closed.[2] Blyden recommended an apostolic Coloured missionary in the Gold Coast, who visited Lagos and ordained three local candidates, D. A. Jones, J. A. Bright, and J. G. Campbell,[3] the last two being recent candidates from outside the U.N.A. who were expected to uphold a monogamous ministry.

John O. George, the weakest of the elders and a compromise between the two factions, was elected president by the General Committee. His presidency was divided into two distinct periods 1897–1900 and 1900–5. During the first period congregation elections followed the pattern set in 1896. The U.N.A. now possessed three churches—Ijero in Ebute Metta, Erelu among Lagos aboriginals, and the mother church, Jehovah Shalom.

[1] U.N.A. Minutes, 4 Sept., 23 Oct., 30 Oct. 1896, 21 May and 5 Nov. 1897, pp. 221, 224, 227, 250 and 275.

[2] U.N.A. Minutes, July 1897–June 1898, pp. 260–93; Hughes, *Charge Delivered to the U.N.A. Conference*, 1922. The A.M.E. Church of America was at the same time successfully negotiating affiliation with the Ethiopian Church of South Africa. Affiliation in 1896 was followed by an enthusiasm which raised the membership to 10,000. Although American Negro, the A.M.E. was still subject to attack as a foreign organization, and schisms followed. The U.N.A. did not experience either the massive inflow of members or subsequent schism. Judged, however, by customary standards, A.M.E. affiliation brought real benefits to the Ethiopians, such as support from the intelligentsia, which the U.N.A. was unable to claim. Sundkler, *Bantu Prophets*, pp. 40–41, 81, and 86.

[3] Oke, *History of the U.N.A. 1891–1903*, p. 8; U.N.A. Minutes, 23 Apr. 1899, p. 327.

Upon the death of J. W. Cole in 1897 the financial base of the U.N.A. disappeared. A determined effort ensued to persuade the general membership to assume greater financial responsibility. As it proved, this was possible, but at the expense of an increase in local autonomy expressed through the parish committees. Elder Williams of Jehovah Shalom attempted to halt this development, but Caulcrick at Ijero and George at Erelu (the branch churches) continued to assert their independence.[1]

In 1900 the General Committee sanctioned a trend it was unable to halt. It recognized the parish committees and instructed them to take over responsibility for the local church and school, and pay agents and teachers. They were also required to give half of the revenue they raised to the General Committee, which was to pay, and have full power over, the clergy.[2]

Congregational influence expressed through the parish committee continued to undermine the unstable oligarchy in the second half of George's presidency (1900–5). In addition, the three ordained clergy were threatening to usurp the dominance of the General Committee in the affairs of the organization.[3] The clergy sought greater authority in the interests of a more vigorous evangelical programme in the interior. Campbell, like the members of the Agege school, was a product of the revivals of the 1880s when he personally dedicated his life to God's work. He was disturbed by the indifference of the lay leadership to evangelism.[4] As a true Evangelical, he sought to have the U.N.A. state its acceptance of polygamy, which to date it had tolerated in practice, but ignored officially.

The power of the clergy grew at the expense of the elders, who were divided. Even Caulcrick and Williams, who customarily stood together and even now opposed Campbell's views on polygamy, were estranged over the relationship between centralized control and local autonomy. But all the elders agreed on one thing—the paramountcy of the laity. They finally united against the clerical bid for power. Fearing to challenge the clergy before the congregation,

[1] U.N.A. Minutes, 15 Oct., 5 Nov. 1897, 4 Mar., 29 Apr. 1898, and 23 Apr. 1900, pp. 268, 275, 281, 287, and 352.
[2] U.N.A. Minutes, 23 Apr., 1 June, and 10 Aug. 1900, pp. 352, 361, and 367.
[3] U.N.A. Minutes, 23 Apr. 1899, 1 May, 25 July 1902, pp. 327, 398, and 401.
[4] U.N.A. Minutes, 27 Apr. 1900, 24 Sept. 1901, pp. 355, 372, 383; 'The Origin of the Building of St. Stephen's', W.A.E. Minute Book 1903–1939; Campbell, *The Origin of the Thirty-six Articles of Faith*, Lagos, 1945, pp. 2–3.

the elders suspended the general elections for three years, and returned to the earlier system of enlarging the General Committee by nomination.[1] Then, unable to control the General Committee, the elders created an Executive Committee of themselves and refused to convene the General Committee. During this time the elders carried the full financial burden of the organization, since the parish committees under congregational influence were withholding their support in protest.[2]

Finally Campbell and Bright decided upon a test of strength. A new congregation had grown up under J. B. Kester at Ikorodu. The clergy repeatedly sought Kester's ordination in the interests of evangelism. The Executive Committee continued to stall, unwilling to add to clerical strength. Bright and Campbell, with a number of the Lagos laity, proceeded to Ikorodu and ordained Kester in May 1903. The Executive Committee dismissed both Campbell and Bright and declared Kester's ordination invalid. Jones threatened to resign in protest.[3]

The suspension of the elections, the ignoring of the General Committee, the arbitrary rule of the Executive Committee, and the threat of losing all their clergy united the opposition against the elders. In a stormy general election in November 1904 the junior leaders under Robert Williams won all the executive positions in the General Committee and either subordinated the elders or failed to re-elect them. The elders became passive and withheld their financial contributions. Soon the General Committee faced an empty treasury and financial collapse. Three months after the election the junior leaders sought reconciliation, Robert Williams admitting that—

[1] U.N.A. Minutes, 25 Oct. 1901, 11 Dec. 1903, pp. 387, 420; F. Cole to J. K. Coker, 30 Nov. 1903, *Coker Papers.*

[2] No U.N.A. Minutes recorded between Apr. 1902 and May 1903, see U.N.A. Minute Book, pp. 401–2; Oke, *History of the U.N.A. 1904–1924,* p. 2; U.N.A. Minutes, 3 Mar. 1905, pp. 440.

[3] U.N.A. Minutes, 8–10 May and 10 July 1903, pp. 402–7 and 408. Campbell, like Vincent, found his leadership ability hemmed in by the strictures of lay control. He might have led half of the U.N.A. membership into schism, but refrained from doing so. His subsequent actions proved the sincerity of his eagerness for evangelism. He established another church (the W.A.E.) in the heart of Lagos pagandom eschewing the policy of 'sheep stealing'. Since he had no ready-made congregation, he worked as a contractor for the money to purchase land and build a church. Campbell made absolute clerical control a cardinal principle of the W.A.E. He believed it was essential to a denomination devoted to vigorous evangelism. Origin of the Building of St. Stephens, 1903, W.A.E. Minute Book; Campbell, *Origin of the Thirty-six Articles of Faith,* pp. 2–3.

... it is not natural ... [for] Africans who had been appointed to a high office to be elected to a subordinate one or to be superseded during their lifetime.[1]

Through the humility of Robert Williams, the effort of the clergyman, D. A. Jones, and the forbearance of G. A. Williams, who though an elder, had continued to sit in the General Committee in a subordinate position, reconciliation was effected. Elder Oke admitted their failings and 'expressed the need for a renewal of the spirit of prayer in our leading men such as had existed in the early days of the church'.[2] After two joint prayer meetings, the junior leaders stepped down and the elders resumed their former executive positions under George. Co-operative action was immediately taken to restore the unity of the church and repair its finances.

In the following general election the elders were re-elected to the executive. G. A. Williams replaced George as president, since his attitude during the young men's revolt gave him influence with both the elders and junior leaders. The new General Committee passed two resolutions to prevent a recurrence of the past troubles. It was made mandatory to convene the General Committee at least once a month, and in future it would choose its own executive from the members which the congregation had elected.[3] These two measures ensured that in future the junior leaders would not be ignored and the executive would remain in the hands of the elders.

By rejecting limited clerical authority the U.N.A. turned against the most natural method of achieving organizational unity. Lay control expressed through the parish committee would eventually lead from local autonomy to local independence. The only way in which the General Committee could maintain its power was to become representative of all the local churches, but transportation and other difficulties prevented this development. Between 1905 and 1917 the power of the General Committee was further whittled away by the local churches.

A centralized organization required a financially strengthened General Committee, but Ijero church at Ebute Metta refused to support any scheme which aimed at strengthening the General Committee at the expense of the local churches. For this reason Ijero led

[1] U.N.A. Minutes, 16 Dec. 1904, 3 Mar. and 6 Apr. 1905, pp. 437, 440, 450.
[2] U.N.A. Minutes, 3 Mar. 1905, p. 440.
[3] U.N.A. Minutes, 10 Aug. 1905, 27 Apr., and 10 Aug. 1906, pp. 464, 475, and 482.

in the development of parish committees. Ebute Metta possessed a strong local patriotism. It was a chronic complaint that Lagos ignored the sister churches. Ijero described the U.N.A. as a group of sister (and thereby equal) churches with the General Committee at its head. In contrast, Lagos, favouring more centralized control, referred to Jehovah Shalom as the mother church, others as branches.[1] The mother–sister terminology was used to express the division over the degree of centralized control. It was a common argument in the African Church Movement and not confined to the U.N.A.

Ebute Metta had developed as a mission station of Lagos, but Porto Novo had sought affiliation with the U.N.A. after a schism from the Methodist mission. It was itself a mother church to outstations in Dahomey. Porto Novo jealously guarded its independence, believing that it was in every sense of the word a sister church.

In 1903 the U.N.A. ordained D. H. Kukui for Porto Novo upon the recommendation of its parish committee, a privilege later denied to Ebute Metta. In 1910 Porto Novo dismissed Kukui. The General Committee divided: Lagos and the clergy believing that Porto Novo was acting too independently; Ebute Metta defending the right of local autonomy. The General Committee was powerless. It hesitated to force a pastor upon an unwilling congregation, and transfer was impossible, since there was no other French-speaking priest. The outstations in Dahomey were too poor to support Kukui, and the General Committee could not subsidize him. Porto Novo's action was allowed to stand, after the parish committee admitted it had acted in excess of its powers.[2] But the precedent had been set.

Kukui's fate was an illustration of the precarious position of clergymen employed by the parish committees. E. Z. Bankole offered for Porto Novo on the understanding that he be paid by the General Committee—an example of the pressure which the clergy exerted towards centralization. Porto Novo agreed to pay an assessment to the General Committee. Through the double exchange rate from French into English and back into French currency, one-quarter of the assessment was lost. Porto Novo paid half the assessment—the half collected in English coin. Thereafter the General Committee allowed the parish committee to pay Bankole's salary. Lagos maintained the

[1] U.N.A. Minutes, 21 Aug. 1917, pp. 179–82.
[2] U.N.A. Minutes, 31 Dec. 1910, 25 Mar., and 30 Dec. 1912, pp. 555, vol. ii, pp. 15 and 42.

procedure was unconstitutional, but in the circumstances there was
no alternative.[1]

While Ebute Metta and Porto Novo resented the 'mother church'
theory, the interior churches in need of financial help were more willing to accept it. The Ikale churches of Southern Ondo accepted
U.N.A. policy without complaint, since no foreign missions were at
work there, and their principles of grants and assistance were unknown. But elsewhere the interior churches expected to rely upon the
U.N.A. as others relied upon the C.M.S., the Wesleyans, and the
African Church Organization. The Ijebu churches, upon the urging
of the Superintendent (D. A. Jones) and in the interest of orthodox
financing, kept all of their moneys in the general fund in Lagos. The
General Committee instructed Ijebu to make arrangements for the
handling of their own funds, since they withdrew in excess of their
deposits. Ijebu was informed that '. . . all churches founded are expected to be self-supporting'. When the Superintendent charged the
Ijebu churches with insubordination the General Committee '. . . objected to holding our branch churches in bondage as foreign churches
do. . .' Finally, Ijebu asked to be a 'mission' rather than a 'church'.
The General Committee refused, insisting that 'It is not the policy of
the U.N.A. Church to take up missions. . . .'[2]

The General Committee's sole concern was the clergy, who were
employed, ordained, paid, and transferred at its command. The system had advantages. It developed a spirit of sturdy self-reliance in the
interior, the lack of which the missionaries tended to bemoan in their
organizations. It encouraged individuals to accept their duty as evangelists, since the organization did not formally concern itself with this
aspect of the work. The result was the patronage system discussed in
an earlier chapter. The development of the Porto Novo outstations
indicated the success of local church and individual efforts.

There were disadvantages. Poverty in the interior meant years
without a priest for many churches. Despite the ceaseless travelling
of the superintendent, the U.N.A. churches received the sacraments
less frequently than the missions. By 1919 the ratio of clergy to members was the lowest of any Christian organization. The slow growth of
the clergy was partly the result of an excess of local feeling encouraged by Ebute Metta and Porto Novo. The General Committee was

[1] U.N.A. Minutes, 17 Mar., 27 Oct. 1916, and 27 Apr. 1917, pp. 139, 152, and
157.
[2] U.N.A. Minutes, 31 Mar. 1905, 3 May 1907, 4 Aug. 1908, pp. 446, 493, and
513.

even more to blame for timidity in not ordaining vernacular agents who could have been employed at rates within the reach of the interior churches. This conservatism with regard to educational qualifications on the part of a General Committee which permitted polygamous priests appeared unusually contradictory. The Evangelicals always argued that the employment of vernacular agents might imply the ordination of polygamists. The U.N.A. policy of accepting polygamists and rejecting vernacular speakers appeared particularly senseless.

Prior to 1911 only Lagos, Ebute Metta, and Porto Novo could afford resident priests. Superintendent D. A. Jones was responsible for administering the sacraments to Ikale, Ijebu, Ibadan, Agege, and eventually Kano. He was not paid a salary, but requested that the General Committee pay his travelling expenses. A superintendent's fund was opened and the local churches assessed. The interior responded quickly.[1]

Prior to 1912 the General Committee asked for one-half of the parish revenues. Ebute Metta and Porto Novo never co-operated. The success of the superintendent's fund encouraged the General Committee to set assessments according to the type of agent the local church employed. An agent's promotion partly depended upon his ability to raise his assessment. This encouraged him to build up his parish contribution to the General Committee. The system was accepted, and by 1920 four interior churches were paying for priests —Agege, Ikale, Ibadan, and Kano.[2]

Upon the assumption of the presidency by G. A. Williams in 1905, the oligarchy of five elders gradually dissolved. Jones became superintendent and Oke removed to Ibadan. Caulcrick and George died. G. A. Williams became the chief and only elder, like J. W. Cole in the past. Like Cole, he held the property deeds. Two junior leaders, T. B. Jacobs and Robert Williams, occupied positions much like that held by G. A. Williams in his younger days under Cole.

[1] U.N.A. Minutes, 21 Jan. 1898, 11 Aug. 1904, 15 Feb. and 5 July 1918, pp. 277, 435, 195, and 202.
[2] U.N.A. Minutes, 29 Mar. 1912 and 15 Feb. 1918, pp. 20, 195. In South Africa both the 'African' and 'Aladura' organizations have suffered endless splintering. While the African churches of Nigeria reversed this trend, the Aladura conformed to the South African pattern. Sundkler (*Bantu Prophets*, pp. 161–79) discusses the causes of fission in sociological terms. He does not discuss what I stress as the major causes of decentralization—inadequacy of central finance, communication difficulties, and parochialism.

Robert Williams had led the young men's revolt of 1905 which overthrew the oligarchy of the elders. Between 1905 and 1919 Williams and Jacobs agitated for a number of reforms; increased clerical staff, both of priests and superintendents, a monogamous clergy, and a new constitution to democratize the organization and provide for an independent clerical authority.

The leadership of G. A. Williams was more subtle than that of J. W. Cole. He was a skilled diplomat and compromiser. His main preoccupation was to hold the U.N.A. together, to preserve its unity. How much of his manipulation of the General Committee by the various means open to him as chairman was the result of his own convictions and how much it was the result of his judgement of the mood of the church was difficult to discover. Seldom did he offer his own personal opinion. But he used all his influence to delay the reforms which Robert Williams and Jacobs proposed, including those on a monogamous clergy which he was known to favour. A monogamy–polygamy dispute could readily lead to division.

In 1918 D. A. Jones, the superintendent, died. According to custom, age, and experience, D. A. Hughes was the logical successor. Like Jones, he had a private income and would continue the honorary superintendency. Hughes was polygamous. Jehovah Shalom supported their young priest, G. A. Oke, for the position.[1] Both Jones and Hughes were from Ebute Metta, a church which half-heartedly supported the organization. Oke was solely dependent upon his salary, and therefore likely to be amenable to General Committee control. He was a monogamist. This combination of local chauvinism, clerical subservience, and polygamy created an issue capable of destroying the tenuous bonds of unity in the organization.

At the same time G. A. Oke began a magazine, the *African Hope*, with an editorial staff of young reformers. Robert Williams (brother-in-law) and Jacobs, in their desire to reform the polygamist ministry, backed Oke and the *African Hope*. The General Committee, fearing the new periodical might become a militant organ of reform, refused to recognize it as the official publication of the U.N.A.[2]

G. A. Williams deferred the vote on the new superintendent four

---

[1] G. A. Oke, Interview, 10 Nov. 1961. G. A. Oke was a nephew of Elder E. H. Oke mentioned earlier.

[2] U.N.A. Minutes, 28 Apr. 1919, p. 247, Minute Book Board of Editors, *African Hope*, 18 Jan.–5 Apr. 1919, *Oke Papers*. Horatio A. Williams, son of Robert, was for a time editor of the *African Hope*.

times in the General Committee to avoid open strife.[1] Jehovah Shalom threatened to boycott a referendum. Schism appeared inevitable. Suddenly in May 1919 G. A. Williams died. Both the clergy and elders were left leaderless. Robert Williams, the vice-president, succeeded to the chair and Jacobs became vice. They promptly appointed Hughes as superintendent and Oke as assistant superintendent[2] to guarantee his succession after Hughes' death or retirement.

Williams and Jacobs now had the opportunity to initiate the reforms for which they had been agitating. The constitution of 1891, which operated 'like the Methodists', was open to the kind of manipulation which had frustrated their efforts in the past decade. A proper written constitution to limit the power of the elders and insist upon monogamy among the clergy was an urgent necessity.

G. A. Williams and the elders had placed every conceivable object in the way of the constitution. It was ten years since a drafting committee had been appointed. Presented to the General Committee in 1911, it was relegated to a review sub-committee, rejected, and again put under review. After a year in the hands of a translation committee it was sent to a lawyer who died (fortunately for the elders) and not recovered from his estate for another year.[3]

The clergy favoured a new constitution because of the provision it was expected to make for independent clerical power. They had quietly asserted themselves through their Ministers Committee, which had been temporarily abolished at one time for acting too independently.[4] The test of strength of 1903 when Campbell and Bright were dismissed was a warning against haste. Over the years it became customary for the Ministers Committee to recommend candidates for holy orders. G. A. Williams permitted this delegation of power, but was unwilling to give it legal force under a constitution. In 1911 precedent was set aside, and over the protests of the clergy the General Committee recommended a man for priesting who subsequently failed as a minister. The Ministers Committee continued to refer to this lay misjudgement, until four years later the General Committee

[1] U.N.A. Minutes, 3 Mar., 17 Mar., 28 Apr., and 9 May, 1919, pp. 234, 239, 247, and 252.

[2] U.N.A. Minutes, 27 June 1919, p. 265.

[3] U.N.A. Minutes, 22 Oct. 1909, 25 Mar. 1911, 6 Mar. 1914, 22 Jan. 1915, 3 Dec. 1917, and 3 Aug. 1918, pp. 532, 560, 72, 93, 193, and 209.

[4] U.N.A. Minutes, 11 Jan. 1895, p. 160. The full title of the Ministers Committee was the Ministers, Preachers, and Leaders Meeting.

apologized.[1] Now under a sympathetic General Committee, the clergy
determined to have their rights written into the constitution.

When G. A. Williams died the constitution laid before the General
Committee was a product of 1909 and entirely inadequate to the conditions of 1919. The interior churches were given no representation.
On the status of local churches it contrived to say nothing. It referred
to Lagos as the mother church and all others as sisters. The Ministers
Committee was given no power to recommend ordinations. Even its
minor decisions were subject to a veto. It was silent on polygamy, but
the authorized form of Native marriage ceremony was appended.[2]

Both clergy and junior leaders had been pressing for the constitution for ten years, and although it gave them less than they already
possessed, it was ratified immediately after Williams' death. Both
parties ignored it. The General Committee, acting within its constitutional right, recommended a man for holy orders. The clergy
protested and the Ministers Committee forced the General Committee to recognize its customary and prior right.[3] Ratification had
been a gesture to tradition. The policy of a respected and departed
elder must not be so obviously dishonoured. It was pointed out how
long and arduously G. A. Williams had worked for the constitution.
It had been his greatest wish that it should be his privilege to sign it.
Ten years was an uncommonly long time to provide a constitution
not six pages in length.

A motion of revision was tabled immediately. The real struggle
ensued. Robert Williams and Jacobs aimed to give the clergy independent authority in exchange for a reform towards monogamy.
The fatal mistake had been to elevate Hughes before the reform
was carried out. Support among the clergy for a monogamous
ministry vanished. The younger clergy, and especially G. A. Oke,
were unwilling to espouse a cause so obviously in opposition
to their superintendent. The *African Hope* opened its pages to a
discussion of marriage customs, but refused to publish articles
openly hostile to a polygamous ministry. The *African Hope* inevitably
came down on the side of polygamy, since J. K. Coker had financed
it when the U.N.A. refused.[4] Advertised as the voice of the African

[1] U.N.A. Minutes, 23 Sept. 1911 and 20 Aug. 1915, pp. 1 and 111.
[2] *The Revised Constitution of the U.N.A. Church*, Lagos, 1919.
[3] U.N.A. Minutes, 16 Jan. and 30 July 1920, pp. 302 and 320.
[4] H. A. Williams to the editor, *Times of Nigeria*, 6 June 1921; see the *African
Hope*, Dec. 1919 to June 1920 for a series of articles by J. K. Coker, 'Did God
Detest Polygamy'. Interview G. A. Oke, 10 Nov. 1961.

Church Movement, it became, in fact, a vehicle of Evangelical expression.

Williams and Jacobs proposed a gradual reform. Future candidates for ordination would be, and remain, men of one wife. Men already ordained should be prohibited from adding to the number of their wives. These proposals should be written into the revised constitution. Jacobs informed the General Committee in July 1920 that he intended to move a motion of reform. It was tabled in September, and after heated debate defeated, the clergy voting solidly against.[1] The same month the parish committee of Ebute Metta recommended the ordination of a polygamist which the Ministers Committee supported. Williams and Jacobs deferred the decision three times. In February 1921, when Williams was ill and Jacobs in the chair, the General Committee voted to accept the recommendation. Williams and Jacobs resigned.[2]

With the reform party broken, the revision of the constitution was rapidly carried forward and came into effect in October 1921.

In a fairly lengthy foreword the U.N.A. set forth one of the best formal statements ever composed defending Evangelical views on polygamy. The repeated use of the word 'tolerate' did nothing to conceal the straightforward policy of acceptance. The fact that the clergy as a separate class were not mentioned indicated U.N.A. determination to turn its back on the double standard preferred by Churchmen of the Lagos school.

The revised constitution[3] was in accord with the realities of 1921. The organization was expanded by the creation of districts (Ibadan, Ijebu, Dahomey, Ikale, Northern Nigeria) and the intention expressed of creating district or assistant superintendents for each, G. A. Oke and S. Ogunmukomi being the first two. The vote was given to members over eighteen, and an earlier restriction against women holding office was abolished. The interior churches were to be represented in the General Committee by their own elected dele-

---

[1] U.N.A. Minutes, 30 July and 17 Sept. 1920, pp. 320 and 330.
[2] U.N.A. Minutes, 22 and 24 Nov. 1920 and 4 Feb. 1921, pp. 328, 340, and 343; *Lagos Weekly Record*, 25 Sept. 1920; R. A. Williams to the editor, *Times of Nigeria*, 13 June 1921; Obituary of R. A. Williams, *Times of Nigeria*, 10 Oct. 1921; Oke, Report of the Third Triennial Conference of the African Communion, typescript, *Oke Papers;* R. A. Williams to the African Communion, *Nigerian Daily Herald*, 24 June 1921; H. A. Williams, 'The U.N.A. Church Defended', *Times of Nigeria*, 20 June 1921.
[3] *Revised Constitution of the U.N.A. Church*, Lagos, 1921.

gates. The power of the General Committee was curtailed by the right of appeal to an Annual Conference which was to be the supreme authority for the organization.

Clerical authority was strengthened by the addition of an entirely new stream of authority controlled by the clergy parallel to the lay stream already in existence. Prior to this the General Committee would never admit that there was any real difference in the church between matters spiritual and matters secular. By the constitution of 1921 spiritual and secular affairs were separated each under its own stream of authority. Both streams merged at the top in the General Conference. The exclusively clerical bodies, the Leaders Committee in the parish, the Ministers Committee in the district, and the Ecclesiastical Board for the organization, handled ordination and discipline of the clergy subject to appeal to the Conference. On the secular side was the parish committee at the local level, the District Councils, and the General Committee for the whole organization.

The symbols of lay control, chairman of the parish committee and the General Committee remained unchanged, but the new body, the District Council, was chaired by the assistant superintendent. This clerical intrusion into the secular side was of considerable importance, since the District Councils elected the interior representatives to the General Committee. In Lagos and Ebute Metta no District Council was created. Their representatives continued to be elected directly by the membership.

The temporary control over the General Committee which the clergy gained in 1921 as a result of the confusion among the laity gave them the opportunity to draw up and have ratified a constitution which provided for enhanced clerical power. But the change, great as it was, did not represent a fundamental switch of authority. Lay control was a cardinal principle of the U.N.A. Not even the radicals would have favoured clerical authority. Under the revised constitution ultimate authority rested with the conference—a predominantly lay body. In any dispute between the Ecclesiastical Board and the General Committee the Conference could be expected to support the lay body, especially since the president of the Committee was also chairman of the Conference.

The clergy were subjected to the most searching criticism before the Conference. They rarely emerged unscathed. The laity condemned them for the moral state of the parish, the meagre increase in membership, the failure to visit, and the slow progress of the parish

schools. The clergy maintained that their humiliating positions and
poor stipends deterred men of stature from choosing the U.N.A.
ministry as a vocation. Such men chose the African Church Organization, where they were given positions of respect and influence and
not subjected to an annual humiliation by the laity.

The U.N.A. of 1922 was a vastly different organization from what
it had been in 1919. The revised constitution was in advance cf
present needs, but it set forth the goal towards which the church was
moving. The assessment system was providing a more stable financial arrangement. The decentralizing tendencies had been arrested by
the representation of all areas on the General Committee, the assistant superintendents, and the Annual Conference. The clerical staff
corresponded to the church's needs. More authority had been granted
to the clergy, which made them less servants of the organization and
more co-partners, albeit junior partners with the laity.

Only on marriage customs had the U.N.A. turned against the progressive policy. Toleration of polygamy expressed by a monogamous
clergy and polygamous laity was a progressive policy with firm scrip-
tural base. It was a flexible policy which could neither be accused of
making marriage custom a prerequisite of salvation nor standing in
the path of social change. Acceptance of polygamy, besides ignoring
St. Paul's advice for a monogamous clergy, projected an unprogressive image of an attempt to preserve something which, in places at
least, was outdated.

Unfortunately the clergy were unwilling to accept the gradual reform proposed in 1920. The whole African Church Movement had
watched the progress of the debate within the U.N.A. with keen
attentiveness. The divergent policy of the U.N.A. towards polygamy
became the greatest single obstacle to organic union of the African
churches.

The history of the U.N.A. was a story of compromise from its
foundation meeting, which brought together Anglican and Methodist
laymen who employed a Baptist as their first pastor. In ceremony, it
used the Anglican form on Sunday morning and the Methodist on
Sunday evening. It tolerated both sprinkling and immersion in baptism. Often the compromise was achieved after prolonged negotiations. It took eight years to decide upon an ordained clergy, twenty-
eight to produce a constitution, and thirty to lay down a policy on
marriage.

The elders maintained their control by possession of the property,

M

substantial financial contributions, and manipulation of the procedure of the General Committee. Upon the death of Elder Cole the property deeds were passed to G. A. Williams, chief elder of the following decades. The arbitrary action of the oligarchy prior to 1904 was possible because it underwrote the total expense of the General Committee. Twice withheld subscriptions were effective—to block a paid ministry in 1896 and following the Young Men's Revolt in 1904. Elder Cole was clumsy and heavy handed in manipulation of the Committee. Williams' ten-year delay of the constitution indicated his superior skill.

Turmoil and confusion resulted from the void in the leadership at the elder's death in 1897 and again in 1919. On both occasions an oligarchy or co-operative circle of junior leaders produced a rush of changes or 'reforms' for which they had long been agitating. Their impatience, political immaturity, and inexperience in manipulation lost them the confidence of the vestry. They could not, like the elders, rely upon solid pyramids of support in the congregations. The result was the rising prominence of the clergy.

The weakness of lay leadership invited the clergy to strengthen their position. Campbell and Bright failed in 1903, but Hughes was more successful after 1919. Since it was axiomatic that strong eldership produced decentralization, the clergy gained some support by their ability to arrest this trend.

The vestry was twice a decisive factor in policy. In 1896 it supported Cole and eliminated his opposition. In 1904 it defeated the oligarchy and elected the young men. Customarily the vestry pursued compromise but stopped short of imposing a settlement by unseating prominent elders. After the elections of 1896 and 1904 compromise was effected and the defeated parties resumed their original positions. The 'stepping down' of the young men in 1905 was the kind of compromise gesture which won universal support.

Vestry pressure favoured local autonomy in disputes between the parish and general committees. Local autonomy was the natural result of provincialism, distance, and costly communications. The U.N.A. barely succeeded in overcoming these difficulties. Had the colonial government consciously or unconsciously added to them, multiplication of independent churches from the common U.N.A. origin would have followed. Where colonial governments in other parts of Africa were not as disinterested, African churches were less

CHIEF J. K. COKER

successful in developing organizations which held the allegiance of members over large geographic areas.

It was symbolic of the difference between the U.N.A. and African Church Organization that while the former took thirty years to formulate its policy on polygamy, the latter took six months. The problems which faced both organizations were the same. Their manner of solution could not have been more dissimilar. It was difficult to believe that these churches operated in the same society, in the same decades, and one block apart in the same city. The African Church Organization was created out of the most energetic section of the most dynamic C.M.S. church in Lagos—St. Pauls Breadfruit. Its homogeneity was a disadvantage. It had not the experience in self-government which the Methodists and Baptists brought to the U.N.A.

Its dynamism was its downfall. In the first four years of its existence the African Church sought to solve all its problems: establish a ministry, ratify a constitution, define the status of the local churches, and codify its attitude to polygamy. The result of this speed was a four-way division.

Within the leadership the same groups appeared—the elders and junior leaders—fulfilling similar roles as in the U.N.A. The two most prominent elders were J. K. Coker and A. W. Thomas.

J. K. Coker (1865–1945) was the eldest son among the twenty-eight children of Ajobo Coker, the Jaguna of Iporo and prosperous cotton farmer of Abeokuta, who had begun an import–export business in Lagos in 1870. James Johnson was the formative influence and instrument of Coker's conversion in the revivals of the 1880s. Coker appeared unaffected by Crowther, but he bore for Johnson affection verging on reverence. It was Johnson's influence which caused Coker to pause in the secession from Breadfruit in 1901. When Tugwell pushed the disaffected out of St. Pauls the schism placed the two friends, Coker and Johnson, in mutually hostile organizations. The friendship survived the schism. Bishop Johnson wistfully preached the reunion of Christendom, while Coker managed Johnson's farm at Agege and made his annual contribution to the endowment fund, which he firmly believed a futile effort the C.M.S. would never honour.[1]

[1] J. K. Coker, 'The African Church', *African Hope*, Mar. 1922; J. K. Coker, 'Diary and Account Book, 1905–7', and J. K. Coker to the editor, 1916?; *Coker Papers*.

By 1901 Coker was managing his father's estate. In 1903 he placed the Lagos business under his brother John and went to Abeokuta to oversee the cotton farm. Ajobo died the following year, leaving valuable property but little liquid capital. All of the family responsibilities (seventeen children were minors) fell on Coker's shoulders. After the settlement of the will he placed the cotton farm in the charge of another brother, Ben, and returned to Lagos, to find that John had run the business into £2,000 debt, for which the three European firms, McIver, Miller Brothers, and John Holt were suing him. By financial acrobatics and borrowing from the African merchants, J. H. Doherty and A. W. Thomas, he arranged satisfactory terms of repayment. Coker then turned to his Agege plantation to make it produce. By 1910 he was out of debt. Beginning in 1912 and continuing until 1920, Coker became a very wealthy man. The commodity prices crisis of 1921 again almost ruined him.[1]

A. W. Thomas (1856–1924) was born in Oyo, his father was a close relative of the Alafin (the paramount ruler of the Yorubas). He was baptized by D. Hinderer, the pioneer missionary in Ibadan, where he received his early education. He first became a mercantile clerk and then joined the civil service. Finding favour with Governor Moloney, he rose to become Deputy Registrar of the Supreme Court. He accumulated wealth and visited England. He was a member of the Lagos *élite* and a worshipper at Christ Church. He educated two of his sons as lawyers. His daughter married one of the wealthiest men of Lagos.

Thomas' influence was the result of the prestige of his birth and his position among the Lagos *élite*. J. W. Cole was the only other of this class to join the African Church Movement. Thomas used his wealth in the accepted manner to create a following within the church. He built himself a large residence, Ebun House, decorated with fine plaster work by the Brazilian craftsman, Balthazar. In 1915 he won the auction contract to dispose of the German assets from the Cameroons. Thereafter he spent £2,000 on the building of Bethel African Church in the heart of Lagos.[2]

Thomas and Coker were the two wealthiest men in the African

---

[1] Coker's statement in Supreme Court, suit no. 93 of 1906; J. K. Coker to my lawyer, 1906?; A. Folarin to J. K. Coker, 11 Dec. 1922, *Coker Papers*.

[2] Deniga, *African Leaders*, pp. 31–33; N. S. Miller, 'The Beginnings of Modern Lagos', *Nigeria Magazine*, Aug. 1961, pp. 110 and 163; Macmillan, *Red Book*, pp. 103–4.

Church. The peaks of their affluence came at different times—
Thomas' before 1916, Coker's after. Both suffered severely in the
economic crisis of 1921. There the similarity ended. Thomas was in
commerce, Coker in agriculture. The former was of the city and enjoyed the society of the *élite*, while the latter was of the country and
mocked the *élite*'s artificiality. Thomas was a 'civilized African',
Coker gloried in being 'an African'.[1] In the church they were
protagonists of two extreme views. Thomas was the conservative
Churchman, Coker, the radical Evangelical.

In 1901 Coker emerged as chief of the founders of the African
Church and principle elder at thirty-five years of age. He financed
the litigation in the St. Judes property case, but his financial limita-
tions prevented it from reaching the Privy Council. Then came his
difficulties, his absence in Abeokuta, bankruptcy, and dissension in
the family over the settlement of the estate.

Thomas was not an original seceder. In the beginning he had been
hostile to the African Church, but through the influence of Coker he
was persuaded to seek membership. Thomas' prestige and wealth led
him to usurp Coker's position after 1905, when Coker was forced to
seek his financial assistance. It seems likely that Thomas pro-
pounded lay control and local autonomy from conviction. But in any
case these issues provided him with a popular ideological base from
which to challenge Coker.

From the beginning Coker and Thomas held opposing views. It
became evident that the disagreements indicated a fundamental
cleavage of beliefs and aims between two distinct schools of thought.
As the junior leaders lined up behind the two elders, the line of
division emerged of what later distinguished Churchmen from
Evangelicals. On marriage customs where they agreed upon the dual
standard, it later became apparent that their motives were different.
Churchmen tolerated polygamy as an expedient. To Evangelicals it
was the first step towards full acceptance. As each decision was taken
there was an exodus of members back to the C.M.S. Between 1905

[1] The leading Anglican member of the Lagos *élite* referred to Coker as an
'obscure person', 'pseudo politician', and 'farmer' who gives *us* 'the impression
of a chimpanzee at the zoo'. *Nigerian Pioneer*, 5 Dec. 1919. An African Churchman replied that the editor of the *Pioneer* and his associates did not know Coker
because he was not an attendant at Government House, ballroom concerts, lodge
rooms, and race meetings. Coker's retort was characteristic. 'I am proud of it.'
O. T. Somefun to the *Standard*, 9 Dec. 1919; J. K. Coker to the editor, 9 Dec.
1919, *Coker Papers*.

and 1907 the two groups hardened. Compromise became steadily more difficult, and finally impossible.

The 'sign of the cross' dispute has been discussed in another context.[1] It was the first issue to divide Coker and Thomas and, although settled amicably, some of the Thomists (notably Dawodu and Oguntolu) were unhappy with the decision. The arbitrary action of the clergy during the dispute left a legacy of ill-will which was apparent when J. S. Williams and S. A. Coker requested consecration.

Many opposed the creation of an episcopate. It was an unbridled bishop who had pushed them out of Breadfruit. It was ecclesiastical tyranny against which they protested in the Anglican Church. Two weeks of fierce dispute ended in a compromise whereby superintendents or presbyter bishops were to be created—a careful distinction being drawn between the powers of presbyter bishops and the historic bishops of the apostolic succession. Coker and Williams were elevated. The creation of two superintendents, one from Lagos and one from Ebute Metta, indicated that Lagos domination, as in the U.N.A., was already an issue in Ebute Metta. Three were ordained: D. C. Coates for Bethel, J. A. Lakeru for Jehovah Jireh (Ebute Metta), and A. O. Ijaoye for Ijebu.[2]

The U.N.A. governing authority began as a committee of the founders. In the African Church the General Committee was composed at first of all those who wished to attend. It included a number classed as sympathizers, who had not broken from the C.M.S. When St. Judes joined it was given a representation of six, which was the first limitation on the General Committee's amorphous form. By 1903, when the secession had become schism, the sympathizers were less welcome. They were expected to take a stand. Particularly those who wished to 'distinguish the camp' became hostile to the C.M.S. influence which the sympathizers brought to bear. At Easter 1903 sympathizers were allowed to attend the General Committee on invitation only.[3] This action was logical, but it was a blow to Thomas, for those with C.M.S. ideas were his natural allies. However, it removed a fluid element. Those who remained could be brought more readily within the elders' pyramids. The lines were hardening.

[1] See above p. 129.
[2] A.C. (Bethel), *Conference Proceedings 1901–1908*, p. 81; J. K. Coker, The First Five Years of the A.C. 1901–1906, *Coker Papers;* S. A. Coker, *Three Sermons on the Christian Ministry*, London, 1904.
[3] Coates *vs.* Thomas and others, Chief Justice Record Book, vol. 41, Oct.–Nov. 1904, p. 400, and vol. 42, Nov. 1905–Jan. 1906, pp. 29–44.

BETHEL CATHEDRAL OF THE AFRICAN CHURCH, LAGOS

As early as 1902 Bethel organized a parish committee elected by the membership. The General Committee instructed that it should 'appoint officers and agents and maintain them'. Bethel interpreted this so as to give the broadest local autonomy and to include the clergy. The General Committee claimed that was not its intention.[1] The parish committee became a stronghold of the Thomists, who used it to place a brake on what they considered the radicalism of the General Committee.

An example of this radicalism was the inclusion of women members in the General Committee and the appointment of a deaconess. Here again was an Evangelical triumph considered scandalous by Churchmen. The women tended to be traditionalists who would ordinarily have been Thomists. For example, they had opposed tampering with the sign of the cross. But Coker had scored another victory. The women enthusiastically supported this innovation.

In 1904 the Thomists sought to promote a constitution. They designed it to attract widespread support. It proposed to provide lay control by the appointment of a lay president and lay chairman of the parish and General Committee as in the U.N.A. It provided for equal representation popularly elected for Lagos and Ebute Metta, an attractive item in the latter city. Coker's party and the clergy combined in their own interests. In the compromise the Thomists gained one significant concession—the popular election of all lay delegates to the General Committee.[2]

The first election to the General Committee was a trial of strength between Coker and Thomas. Coker had a number of advantages. He had the prestige which followed him throughout his life of being chief of the founders of the African Church. He had gathered around himself a group of talented young men devoted to creating a church worthy of the race. He had the support of the clergy. But Coker was not then the wealthy man he later became. His supporters more resembled a co-operative circle than a pyramid. Finally, his bankruptcy and the division within his own family weakened his hold over the 'hangers-on'. Coker faced this popular test of strength with little but the force of his ideas. The past policies of the General Committee (which were his policies) had each in turn alienated

---

[1] See Judgment of Chief Justice Nicol in A.C. (Salem), *Conference Report,* 1907, pp. 35–43.

[2] Coates *vs.* Thomas and others, Chief Justice Record Book, vol. 41, pp. 400–14, and vol. 43, pp. 1–9; J. K. Coker to Ajasa, 1905?, *Coker Papers.*

sections of the membership. The election was a test of their popularity.

Over the previous four years Thomas had used his wealth to build himself a solid pyramid of support in Bethel. He added to this his personal conviction that Coker was steadily abandoning the principles which had inspired the organization's birth—an enhanced place for the laity in the church, local autonomy, and an end to bishops and their tyranny.

The elections were held at Easter 1905. The Thomists, some vaguely threatening to remove Bethel from under the General Committee, swept into all offices of the church. In the first flush of victory they set up a special Interior Committee charged with managing the evangelistic activities of Bethel Church. It behaved like a General Committee and was accused of schism. Bethel vestry repudiated the Interior Committee and dismantled it. This encouraged Coker and the Clergy to believe that the Thomists had gone too far and lost the support of the church.

The miscalculation led Coker to take the first illegal step which culminated in a flood of illegality so complicated that legal argument could not possibly untangle the confusion. Coker and his supporters refused to vacate their General Committee seats for the newly elected Thomists.

Thomas claimed Coker was creating another form of Anglican oppression. Coker was as firmly convinced that Thomist policies were designed to reproduce the impotence of the U.N.A. in the African Church.

The whole church became involved.[1] The bitterness of feeling surpassed anything before or after in the African Church Movement. There was no alternative to Coker or Thomas—no one big enough to command respect. The clergy were too involved on Coker's side. The elder concept was in direct opposition to the majority principle. It was as useless for Coker to stand in the way of majority opinion as it

---

[1] The whole story of the crisis is told from one side in A.C. (Bethel), *Conference Proceedings 1901–1908*, and from the other side in A.C. (Salem), *Conference Report 1907*. The latter prints a number of important documents and letters. Coates *vs.* Thomas and others, Chief Justice Record Book, vols. 41–43. From the *Coker Papers* the following: (*a*) Testimony by A. W. Thomas, n.d.; A. O. Ijaoye to the Superintendents, Sept. 1905; J. K. Coker to Ajasa re C. C. Cole, 1905?; J. K. Coker's testimony, 1905?; O. T. Somefun to J. K. Coker, 5 Sept. 1905; D. J. Sorinolu to J. K. Coker, 7 Aug. 1905; Campbell, 'Something We Ought to Take Note Of', *Times of Nigeria*, 29 Aug. 1921.

was for Thomas to believe he could replace Coker and set him aside as chief elder.

An outside attempt at mediation, led by M. L. Stone of the Baptists and assisted by U.N.A., C.M.S., and Methodist laymen, failed. Both Thomas and Coker agreed to it, but although Thomas with his wealth could impose a settlement on his party, Coker in his financial difficulties was no longer the leader, but the spokesman for his supporters, who repudiated the arbitration. After this initial setback the arbiters retired.

The Thomists used the parish committee to govern Bethel. The General Committee attempted to control the parish committee through the minister, D. C. Coates, in his capacity as chairman. The parish committee invited A. O. Ijaoye, a deacon working in Ijebu, to replace Coates as pastor. Coates was suspended and then dismissed. He ignored the dismissal and continued to officiate in the church.

Force replaced political manœuvring. With a police posse outside, Coates forced himself into the church. He was thrown from the chancel as Ijaoye entered. The sidesmen carried him bodily out the main door. The congregation divided into fighting factions, ending when Coker's party escaped through the windows. The Thomists assaulted the women who retaliated, marching through the streets of Lagos singing songs of condemnation of Thomas and the anti-feminists. The African Church never recovered from the damage done to its prestige. It was hardly an enviable image of African leadership.

Violence was followed by a long series of lawsuits by and against the pastor, D. C. Coates, to determine whether the parish committee or General Committee held the power of dismissal. The court ultimately ruled that the basic cause of the establishment of the church had been the forcing of an unwanted clergyman upon an unwilling congregation. Since the church had not adopted a constitution, the congregation had not delegated its authority to choose or dismiss its clergyman to either the parish committee or the General Committee, the congregation must still make its decision regarding Coates.

Violence again flared as both the parish committee and General Committee sought to get a favourable verdict from the congregation. The General Committee disconnected the Thomists from membership. The parish committee retaliated against Coker's party. Fisticuffs developed at the door of the vestry meetings, over which membership cards were valid. The result was vestry resolutions for and against Coates according to whom had convened and chaired the meeting. Case followed case before the courts, Coker financing one, Thomas the next. Anonymous threats against life were made, adverse resolutions not recorded, and minute books disappeared.

After an unsuccessful scramble to purchase the leased property on which Bethel was built, Coates and Coker locked the building and took the keys. The Thomists broke it open, changed the locks, and slept in the building. The Thomists finally prevailed. The court ruled that Coates had been properly dismissed by the Bethel vestry. Superintendent S. A. Coker and D. C. Coates withdrew with the minority and formed Zion Church a few blocks from Bethel.

The General Committee virtually ceased to function for a year. In 1907 the Ebute Metta church, which had remained neutral during the crisis, instructed its pastor, J. A. Lakeru, to call a reconciliation conference of all the churches of the organization. Bethel refused to attend. Dominated by Coker's party, the conference organized the African Church (Salem) under a constitution which gave ultimate authority to the clergy. An abortive mediation attempt by the interior delegates failed. The Thomists had already moved to call a rival conference which organized the African Church (Bethel). This conference ratified the constitution of 1904, and under the influence of the extremists led by T. B. Dawodu, eliminated the last vestige of clerical influence and defined local autonomy in terms of absolute independence.

Jehovah Jireh Church of Ebute Metta had remained neutral to prevent division. Its attempt at reconciliation had resulted in the creation of two African church organizations which forced Ebute Metta to take a decision. The church divided peacefully. Since Jehovah Jireh was a temporary structure, both the majority under the pastor J. A. Lakeru and the minority under T. B. Dawodu left to form new churches. The majority formed Salem, which affiliated with Zion in Lagos and supported the A.C. (Salem). The minority formed Bethlehem and joined Lagos Bethel to support the A.C. (Bethel).[1]

Both organizations made strenuous efforts to gain the allegiance of the interior churches. Delegations on tour argued their respective philosophies, which provided an education in church government to the less sophisticated interior. Both new constitutions offered the

[1] A.C. (Bethel), *Conference Proceedings 1901–1908*; A.C. (Salem), *Conference Report*, 1907.

interior churches direct representation on their General Committees, a step in advance of any of the other African churches.

The delegations offered an excellent opportunity for the interior to ventilate its peculiar grievances, which had nothing to do with laity versus clergy. The delegations were thoroughly reproved for the image of African leadership which their childish behaviour in Lagos was projecting to the interior. The result had been a steady loss of membership to the C.M.S. What did the pros and cons of laity and clergy mean to the interior churches which had no clergy? They had not seen a superintendent in the past three years. The interior was becoming tired of what one church described as adultery, 'from one husband to another', from the C.M.S. to Bethel, from Bethel to Salem.[1]

Many churches sullenly refused to attend either of the rival conferences. They listened to the competing delegations and refused to declare for either. This mood was a warning that repeated crises of leadership would forfeit any claim which Lagos had to leadership. The interior's reaction had a sobering influence.

The decision of the interior rested upon two considerations—the attractiveness of local autonomy under the Bethel constitution as against the hope of financial support under the constitution of Salem. On this basis the stronger joined Bethel and the weaker, Salem. The cities chose Bethel, the villages, Salem. Fortunately the organizations did not foment schism and accepted the majority decision in all but one case.

Coker's party had been called the minister's party. Coker with some justification denied this. Of the five clergy, only Lakeru and Coates joined the A.C. (Salem). Superintendent J. S. Williams and the deacon, Ijaoye, stayed with the A.C. (Bethel). Superintendent S. A. Coker set up his own organization.

Both A.C. (Bethel) and A.C. (Salem) drew up constitutions in 1907. In the A.C. (Bethel) the General Committee dominated by the laity held wide theoretical powers. But since the parishes paid their clergy, the General Committee held power over the superintendents only. By 1921 the local churches were raising £4,000 a year, out of which they paid a 2½ per cent. assessment. This provided the General Committee with a yearly budget of around £100. The central authority was so weak that the A.C. (Bethel) might have been

---

[1] J. J. S. Nicol to J. K. Coker, 7 Mar. 1907; Nicol to J. K. Coker, 19 Apr. 1907; J. A. Daniel to J. K. Coker, 15 July 1907, *Coker Papers*.

accurately described as a confederation of churches. Section six reflected the spirit of the constitution. The individual churches shall be:

. . . independent, self-governing, self-supporting and self-extending, making their own arrangements, raising their own funds, controlling their own finances, appointing and dismissing their ministers, ordained or unordained.[1]

In contrast, the General Committee of the A.C. (Salem) was the most powerful body in the organization, with an annual budget around £1,000, responsible for the salaries of all the clergy and half of the expenses of evangelism.[2] Combined with the power of the superintendent over matters spiritual, the result was a highly centralized organization.

In this regard the A.C. (Salem) was unique in the African Church Movement. It faced unique problems. Since evangelism was half financed by the General Committee, the organization was carrying out what appeared to be a missionary programme. Providing the finances inevitably led to charges of interfering with local autonomy, of promoting mission-churches held in bondage, and of behaving as a foreign society.

The A.C. (Salem) carefully drew the distinction between mission-churches and their own system of dependent-churches. 'To nurse to independence' was a favourite slogan. The nursing often appeared like prodding. Like the U.N.A. Ijebu churches, which asked to be classed as 'missions', the interior welcomed financial assistance in the early years. There came a time when finance became the secondary, and local autonomy the primary aim. Customarily the dependent period lasted less than ten years, after which they were thrown on their own resources. If the church collapsed the town was abandoned. Surprisingly few collapsed.

Critics of the foreign societies usually agreed that there was nothing basically wrong with the mission system except that the period of tutelage and dependence was far too long. The African churches, however, challenged the whole idea and tended to be critical of even a ten-year period. Christianity either spread by conviction or by money. The A.C. (Salem) policy of bolstering conviction by even a little money was a denial of the principle. The implication was that if

---

[1] A.C. (Bethel) Minutes, 15 Dec. 1921, iii, pp. 223–7: 'The Constitution for the General Government of the African Church [Bethel]', *Conference Proceedings 1901–1908*, pp. 10 and 39.

[2] The General Committee in Account with J. K. Coker, 1916, *Coker Papers*.

Salem had the resources of the foreign societies it would mix God
and Mammon for longer and longer periods.

The A.C. (Salem) countered its critics by declaring that the organization had a duty to bring the sacraments to its members and teach
them to read the scriptures in the vernacular. This was no less a duty
because they were unable to pay for these services. The vital test was
that the local church could at any moment it felt oppressed pick up
its material possessions and join another organization.[1] None had
done so, although some had joined the A.C. (Salem) because of neglect by other African churches.

The question of raising adequate central finances had not been
solved by the U.N.A. The A.C. (Bethel) followed the U.N.A. pattern. What success A.C. (Salem) achieved was due first to the evangelistic fervour which that organization was able to maintain, and
second, to the smooth working of its leadership. Nothing had such an
adverse effect upon central income as strife within the General
Committee.

Between 1907 and 1910 the coastal churches paid subscriptions to
the general fund to defray the cost of the superintendent's visits to the
interior churches. By 1913 all of the local churches were paying
regularly into this fund. Between 1913 and 1915 Associations for
Evangelism were formed in all the churches, some of which accepted
the financial liability for specific dependent churches.[2] Prior to 1914
the general fund for clerical salaries had been collected by a system
whereby the local churches remitted one-quarter of their collections.
In 1914 this was changed as in the U.N.A. to fixed assessments, in
order that the General Committee had some idea of its budget for
planning purposes. The response from the churches was satisfactory.
The General Committee paid the clergy and nine unordained
evangelists.

Between 1914 and 1917 inflation and the rapid increase in membership in the interior caused the first real financial crisis. More money
and inadequate funds became a preoccupation of the General Committee. In 1917 the General Committee took drastic action by ruling
that only subscribing members could vote in elections and that agents

[1] A.C. (Salem) Minutes, 10 Feb. 1919, *iv*, pp. 172–8; Circular, 14 July 1925,
Coker Papers.
[2] A.C. (Salem) Minutes, 19 Sept. 1910, 8 Apr. and 6 May 1913, 12 Jan. 1914,
8 June 1915, and 26 June 1917, *ii*, pp. 81, 141, 143, and 160, and *iv*, p. 31, and
rough minutes in *Coker Papers.*

must supply lists of members and the amount of their subscriptions to the General Committee. Furthermore, churches not paying at least £15 a year were threatened with the loss of their school teacher. The General Conference of 1917 was shocked at these tactics and recommended that the General Committee hold its 1918 budget to the 1917 level.[1]

The stringent economic measures produced a mild revolt in the Abeokuta district where the African Church had been making phenomenal progress between 1916 and 1920. The churches of Abeokuta rather peremptorily announced their intention to form a District Council to organize and finance evangelism in the Abeokuta district.

Instead of charging Abeokuta with insubordination, J. K. Coker persuaded the General Committee to accept the District Councils with good grace, and to formulate a constitution to guide this handing over of General Committee power. The Council was to be under the chairmanship of the superintendent or senior minister. It would include all ministers and agents and two to four delegates from each local church. It would have authority over all unordained agents and education. It would make recommendations to the General Committee with regard to the clergy. The District Council was to control all finances raised by dependent churches within its area of jurisdiction. The General Committee by this innovation was turning over its evangelistic activity to the local churches where they were financially able to bear the responsibility. In new areas the General Committee continued to act as the major source of finance and inspiration. The strength of the tendency to decentralize and the intensity of local feeling was exemplified by the popularity of the District Council. Within a year three more had been formed—in Akoko, Ilaro, and Ekiti.[2]

The District Councils were supposed to lift the financial burden from the general fund. But the General Committee's budget continued to rise, as the statistics below indicate. These figures show the part of the budget raised by the church. The main financial support came from patrons. For example, in 1916 the church-raised budget totalled £409. J. K. Coker personally added £757 to raise the central

[1] A.C. (Salem) Minutes, 13 Aug. 1917 and 21 Jan. 1918, *iv*, pp. 102 and 113.

[2] A.C. (Salem) Minutes, 8 May 1917, 21 Jan. and 19 Nov. 1918, *iv*, pp. 93, 113, and 161: J. K. Coker, Constitution of the A.C. District Councils; Sodeinde to J. K. Coker, n.d. 1917; Minutes of the Second Meeting of the Ekiti District Council, 2 Oct. 1918; Sodeinde to J. K. Coker, 30 Oct. 1918, and Report of the Work of the General Committee for 1917, *Coker Papers*.

fund to £1,166. The dependence of the church upon the planter patrons of Agege was a source of weakness. The collapse of primary produce in 1921 bankrupted the planters and destroyed the elaborate structure of the A.C. (Salem).

Budget of the G.C. of the A.C. (Salem) Raised by Assessments [1]

1914	1915	1916	1918	1919	1920
£293	£222	£409	£504	£660	£720

In contrast with the U.N.A., the history of the African Church was one of confusion. In the U.N.A. crises developed slowly. The issues were clear and the leadership moved within defined constitutional limits. In the African Church all the issues exploded between 1905 and 1907. The leadership was unstable and the line blurred between constitutional and unconstitutional behaviour.

The schism of 1901 had been in the nature of a young men's revolt against the elders of Breadfruit. Secession had been unpremeditated, and Coker, almost in surprise, found himself its leader. Had A. W. Thomas been among the seceders, he would naturally have become their chief elder. By the time he joined, Coker enjoyed the prestige which surrounded his title, 'chief of the founders'. His replacement required delicate manœuvring. It might have been facilitated if he and Thomas had shared similar ideologies.

Neither by age (thirty-six in 1901) nor wealth was Coker prepared for eldership. He possessed little capital, and after his bankruptcy, none. Thus, unlike J. W. Cole, he did not hold the property deeds. Passive membership and withheld subscriptions were not weapons he could use. He was, in fact, a brilliant junior leader with radical ideas, personal charm, and ceaseless energy unparalleled among African Church laymen. But like the younger men of the U.N.A., he lacked political maturity and the art of manipulation and compromise. His appeal to the civil courts against his fellow members (a grievous sin in African eyes) lost him the sympathy of the uncommitted. Leadership of a co-operative circle rather than a pyramid compelled him to assume rigid postures. The refusal of the circle to abide by the arbitration he had accepted embarrassed him and brought his word into question.

The crisis was complicated by the action of the clergy in using the

[1] *Proceedings of the Ninth General Conference of the African Church* (Salem) *December 1916*, Lagos, 1917; The General Committee in account with J. K. Coker, 1916, *Coker Papers*; A.C. (Salem) Minutes, 13 Apr. 1915, 22 Oct. 1918, 30 June 1919, and 16 Feb. 1920, *iv*, pp. 28, 155, 197, and 233.

confusion among the laity to enhance their prestige and power. They sacrificed their impartiality for Coker's support. The Thomists retaliated by limiting their influence. Superintendent J. S. Williams, possibly because of his maturer years, was the only one to remain neutral and impartial. Had the clergy imitated him, they might have achieved their objective in the role of mediators.

The first general election at Easter 1905 was a rebuke to Coker. The vestry momentarily turned away from its conciliatory role. It immediately indicated its repentance by rebuffing the Thomists (at Coker's request) by dismantling the Interior Committee they had created as a rival to the General Committee. Coker did not reciprocate the gesture, but turned to the civil courts, hoping to get a legal judgement based on Anglican custom and procedure. The courts, however, ruled in favour of the majority principle, requesting the vestry to pronounce a verdict totally out of keeping with its normal role. Neither party accepted the majority principle. So followed the violence as both factions sought legally and illegally to procure a vestry decision. Once Thomas had been vindicated, a gesture of conciliation would have prevented division and won him universal applause. He chose not to make the gesture.

The crisis encouraged the desire for local autonomy, and introduced the 'mother–sister argument' to the organization. Thomas championed the parish committee and local autonomy, against the central authority. Furthermore, it was not surprising that the crisis aggravated jealousy and suspicion between Lagos and Ebute Metta— a significant factor in U.N.A. history as well. In the division they chose opposite organizations. Lagos became the headquarters of the A.C. (Bethel), Ebute Metta of the A.C. (Salem). When new constitutions were drawn up both found it necessary to guarantee local autonomy to woo the interior churches.

Decentralization in the A.C. (Bethel) (to be discussed later) was a marked trend in the next decade. The A.C. (Salem), through the dependent-churches' theory, maintained a strong central authority. In essence, the interior submitted to Lagos direction as long as that city carried the financial burden. The moment it grew beyond the resources of Lagos alone and the wealthier interior churches were requested to assist, they pressed for decentralization. Rather than share the burden of the rising budget, the Annual Conference froze central expenditure in 1918. If the interior churches were to contribute more for the spread of the organization they preferred to do it through local bodies. The District Councils resulted, initiated not unnaturally by the wealthiest interior church—Abeokuta.

Even before the African Church was fully established in 1902, the editor of the *Lagos Standard*, G. A. Williams of the U.N.A., called for the co-operation of the St. Pauls' secessionists with the U.N.A. to form a national church. Blyden supported the proposal and others suggested an amalgamation of the African churches of West Africa, to be arranged at a conference in Cape Coast. A church union committee was set up in Lagos.[1]

Mojola Agbebi was the only leader of sufficient inter-colonial stature to lead an amalgamated church. In December 1902 he was guest speaker at the African Church organization's first anniversary. During his lecture he replied to Blyden and the *Lagos Standard* by describing the amalgamation as a non-essential which could bide its time. Agbebi reflected the views of his own organization—Ebenezer Baptist—which had never considered itself an African church. Furthermore, Agbebi had just created a Baptist union embracing independent Baptists from Sierra Leone to the Cameroons.[2] Baptist principles were important to Agbebi. They would be lost in an amalgamation. For the moment his anniversary lecture dashed the hopes of the promoters.

A year later the U.N.A. and African Church were still talking of 'our intended purpose to amalgamate'.[3] But schisms were more popular than unions. Two in 1903, followed by three in the crisis of 1905–7, produced seven warring and hostile denominations. It was a sorry spectacle for the idealists and spurred the efforts of those who felt that amalgamation was the only method by which the tarnished image of the movement could be restored.

At the close of 1907 the A.C. (Bethel) invited M. T. Euler-Ajayi, a U.N.A. clergyman, to deliver their anniversary lecture. He raised the issue again, no longer as amalgamation but as federal union.[4] Little but discussion followed.

[1] *Lagos Standard*, 19 Feb. and 6 Aug. 1902; Theophile, 'Exodus from Spiritual Bondage', *Standard*, 9 Apr. 1902; Letter from Sierra Leone to Agbebi, 9 July 1902, in the *Standard*, 27 Aug. 1902.

[2] Agbebi, 'Inaugural Sermon', *Conference Proceedings 1901–1908*, p. 94; *African Times*, 5 July 1899, p. 100; *Standard*, 26 Apr. 1899; *Agbebi, An Account of Mojola Agbebi's Work in West Africa*, Lagos, 1903.

[3] Francis Cole to J. K. Coker, 30 Nov. 1903, *Coker Papers*.

[4] M. T. Euler-Ajayi, 'Annual Sermon 1907', *Conference Proceedings 1901–1908*, pp. 20–21; Winfunke, *Causes of Indigenous Churches*, p. 15.

N

It was obvious that much patient work was necessary to restore amity before any type of union was possible. The U.N.A., which had taken the lead in the past, did so again. Beginning in 1908, it turned its anniversaries into occasions in which all the clergy of the African churches were invited to take part. In 1910 all of the organizations participated. Heartened by this response, the U.N.A. convened a meeting of the clergy and proposed an annual united week of prayer in conjunction with the Evangelical Alliance. The clergy were agreeable, but upon return to their respective organizations discovered that the proposal was coldly received.[1]

The clerical meeting resulted in the formation of a Free Churches Ministers Union. Its aim was to promote amity and interdenominational good will. It was ultimately successful in winning general support for the week of prayer and promoting united appeals for such bodies as the British and Foreign Bible Society.[2]

J. K. Coker was so impressed and inspired by the united week of prayer that he approached the Ministers Union with a proposal for the formation of an African Communion to perpetuate good will throughout the year. The union agreed to convene a meeting of clergy and representative laymen. The first meeting sat in August 1912 and agreed upon the desirability of a Communion, but divided over its aims and the basis of union.

At a second meeting it was agreed that organizations eligible should be those 'of local origin and African management'. A committee of seven was elected to draft a proposed basis of union, and Agbebi was chosen to head the committee.[3] His Anglican and Baptist background was of immense importance for drafting an agreement which would be acceptable to such diverse organizations as Araromi and the A.C. (Bethel).

The basis of union was presented to the third meeting of the delegates on 28 August 1912. It consisted of ten statements, the first nine

[1] U.N.A. Minutes, 28 Aug. 1908, 31 July 1909, and 6 Aug. 1910, pp. 515, 527, and 548. *Evangelical Alliance Programmes for Universal Week of Prayer*, 1909 and 1912, Report of a Meeting on the Week of Prayer sponsored by the Evangelical Alliance, 14 Dec. 1908, and Campbell to Jones and Euler-Ajayi, 18 Dec. 1908, W.A.E. Minute Book.

[2] A.C. (Salem) Minutes, 31 Jan. 1910, *ii*, p. 69; Circular to the African churches, 7 Mar. 1910, *Coker Papers*.

[3] U.N.A. Minutes, 24 July 1912, *ii*, p. 31; A.C. (Salem) Minutes, 11 June 1912, *ii*, 120; J. K. Coker to General Committee, A.C. (Salem), 22 May 1912, *Coker Papers*; Euler-Ajayi, General Report of the African Communion, 1913, *Oke Papers*.

of which were traditional statements of orthodox Protestantism. There was opposition to the word 'communion'. Some preferred African Church Alliance for the name of the organization and Lord's supper for the ordinance. The promoters opposed both as weakening the vital core of the venture—inter-communion. Opposition arose to the doctrinal statement—'justification of sinners by faith'. One group proposed adding 'and repentance'.[1] Another felt literacy should be included; an example of missionary teaching as opposed to biblical example.

The basis of union ended with what became the most controversial of all—statement ten. It was designed to cover the points of dis-agreement on dogma and organization (polygamy, the Christian ministry, and the balance between clerical and lay authority). It was paradoxical that statement ten, fashioned with so much care to avoid friction, was the cause of future ill-will and dispute.

This basis does not involve an assumption to define the limits of Christian fellowship; and no compromise of the views of any member; or sanction of those of others on the points wherein they differ is required or expected; but all are held free as before to maintain and advocate their re-ligious convictions with due forbearance and brotherly love without interfering with, or disturbing the order of polity of any African Church to which its membership belong.[2]

The organization was to consist of a General Council composed of all the clergy and seven delegates from each member denomina-tion. The executive was to be elected at triennial conferences. The influential positions, president, vice-president, and secretary, were to be held by the clergy, the subordinate posts by the laity. The lay-controlled organizations objected to this clerical domination. Amendments added the 'lay heads' to the executive. This in turn frightened clerical organizations. The A.C. (Salem) stressed that this post had created confusion in the past. While J. K. Coker was now being appointed, it was for communion pur-poses only. He held no duties or rights under Salem's constitution. The W.A.E. refused to appoint a lay head. It also refused to tolerate the clergy standing before a lay conference for election. When the proposal that clerical heads should take the presidency

[1] Euler-Ajayi, General Report, *Oke Papers*; A.C. (Salem) Minutes, 24 Sept. 1912, *ii*, p. 129.
[2] Euler-Ajayi, General Report, *Oke Papers*.

in rotation was turned down the W.A.E. refused to sign the basis of union.[1]

Eight organizations participated in the preparatory meetings. Three accepted the basis of union, and the African Communion was formed in 1913, with Mojola Agbebi its first president. Its success in promoting co-operation induced others to join in the following years —A.C. (Bethel), A.C. (Penuel), and U.A.M. (Eleja). Active branches operated in Ibadan and Agege.[2] In 1921 the Communion was at the peak of its power and prestige, uniting six organizations which held the allegiance of 90 per cent. of the African churchmen of the Yoruba country.

The Communion developed admirable co-operation between its members. It arranged for comity and settled disputes on overlapping. The united anniversaries and week of prayer continued under its auspices. United revival conventions were an added event. The Communion clergy led the processions at prominent funerals.[3] They attended each other's ordinations and consecrations.

The U.N.A. took the lead in inviting the bishops of the member organizations to lay hands in the elevation of its superintendent. Upon the establishment of the U.A.M. (Eleja) in 1917 the Communion provided the ministerial functions for that church for three years. When the U.A.M. (Eleja) decided to create its own clergy in 1919 Communion, bishops were invited to ordain. They continued to provide this service until 1938, when the U.A.M. (Eleja) asked the Communion to elevate a superintendent so that they might perpetuate their own ministry.[4]

The Ministers Union continued to function in co-ordination with the Communion, and other subsidiary organizations were created—a Women's Auxiliary and a Choir Union. Joint financial projects were undertaken, such as collecting for Belgian war relief, a Communion

[1] G. A. Oke, Iwasu Isin Adupe ti African Communion Ti a se ni, 25 Aug. 1935, Oke Papers; Sixth Annual Conference, May 1914, W.A.E. Minute Book.

[2] Scott to J. K. Coker, 31 July 1914; Agbebi to J. K. Coker, 28 July 1913; J. K. Coker, African Methodist Church, 1918, Coker Papers, U.N.A. Minutes, 28 Sept. 1912, p. 37.

[3] The Communion held a memorial service for Bishop Johnson, the only mission person ever so honoured. See Communion circular, 18 June 1917, Coker Papers.

[4] Oke, History of the U.N.A. 1904–24, pp. 14–15 and 47–48; U.N.A. Minutes, 3 Apr. 1914, p. 74; U.A.M. (Eleja) Preachers Book, 1921–30; U.A.M. (Eleja) Twenty Fifth Annual Report, 1942, typescript; U.A.M. (Eleja) Vestry; U.A.M. (Eleja) Anniversary Programme, n.d., Coker Papers.

Hymn Book, an Agriculture Institute, and a Theological College. The Communion sought to defend the name of the African churches and sued the C.M.S. for a publication which described their doctrines as 'pernicious'.[1]

In 1917 the Communion organized a day of prayer for the success of imperial arms 'to damp down unrest' and develop love between rulers and subjects. In 1920 another day of prayer sought blessing for the nationalists in the National Congress of British West Africa. The 1920 prayer topics included 'that brotherhood and unity may be increasingly developed among Black men so that those close to the Governor may give just and sympathetic advice', and again, 'that the spirit of hatred towards the Black man may die out in the hearts of the White and the truth that both are the same, grow and develop'.[2] Both were significant. The first reflected the general concern over the reliance of the governor upon the advice of a small coterie of Africans of the establishment. The second indicated uneasiness at the growing racial antipathy which followed the First World War.

The Communion's most important role was an unexpected one. It became a court of appeal for disputes between factions within the organizations. It was natural to expect that it would become an arbiter of inter-organizational disputes. But it was surprising that the organizations permitted the infringement of their sovereignty on matters of a strictly internal nature. Successful decisions were handed down on disputes in the U.N.A., in Bethlehem, and in Bethel churches.[3] In comparison with the civil courts used earlier, the Communion provided a dignified and economical solution to factional disturbances.

The Communion played a definite and positive role in promoting co-operation between the A.C. (Bethel) and A.C. (Salem) which led to their reunion in 1922. The A.C. (Salem) for a number of years professed eagerness to enter into reunion negotiations. The sincerity

[1] G. A. Oke, Report of the Third Triennial Conference of the Communion, 1919–22, *Oke Papers*, U.N.A. Minutes, 23 Aug. 1918, pp. 209 and 217; A.C. (Salem) Minutes, 1 Oct. 1917, *iv*, p. 108; A.C. (Bethel) Minutes, 27 Mar. 1920, *iii*, p. 112.

[2] J. K. Coker to Oke, 23 Jan. 1917; Additional Prayers for the Evangelical Alliance Prayer Week, 1920, *Coker Papers*.

[3] U.N.A., *Thirtieth Anniversary Report*, p. 11; Oke, Report of the Third Triennial Conference, 1919–22; Oke, Iwasu Isin Idupe . . ., 1935, *Oke Papers*; Oke, *History of the U.N.A. 1904–1924*, p. 38; A.C. (Bethel) Minutes, 12 July, 19 July, 15 Sept., and 27 Oct. 1921, *iii*, pp. 172, 176, 191, and 200; *Times of Nigeria*, 13 June and 20 June, 1921.

of its motives were never tested, because the A.C. (Bethel) refused to negotiate. The change of heart of the A.C. (Bethel) in 1921 came as a culmination to multiple problems which beset that organization after 1914.

The power structure within the A.C. (Bethel) was familiar. A. W. Thomas (like J. W. Cole and later G. A. Williams of the U.N.A.) was chief elder, supported by junior leaders—the key figures in his vast pyramid of followers. Policy could not be initiated, far less put into practice, without his consent and active approval. Thomas was more powerful in 1914 than when he challenged Coker in the popular election of 1905. He continued to show a unique ability to espouse popular causes and combine them with the influence of his wealth to weld his pyramid into a formidable force within the A.C. (Bethel).

Thomas emerged the undisputed elder of the A.C. (Bethel) after the crisis of 1905-7. During the following seven years a possible challenge and alternative to his leadership developed around independent junior leaders—the Adeshigbin brothers and the Agege planters, C. C. Cole and Fred Williams.

Dada Adeshigbin (1865-1925) was a commercial agent in Lagos, the sole representative for thirty years of the Singer Sewing Machine Company in Nigeria. He was an active patron of the interior churches He was a modest man, devoted to reform within the church by constitutional means. His son qualified as a medical doctor and his daughter married another prominent African churchman and merchant, Disu Ige, a Moslem convert to Christianity. His younger brother, Akin, established Tika Tore Press in 1910, which became an important publisher of nationalist writings. In the early 'twenties it published the Yoruba weeklies *Eleti Ofe* and *Eko Akete*. In the 'thirties Tika Tore published the *African Church Chronicle*, which Oke Adeshigbin, another brother, edited.[1]

C. C. Cole (1868-1923) and Fred Williams (1867-1918) were planters at Agege, the chief elders of the plantation church, St. Andrews Iju. Cole was also proprietor of Karaole printing press, begun in 1898 in Lagos. His son Aboyade-Cole entered the ministry and in 1962 was elected primate of the African Church Organization. Both Cole and Williams were personal friends of J. K. Coker, chief elder of the A.C. (Salem). They owned adjoining plantations. Their co-operative efforts in the Agege Planters Union brought them into

[1] *African Church Chronicle*, Apr.–June 1936; *African Messenger*, 18 Oct. 1923; Memorial Plaque, Bethel Cathedral; Ikoyi Burial Grounds.

daily contact.[1] Plans for reunion matured on the plantations of Agege.

Three issues aroused controversy in the A.C. (Bethel) between 1914 and 1921. They were the demand for revision of the constitution to give more clerical authority, reunion with the A.C. (Salem), and a dispute over whether the new Bethel Church was to be built as a story or ground structure.

The revision of the constitution towards a clerically controlled organization was supported by those disturbed by the stagnation of the church as compared with the dynamism of the A.C. (Salem). The General Committee was financially too weak to initiate, far less carry out, policy. In contrast, the individual churches were strong. They paid the best clerical stipends in the African Church Movement. Yet this was insufficient to draw candidates to the ministry. Rebel C.M.S. clergy preferred the lower salaries of the A.C. (Salem), where they wielded influence in policy making.[2]

The clergy complained of the low ebb of spirituality among the laity. The result was immorality, self-assertion, and continual strife. They maintained that this corruption was the result of a constitution which controlled its clergy but not its laity. The clergy realized that they either moved in concert or not at all. In the General Committee they argued in favour of constitutional revision, but when a vote was called they voted against it, wisely realizing that the laity, and especially Thomas, held power over them.[3]

Some of the laity, led by A. A. Obadina, favoured the clerical argument, pointing out the evils of an excess of local autonomy and the narrow limits to General Committee power. It could not ordain, transfer, or dismiss clergy except upon the recommendation of parish committees. In one instance two priests were charged with disobeying the General Committee. The clergy boycotted this meeting in protest against condemning ministers who obeyed their parish committees, as was their duty under the constitution. Sufficient laity agreed with them and the charges were dropped.

The General Committee could not even compel a minister to appear before them. When Ijebu Ode District Council forbade its ministers to appear before the General Committee many of

[1] Interview, Rt. Rev. A. Aboyade-Cole, 27 Feb. 1962; A.P.U. Minutes, 27 July 1912, *Coker Papers;* Isaac O. Williams, 15 Jan. 1962 (interview).

[2] See Table VI, part III, p. 123.

[3] A.C. (Bethel) Minutes, 7 Mar. 1917, 27 Sept. and 18 Dec. 1919, and 16 Dec. 1920, *iii*, pp. 1, 94, 108, and 147.

the elders in helplessness talked of halting the trend of decentralization.[1]

T. B. Dawodu, president of Bethlehem and Thomas, president of Bethel, supported by the interior churches, especially Ijebu Ode, opposed meddling with the constitution. They blamed clerical control for the schism from Breadfruit in 1901 and the crisis of 1905–7. It was an emotionally charged issue.[2] The interior, as always, associated clerical control with Lagos domination.

For the clergy, reunion with the A.C. (Salem) would achieve the same end. That organization was unlikely to submit to a reunion constitution which denied clerical authority. Since only one of the twelve ministers had experienced either the schism of 1901 or the crisis of 1905–7, they had no personal bitterness arising out of the past. Reunion was a popular proposal, especially for the younger laity, even those within Thomas' pyramid. They talked of its inevitability, of the two visible branches of the one spiritual African Church, and the scar which division continued to implant upon the image of the church. They hoped reunion would provide an institution of secondary education and theological training, from which some, no doubt, hoped to benefit personally. The youths admired Coker and the militancy of the A.C. (Salem). Coker wooed them sedulously with popular gestures—a generous donation to a worthy cause, an invitation to a lavish festival on his plantation.

The Agege planters, A. A. Obadina, C. C. Cole, and Fred Williams, were party to the conspiracy to undermine Thomist strength. On 11 December 1916, as a gesture of gratitude for his fiftieth birthday, Fred Williams issued an appeal to both organizations to appoint seven delegates each to sit as a committee of reunion. In sub-sections of the appeal Williams provided for an endowment of £500 and fifty acres of land to be invested for the joint use of the African churches (Bethel and Salem) and the U.N.A.[3] Williams died before the advantageous moment could be utilized by the union party. But the appeal stood as a rallying point. When the union was ultimately consummated tradition gave the major share of the credit to Fred Williams.

The third problem was the new Bethel building. The majority of the congregation voted for a tall, story building. The minority, which

[1] A.C. (Bethel) Minutes, 7 Mar. 1917, 28 Apr. 1917, and 27 Mar. 1920, *iii*, pp. 1, 8, and 147.
[2] A.C. (Bethel) Minutes, 7 Dec. 1917, *iii*, p. 50.
[3] A.C. (Bethel) Minutes, 12 Dec. 1916, *iii*, pp. 75–80.

included the elders, wanted a modest one-story edifice. Since the
elders would shoulder the costs, they expected their wishes to prevail.
Normally they would have. But A. W. Thomas reversed himself and
joined the 'poor majority'. He determined to erect the tallest building
in Lagos, which would look down upon the mission churches—especially Christ Church. Thomas declared he would build a church
worthy of his name to demonstrate his zeal and love for the work of
God, the African Church, and the race.

The congregation subscribed £200. Thomas loaned £800 and construction began. Dada Adeshigbin led the 'wealthy minority', who
questioned the elaborate structure and doubted whether the congregation could afford its future upkeep. He foresaw that the total cost
would run to £10,000, no more than 10 per cent. of which could be
expected from the congregation.[1]

No one doubted that Thomas could build the church without the
assistance of the elders. But they feared, and rightly, that this was
designed to strengthen Thomas' control, which was being threatened
by the clergy, by demands for constitutional revision, and by the
Williams' appeal for reunion.

It was customary for elders to use the device of a loan to maintain
their control. J. W. Cole, for example, 'gave' the U.N.A. their first
building in 1891, but the title deeds were in his name and possession.
Before his death he turned them over to G. A. Williams, who succeeded him as chief elder. If there was no threat to Thomas' position
within the organization the loan would never be collected. If, on the
other hand, he was challenged he could (in an extreme case) sue the
church and seize the building.

Thomas' position appeared secure. He demonstrated repeatedly
that he had popular support. Ebute Metta and the interior defended
the constitution and Bethel supported the story building. Reunion
was popular everywhere, but impractical as long as the constitution
remained unrevised and the Bethel building incomplete. Most wanted
the story building and reunion too. Thomas made this impossible. In
1917 he held a mortgage on Bethel for £2,000. If his opposition ever
combined to revise the constitution and push reunion he could
threaten to foreclose.

[1] 'Quiet Worshipper', *African Messenger*, 7 July 1921; A.C. (Bethel) Minutes,
16 Dec. 1920, *iii*, p. 147; Brief of the Minority Party to the African Communion,
19 Dec. 1916 and Fred Williams to Congregational Meeting, 6 July 1914 (Document A), Communion File, *Oke Papers*.

Thomas, like a clever diplomat, never openly expressed his hostility to the measures he opposed. As president of the General and parish committees, he used all the prerogatives of his office to his advantage—postponing the vote, suspending discussion, pleading no quorum, and crossing out unsatisfactory resolutions from the minutes.[1] The wealthy minority fought back by refusing to contribute to the building funds. A number of times transaction of business was halted in deadlock. Thomas usually resigned. The result was his massive re-election by the congregation. The vestry finally passed a resolution that he should hold office without re-election until the building had been completed.[2]

When Fred Williams issued his appeal in 1916 Thomas insisted that it should take precedence over constitutional revision. He argued that since the reunited organization would have to fashion a new constitution, to revise the present one was unnecessary duplication. Thus he sought to ride the popular issue of reunion—at least not to appear as opposing it.

A committee of reunion was elected by the General Committee. Thomas' nominee, T. B. Dawodu, a strong opponent of both revision and reunion, was selected to head it. Dawodu stalled the work of the reunion committee for two and a half years, once declaring the appointments irregular, then calling for new appointees, and finally complaining of the inadequate representation of the interior churches. When requested to report the committee's progress he pleaded illness and failed to attend the General Committee.[3]

The opposition united after the partly completed structure of the church collapsed in 1917. The wealthy minority withheld their contributions and boycotted the Sunday services. The clergy, aware of the futility of individual opposition, joined their superintendent in refusing to attend the General Committee until revision of the constitution was begun. United action brought them one minor gain. For the first time (in 1918) the A.C. (Salem) was invited to participate in their anniversary celebrations. This was some time after the A.C.

[1] A.C. (Bethel) Minutes, 22 Nov. 1918, 27 Mar. and 26 June 1920, *iii*, pp. 65, 112, and 116.
[2] Pope, 'The African Bethel Church in Travail', *African Messenger*, 30 June 1921.
[3] A.C. (Bethel) Minutes, 7 Dec. 1917, 28 Mar. and 12 Dec. 1918, and 27 Mar. 1920, *iii*, pp. 50, 55, 75, and 112; Dawodu to J. K. Coker, 22 May 1918, *Coker Papers*.

(Salem) had extended a similar invitation. For years now both clergy had been mingling in U.N.A. services.[1]

To restore peace, the African Communion was asked to arbitrate. The collapse of the building had been a heavy blow to Thomas. His £2,000 had accomplished nothing. During the arbitration he offered to reduce the loan by £500 and make another loan to begin rebuilding if the elders would recommence their subscriptions. The Communion supervised the vestry meeting, where Thomas once again received overwhelming support. His gift of £500 and his offer of a further loan were accepted.[2]

The arbitration failed. The wealthy minority had sought a written agreement from Thomas stating the terms of repayment. Thomas promised that it need not begin until after the building was completed. There would be no interest charge. The annual payments would not be oppressive. The elders pressed for a legal agreement. The vestry rejected this demand as demeaning to Thomas' public word.

The wealthy minority resumed attendance. Quietly they began contributing to a private fund in the hands of Dada Adeshigbin. He offered to contribute £100 to the Bethel building fund every time that Thomas reduced his loan by £200.[3] Thomas ignored the offer.

Many had become aware of the political game which Thomas was playing, even before the economic crisis of 1921. By the time Thomas began to feel financial embarrassment T. B. Dawodu, the strongest and most influential leader in the pyramid, had died. When the Adeshigbins again brought the General Committee to deadlock Thomas made the tactical mistake of resigning (as was his habit) to gain vestry support. He failed to get it. His pyramid had crumbled with his affluence. Presumably Adeshigbin offered the substantial sums in the private fund to the congregation in exchange for its acquiescence in Thomas' resignation. Adeshigbin was the only one capable of getting construction moving again. Without serious vestry objection, the General Committee dismissed Thomas and two of his supporters from membership. Thomas

---

[1] A.C. (Bethel) Minutes, 16 Dec. 1920, *iii*, p. 147; A.C. (Salem) Minutes, 10 Nov. 1913, *ii*, p. 158; J. K. Coker to Thomas, 12 Nov. 1913; Akiola to J. K. Coker, n.d., 1917?, *Coker Papers.*

[2] Minutes of [Arbitration Board] Meeting with A.C. (Bethel) delegates, 29 Oct. 1917 and 2 Nov. 1917, *Coker Papers.*

[3] A.C. (Bethel) Minutes, 16 Dec. 1920, *iii*, p. 147.

immediately sued Adeshigbin and others in the civil courts for £1,500.[1]

Upon the dismissal of Thomas in July 1921 the General Committee immediately ordered the revision committee to rush its proceedings. The revised constitution was sent out to all churches in September. Bethlehem Church of Ebute Metta objected and dismissed its ministers who openly supported it. It was passed by the General Committee on 2 December 1921 over the unanimous protest of the Bethlehem delegates.[2]

The revised constitution, which embodied the principle of clerical control from the parish to the organization level, was brought before the Annual Conference, 13 December 1921. Superintendent J. S. Williams was for the first time invited to take the chair. The opponents held up the ratification vote for three hours by numerous questions, cat-calls, and rowdiness. A. A. Obadina, who shepherded the vote, kept his temper, answered questions, and proved the constitutional nature of every step taken. He finally carried the ratification on a vote of thirty to sixteen.[3]

It was an historic occasion, one of those rare times when policy was initiated on a majority vote. But it was a dangerous occasion. The ratification vote was a clear-cut triumph for Lagos at the expense of the interior—Lagos domination in its most naked form. That Lagos could dominate a conference against the wishes of Ebute Metta and the interior on a vote of thirty to sixteen indicated the bias in the representative system. Seventy per cent. of the membership controlled one-third of the representatives.

Immediately after the vote the Bethlehem and Ijebu delegates walked out. Bethlehem school was locked against the conference. In the months ahead Bethlehem, Ijebu, and surprisingly enough Agege sent no representatives to the General Committee. All of the interior churches withheld their assessment rates.[4]

Once the conference had ended, the reunion committee began

---

[1] Thomas won the case in the courts which set out the method of repayment. Thomas then forgave the debt, turning it into a gift or donation. A.C. (Bethel) Minutes, 12 July and 15 Sept. 1921, *iii*, pp. 172 and 191; the letters of dismissal were published, see *African Messenger*, 11 Aug. 1921; A. W. Thomas *vs.* Akinoso and Adeshigbin, in the Supreme Court of Nigeria, 23 Dec. 1921, *Coker Papers; Lagos Weekly Record*, 1 Jan. 1921.

[2] A.C. (Bethel) Minutes, 12 July, 15 Sept., 27 Oct., and 2 Dec. 1921, *iii*, pp. 172, 191, 200, and 211; *Times of Nigeria*, 20 June 1921.

[3] A.C. (Bethel) Minutes, 13–15 Dec. 1921, *iii*, pp. 215–19.

[4] A.C. (Bethel) Minutes, 21 Feb. and 20 June 1922, *iii*, pp. 234 and 288.

regular sittings. On 24 November 1922 it declared its intention to re-
unite the two organizations. In December an amalgamated conference of the A.C. (Bethel) and the A.C. (Salem) was held, where
reunion was ratified by a unanimous vote. The conference elected a
committee to draw a constitution for the reunited organization.
Before the committee had even begun its sittings the reunited General
Committee sat for the first time on 18 March 1923.[1]

What caused such remarkable speed? The dismissal of Thomas and
the death of Dawodu disorganized the opposition. J. K. Coker had
gained immense prestige by his offer (not accepted) to repay Thomas
his loan.[2] The clergy favoured reunion. They controlled both organizations. Once the hierarchical ladder was adjusted to the satisfaction
of all, few other obstacles remained. The dangerous defection in the
interior was demanding immediate attention. Possibly a reunited
church could win back its allegiance.

A last-minute hesitation arose in the A.C. (Salem). As late as
February 1923 (the United General Committee sat in March) that
organization was talking of the reunion being perfected in four years.[3]
After all, the union would swamp Evangelical principles and their
defender—J. K. Coker. But the economic crisis of 1921 was embarrassing Coker as well as Thomas.

The A.C. (Salem) was on the verge of financial collapse. The
ministers had not been paid. Some threatened to resign, others asked
for an honourable release to take up work elsewhere. Coker and the
other Agege planters were broken. Coker proposed calling upon the
A.C. (Bethel) for assistance. Thus the reunited General Committee
met for the first time.[4] The arrangement became permanent.

The new constitution[5] created a primate (a symbol of clerical
authority) and three bishops with territorial jurisdiction. The same
two streams of authority were developed as in the U.N.A., except that
the clergy presided over all committees. While the lay stream was

[1] Declaration of Union, 24 Nov. 1922; United General Committee Minutes,
18 Mar. 1923, *Coker Papers*; 'Programme of the Conference of the Amalgamated Organization', 10–18 Dec., *African Messenger*, 7 Dec. 1922; *Revised Constitution of the African Church*, Lagos, 1951, preamble.
[2] John to J. K. Coker, 3 Aug. 1917; Akiola to J. K. Coker, 15 July 1918, *Coker
Papers*.
[3] A.C. (Salem) Minutes, 12 Feb. 1923, Rough notes, *Coker Papers*.
[4] A.C. (Salem) Minutes, 12 Feb. 1923, Rough notes; J. K. Coker to Fisher,
21 June 1922, Opebi to Adefolu, 30 Jan. 1923, *Coker Papers*.
[5] Revised Constitution of the African Church, 1925; J. K. Coker, History of
the African Church, 1941; J. K. Coker, Memorandum, 1935?, *Coker Papers*.

subordinate to the General Conference, the clerical was not. District Councils, a compromise form of local autonomy, were given enhanced powers, including responsibility for clerical stipends. The new constitution did not operate perfectly, but no major division took place which suggested that a workable balance had been found.

The A.C. (Bethel) was a classic example of the interaction among the four major factions in an African Church governing authority. A. W. Thomas was the prototype of the powerful chief elder opposed by junior leaders devoted to constitutional action to isolate him. The clergy acted as a unit and attempted to remain detached from the struggle among the laity. The vestry, while urging compromise, was unwilling to upset the delicate balance in the leadership by unseating either of the factions.

Thomas combined the attributes of eldership of J. W. Cole and G. A. Williams of the U.N.A. Like Cole, his vestry support depended upon his pyramid of supporters and the popularity of the story edifice he was prepared to provide. Like Williams, he possessed superb skill in manipulating the procedures of the General Committee. By the device of having his priorities accepted, he made the popular issue of reunion dependent upon the unpalatable revision of the constitution and a one-story edifice. The appointment of Dawodu, an avowed opponent of revision, to head the reunion committee assured that it would never reach the stage of committee debate.

Dada Adeshigbin led the co-operative circle of independents which sought by constitutional means for seven years to break the elder's power. On occasion he succeeded in isolating him in the General Committee, but each time Thomas returned with a fresh mandate from the vestry. Passive membership and withheld subscriptions brought Thomas to arbitration, but it was the special fund during Thomas' economic embarrassment in 1921 which was ultimately effective. The device of a special fund had first been used by G. A. Williams to undermine Elder Cole in 1895 in the U.N.A.

The clergy remained detached from the quarrel among the elders. Particularly after they had achieved unity among themselves, they openly supported Adeshigbin's faction. In crucial decisions, however, they voted with Thomas. An oligarchy succeeded Thomas in 1921, as it had Cole in 1897 and G. A. Williams in 1919. The usual rush of changes took place. As in the U.N.A., the clergy seized the opportunity to enhance their influence and power.

The vestry repeatedly urged its leaders to compromise. Its support

for Thomas had been emphasized. It was also noteworthy that the
vestry re-elected his opposition each year. It refused to impose a
settlement by unseating either Thomas or Adeshigbin.

The operation of the governing authority was seen at its best in the
A.C. (Bethel) between 1914 and 1921. During a compact period of
seven years one crucial episode began and ended. The participants
remained throughout, with no major change in their economic and
social circumstances. The four power groups—elders, junior leaders,
clergy, and vestry—acted within constitutional limits. With the major
outside influences stable, the governmental structure operated with
unusual simplicity and clarity. It was the ideal example of African
Church government procedure in the early twentieth century.

Decentralization reached the last stage before secession, if indeed
the revolt of the interior in 1921 was not secession. The doctrine of
local autonomy so effectively used by Thomas against Coker in 1907
was turned against him by Ijebu Ode a decade later. By 1918 even
Thomas would have welcomed a 'tightening up' of the A.C. (Bethel)
had it been consistent with lay authority. The reunited church of 1922
realistically tackled the problem of the interior. The union constitution made strenuous efforts to broaden the organization from its
narrow base in Lagos to the whole of Yorubaland. With greater
attention to representation according to membership, District Councils with firm rights and responsibilities, and the appointment of
resident interior bishops, the African Church could rightly feel that
organizationally it had matured.

In surveying the African Church Movement as a whole between
1913 and 1922, three major events achieve prominence—the creation
of the Communion, the reunion of the African Church Organization,
and the U.N.A. ruling on polygamy.

The Communion had been the product of Evangelical agitation.
It was the most imaginative and inspiring development after the
schisms which began the African Church Movement. Evangelical influence was smothered in the reunion of 1922, and support for the
Communion in the African Church Organization withered away. The
U.N.A. was not blameless. After years of patient effort to establish
the Communion it destroyed its creation with a hard and inflexible
policy on polygamy.

Following the U.N.A. decision to accept a polygamous clergy, the
African Church, U.A.M. (Eleja), and Araromi Baptists withdrew
from the Communion. Had Agbebi lived, he might have averted this

crisis. No leader of his stature succeeded him. G. A. Oke of the U.N.A., the obvious choice, was admired, personally, but the majority would not tolerate the policy of the organization he led.

By 1925 the Communion had been abandoned. It was revived in less-effective forms on a couple of occasions and is still in existence. Since 1925 it has never won wholehearted support and its influence has been negligible and sporadic. Higher education and theological training have suffered as a consequence.

The educated *élite* of modern Nigeria, whether Christian, Muslim, or Pagan, judge church organizations by the amount and quality of the education they have provided in the past. On this criterion, the *élite* has pronounced the African Church Movement a failure. For this reason missions employ the majority of their foreign staff in educational work. Favours which the *élite* will be prepared to sanction in the future will be bestowed on churches in recognition of their educational efforts. The African churches will not qualify.

In the past the African churches fell heir to leaders of quality because of the limited opportunities in civil life and the reticence of the missions to tolerate a challenge to European authority. But what of the future? The result may be a sharp deterioration in the quality of African Church leadership.

A revived African Communion could promote education and provide the basis for future organic union. African Church union is more urgent than ever before, since the missions are negotiating their own union scheme. Regardless of mission policy, churchmen cannot be satisfied until the plans first formulated in 1891 by Johnson and Blyden are consummated in a National Church. It is within the realm of the possible for the African churches to create the largest single Christian organization in Nigeria. When the African churches become *the* African Church the reformation of 1888–1922 will command the attention denied it in the past, and churchmen will have fully justified the faith of the founding fathers in African leadership.

Conclusion

THE African Church Movement was the result of a positive impulse generated by the revival movement of the 1880s in Lagos and a reaction against the change of mission policies which had radically altered from the theories common in the earlier nineteenth century to ones more compatible with the changed circumstances of the impending European penetration and occupation of African territories. Under Henry Venn, C.M.S. policy had been sincerely based upon efforts to create a self-supporting, self-propagating, and self-governing church in Africa. The missionaries took for granted that this church would resemble its parent denomination overseas in its rituals, doctrines, and governing institutions. The heart of the transfer to self-government was the gradual rise of Africans to supersede Englishmen in the hierarchy of the mission church. Venn's most important step in this direction had been the appointment of S. A. Crowther as missionary bishop on the Niger. Venn looked forward to an early independent diocesan bishop for Yorubaland.

After the death of Venn his whole policy was undermined by a group of younger Englishmen more hostile to African ambitions. When Crowther died the settlement which followed was a definite turning away by the C.M.S. from the policy advocated by Venn. Since the Anglicans were predominant in Yorubaland, Anglican policy was crucial for all Christian Yoruba regardless of their denominational affiliation. The Methodists and Baptists moulded their own policies to conform to the new C.M.S. practice.

Following the settlement of 1894, self-support was paraded as the *sine qua non* of self-government. Within the following three decades self-support was achieved and Bishop James Johnson's Endowment Fund was to provide the basis for a financially independent episcopate. The prostitution of the Endowment Fund after Johnson's death exposed the hypocrisy of the new policy. In anticipation of Johnson's success, self-government was tied to a new criterion— moral readiness. The missionaries became the arbiters of African moral readiness for leadership. What followed was a systematic denigration of the Negro race as English bishops and clergy in Africa sought to explain why, with thousands of active church members,

o

schools, colleges, a degreed priesthood fully African financed, further steps towards self-government should be further delayed.

Self-government was interpreted by the nineteenth-century missions to follow the form prevailing in their respective denominations overseas. Anglicans sought to create a hierarchy with powers centred on the bishop. Baptists preached autonomous local churches under congregational control. Following the settlement of 1894, both Anglicans and Baptists raised doubts as to the advisability of the full transfer of the governing tenets of their parent denominations to Africa. Both began to discuss the advisability of adapting to African conditions. The major condition which set Africa apart from Europe or America was the presence of the missionaries. Adaptation meant finding a place for themselves in the church in Africa. They sought to be external to the church, yet in a position of control while giving a semblance of authority to African leaders. Thus Anglicans created assistant bishops. Baptists established a virtually powerless convention with an African president, while a separate American executive controlled the Baptist churches as surely as the English bishops controlled the Anglicans. It was curious to note that since these opposites—Anglicans and Baptists—faced similar problems and sought similar goals, they were able through totally different ideologies to achieve similar ends—full expatriate control of the mission church.

Turning from mission policy and practice to African views, evidence reveals the almost total acceptance by Africans of the early-nineteenth-century goals—Venn's self-supporting, self-propagating, and self-governing church and the working of this policy towards the creation of churches in the image of the parent denomination overseas. Many Africans were as aware of how their denomination overseas was governed as they were of the biblical stories of Christ. Frequently African Christians attempted to defend themselves and uphold their rights by reference to judicial decisions by which the Anglicans were bound in England or by quoting from textbooks of Methodist polity. Adaptation was the missionary's counter weapon. Thus, quite apart from events in the world outside of the missions, African revolts were sure to develop which would ultimately result in the formation of new denominations.

Outside events did intervene. African Christians of Lagos and the Niger Delta were adversely affected by the European penetration of the continent which accompanied mission policy changes. Frequently

Christians were the middle men of the African trade, between the European merchants on the coast and the interior kingdoms. The successful efforts of the European trading houses to penetrate the interior destroyed the African Christians' livelihood. Those who had been trading on the Niger witnessed the intimate connexion between the economic imperialism of the European merchant houses, the change of policy in the C.M.S. Niger mission, and the ensuing penetration of imperial forces. Those trading on the Congo and at Porto Novo had parallel experiences. The African churches drew many of their original supporters from among their ranks. In this sense the African Church Movement was a revolt against imperialism—all aspects of it—religious, economic and administrative.

Since the connexion between the African Church Movement and imperialism has been stressed, it is natural to inquire into its relationship to Nigerian nationalism. This study has consciously not dealt with the African churches and political protest. But a broad view may be permissible. African nationalism is occasionally divided into two manifestations—traditional, as exemplified by King Ja ja in 1887, and modern, dated from the foundation of the National Congress of British West Africa in 1919. The interval between 1887 and 1919 is the formative period of the African churches which links the two. Viewed in this manner, a certain artificiality is created in the academic distinction between the traditional and modern forms of nationalism. Like Ja ja, the African churches resisted European penetration. Like the Congress, they attempted to organize on a West Coast basis. The West African church scheme of 1891, the Baptist Union of 1898, and the West African Episcopal Communion of 1924 were all designed to organize the Christians in coast-wide opposition to the foreign missions.

While African churchmen were conspicuous by their numbers in the political protest movement prior to 1920, church organizations as such remained aloof from political involvements. They were engaged in a more subtle campaign. They produced a stream of books, pamphlets and newspapers in defence and justification of African customs such as Lagos had never before witnessed. It was a necessary preliminary to the success of later political nationalists. The nationalist statesman, Dr. Nnamdi Azikiwe, President of Nigeria, publicly paid tribute to the historic role which the African churches played in Nigerian nationalism.

In policies expansion of African churches sought a massive

ingathering of the Yoruba. Christianity represented salvation for the Yoruba, both as individuals and as a society. For the individual it was to bring freedom from fear. For the society it was to heal the wounds inflicted upon the politic body by the previous century of turmoil. Christianity was to be the new cohesive force binding all Yorubas together in brotherly love and unity. While the missions emphasized the individual nature of Christian life, the African churches stressed its communal responsibilities. The missions preached 'come out from among them and be ye separate'; the African churches sought 'to leaven the loaf'.

Churchmen argued about the future of Yoruba society, and their policies were conditioned by their view of it. They worked for the 'massive ingathering', 'the national church'. They looked with eagerness for a succession of Yoruba Constantines who would do for the various Yoruba states what he had done for the Roman Empire—make Christianity the popular and official religion, compelling the intransigent if necessary. There were occasions when the time appeared opportune for such action in Abeokuta, Ondo, Ijebu, and Ilesha.

It must be admitted that the African churches' success was limited because they would not change their practice sufficiently to conform to their theological position. While emphasizing the communal approach, few bishops would baptize whole compounds at once. They could not face the barrage of mission ridicule which such actions provoked. Occasionally the African churches passed through periods when their conditions for baptism and confirmation were as severe and restrictive as the foreign missions. Too often they became quality conscious—judged in terms of literacy—when they compared their own congregations with the Anglicans or Methodists.

It has been pointed out that the African churches emphasized unity and brotherly love in Yoruba society. Nowhere was the need of this more apparent than in the governing bodies of the church. Indeed, if the machinery of government was to move at all it depended upon amity among the big men or elders, and patience and respect among the junior leaders or progressive elements. Government was in a very real sense a process of continuous compromise. A sincere and strongly held ideology could effect the continuous compromises necessary to keep the system working. When it worked well it produced an unusual dynamism. On the other hand, when divergent views could not be harmonized chaos followed by stalemate threatened the existence of the organization. Part IV of this study, dealing with 'Church Government', provides examples of both the dynamism and the stalemate which the system could and did produce.

When dealing with disputes of major importance the historian is faced with the problem of how far contending parties assume their positions on ideological grounds and how far they are motivated by purely personal or material considerations. The historian frequently discovers that when dealing with western societies a cursory and preliminary observation of the dispute reveals an ideological basis to the views of the contending parties. The opposing groups will go to considerable lengths to cloak their positions in ideological terminology. Deeper probing frequently reveals the hidden personal and material motives. The task of the historian is to decide how much motivation is due to ideological conflict and how much results from personal animosity or expectations of material gain. The result is often a judicious mixture, with the ideology frequently predominating, particularly when religious or humanitarian organizations are under scrutiny.

Confronted with a similar dispute in Yoruba society, the historian finds a different—almost opposite—approach by his source material, whether it be documents or men. Ideology is cloaked or hidden, while personal reasons are emphasized. For example, a prominent man's position *vis-à-vis* the monogamy–polygamy issue is not the result of his view of Yoruba society nor based upon his assessment of the merits of the two marriage customs. It is rather ascribed to the intensity of his emotional drives, his desire for prestige, avariciousness, or childlessness. A man contributes heavily to a church to glorify his name, to bribe a congregation, to get ordination for his son. He pays the salary of the school master to be able to demand favours for his children. Factional disputes are invariably ascribed to the prestige-mania of their leading contenders. Ideology is seldom mentioned.

But it can be found. By careful checking of the membership of factions and the factional position on numerous issues a consistent ideology is frequently unearthed. But it requires a mass of detail which is difficult to uncover and time consuming to assemble and digest. It is almost impossible, for example, to make an accurate listing of the marriage arrangements of the polygamy–monogamy factions within the church. But it becomes obvious at least that it was not necessarily the polygamous man upholding polygamy and the monogamous supporting monogamy.

One of the major historical problems is why the Yoruba consistently clothes his ideological disputes under a screen of personal animosity. Why is he afraid to admit ideological divergence, while western man fears to admit personal animosity lest it discredit his public image? Is it possible to suggest even tentatively that the Yoruba fears an ideological position as being irrevocable? Does he believe that personal animosity, even clash of economic interests, can be overcome, compromise effected, and unity restored, permitting the instruments of government to resume their normal functions? Divergent ideology permits no compromise, brings stalemate and the ultimate collapse of organization.

It may be argued, and perhaps justly so, that the universal Christian church in all its denominational forms among the Yoruba has been harshly criticized in this work. It paints the average missionary as narrow minded and culture bound. It describes the mission clergy as subservient, sacrificing their independence of spirit for the security and prestige of the cloth. It pictures African congregations willing to continue the hypocritical gulf between profession and practice. It has shown the African churches revolting against the missions in loud proclamations of lofty ideals, only to fall back to strict conformity and imitation of their erstwhile masters. With eyes fixed narrowly on the Yoruba scene one could easily ask: What is justifiable in this whole edifice of the Christian church?

But if one compares the church among the Yoruba with the church in Nigeria as a whole one is struck by how far criticism of the Yoruba church must be relative. Compared with its position in other societies, the Christian church in all its denominational parts—mission, African, and Aladura—has embedded itself in Yoruba culture, gaining strength from the culture and in its turn infusing the culture with new vigour. In a sense the screen of hypocrisy was the cloak behind which the Yorubas proceeded to make the church their own, despite the watchful eyes of their paternal overseers. If the alien missionary tends to hold up his hands today in dismay at his inability to change the course of events it is because of the strength of the Yoruba undercurrent. The Yorubas are now engaged in the final skirmish of the battle for their own church.

Major credit must go to the Yorubas themselves, with their cultural pride and remarkable ability to adapt but not discard. In addi-

tion, they were fortunate that their Christian beginnings were nurtured in nineteenth-century mission philosophy. Yoruba Christianity
has never lost the mark of its origins. Neither theories nor practices
of succeeding generations could erase the imprint of its early character.

In most other areas of Nigeria the church is solely a product of the
colonial era and the twentieth century. It is not nearly as Africanized
in personnel. It is not the purveyor of cultural pride. Frequently it
has neglected the vernacular. In the modern age as it seeks to identify
with Africa it has few foundations on which to build. In few institutions is precedent so powerful as in the church. A whole set of pre-
cedents is needed. It is doubtful if they can be built in time to pace
developments in the secular field.

And where do the African churches stand in relation to these
developments? Since the majority of the non-Yoruba areas of
Nigeria unfortunately missed the stimulus of nineteenth-century
mission policies, so also they have missed the African Church Movement, which was a product of the thought of that age. It is noteworthy that the African church has flourished best in those areas
where evangelization was well under way in the nineteenth century,
Calabar, the Niger Delta, and Yorubaland. Elsewhere the African
churches have branches, but they cannot be said to profoundly
influence the Christian situation.

In Yorubaland the African churches posed as the conscience of
the mission churches—constant reminders of the philosophy which
the missions themselves had once held, and which they still professed
to hold, but which had long ago become embarrassing. Furthermore,
the African churches as a strong alternative to the missions became
a guarantor of tolerance within mission Christianity. Their presence
put an end to mass excommunications. They were a powerful check
upon the reforming purist, who was tempted to tear away the façade
of hypocrisy behind which mission Yorubas were working out their
own salvation. They effectively broke the gentlemen's agreements of
comity and forced a more widespread distribution of educational
facilities than the missions were otherwise willing to undertake. They
pioneered the use of the drum in its numerous forms, introduced
rhythm and Yoruba music to divine service, a practice which the
missions ultimately copied. They kept alive an intellectual ferment
through their publications and forced Yorubas of whatever denominational affiliation to ponder the effects which the penetration of

Christianity was having upon their culture. Finally, they stood for a certain kind of honesty which was in danger of being overlooked, another aspect of truth which had hitherto been illustrated as just too simple to conform to reality. The African churches were in fact one of the major reasons why Christianity among the Yorubas possessed a unique character.

Bibliography

A. PRIMARY SOURCES IN THE UNITED KINGDOM

I. *Church Missionary Society Archives, Salisbury Square* (*C.M.S.*)

1. Incoming Papers from the Yoruba Mission 1889–1914 under the classification G3 A2/O.

The main manuscripts of interest are:

(*a*) The Minutes of the Yoruba Finance Committee (later called Executive Committee), which met every six months. Almost all questions except those confined to the bishops were discussed in these meetings. The business in the minutes is conveniently headed under topics.

(*b*) Letters from European missionaries and African pastors to the African Secretary.

(*c*) Yearly reports from the ministers. When a parish begins to be self-supporting these reports no longer come to Salisbury Square headquarters. As the period progresses, there tends to be less and less information available about the activities of the Africans. The Europeans become more involved in training activities, and their reports are of less value in judging the progress of the church.

(*d*) Private letters to the African Secretary. These letters sent by the missionaries for the private perusal of the secretary are unfortunately absent from the files. It is noted, however, that they were received.

(*e*) Autobiographies of Africans accepted for ordination.

Special Categories

(i) The Anglican Communion: In Relation to its Parts, a paper prepared (but never given) by Melville Jones for the Pan-Anglican Congress of 1908.

(ii) Herb. Tugwell, Address to the Diocesan Synod, 1912.

(iii) Private Papers of G. W. Brooke covering 1885–91. Classified under F 4/1–10.

2. Incoming Papers from the Niger Mission 1889–94 under the classification G3 A3/O.

(*a*) All the same categories as in the Yoruba Mission.

(*b*) Outstanding documents in this collection:

(i) Memorandum prepared before Hill's interview with Lagos clergy, 1892.

(ii) Memorial to J. S. Hill by the clergy and laity of Lagos, December 1892.

(iii) Report of J. S. Hill to the Archbishop of Canterbury, December 1892.

(iv) Report of the Deputation to the Niger, March 1892.

3. Minutes of the Group III (Africa) Committee of the C.M.S. (1889–1907) under the classification G3 M, also under Correspondence Committee Minutes (1889–92) and Sub-Committee of Group III Committee 1888–98. All the Minutes of Committees in England are almost useless, being so briefly stated. The resolutions passed are recorded, but none of the discussion. There is, furthermore, no index even as to missions under discussion.

Report of the Ecclesiastical Sub-Committee placed before the General Committee 10 April 1900.

4. Outgoing letters from the African Secretary to the Yoruba Mission. Yoruba Letter Books classified as G3 A2/L7 (1892–1901), G3 A2/L8 (1901–9).

II. *The Methodist Missionary Society, Marylebone Road (W.M.M.S.)*

1. Incoming Papers from the Lagos District 1893–1912 classified under Lagos Original Papers:

(*a*) The most voluminous material is in the Synod Minutes for the various years. For the years 1893–1902 there are separate reports for each circuit. After that it appears as if these reports were condensed into a smaller and less valuable report called Report of the Circuits.

(*b*) As in the C.M.S., the most productive source of information is from the missionaries' letters to the Secretary. The vast majority of letters, however, are from the chairman, and this gives a more one-sided picture than in the C.M.S.

(*c*) Again like the C.M.S., certain letters have been removed or censored, but for numerous reasons this is not as serious as in the C.M.S., for the information comes out in numerous other places. Rev. W. H. Findlay, Methodist secretary in 1900, visited West Africa and wrote a very critical report of the mission. This document is unfortunately not available.

(*d*) The autobiographies of African ministers are only available in the printed form and are not as valuable as those in the C.M.S.

2. Minutes of the General Committee classified under M.G. No. 11 (1897–9), No. 12 (1899–1902), No. 13 (1902–4), No. 14 (1904–6), No. 15 (1906–8), No. 16 (1909–11).

3. Outgoing Papers. Letters from the Secretary to the Lagos District classified under Outgoing Letters Lagos (1885–1913).

III. *Lambeth Palace Library*

1. Letters received and sent to the Niger Diocese and Lagos classified under Benson, I, 11g, 1892, Foreign, and Benson, 12d, 1893, Foreign. One document written by the Archbishop re *the Niger*, which appears to be his scribbled notes before a conference with the Archbishop of York and other bishops, is an extremely useful one. It is hard to see how an adequate understanding of the situation in England in 1892 could be possible without it.

IV. *Trinity College Library, University of Cambridge*

Official diary of Archbishop Benson. Consulted 1892.

B. PRIMARY SOURCES IN NIGERIA

I. *Southern Baptists*

1. Ogbomoso Seminary Library (Ogbomoso):

(*a*) Baptist printed secondary sources and the *Foreign Mission Journal*, *1890–1908*.

(*b*) Statistical information on Baptist pastors, 1941.

2. C. F. Roberson Collection:

(*a*) Minutes: Annual Conference 1850–1940; Nigerian Baptist Convention 1917–44; Women's Auxiliary Union 1919–49; Constitution and Bye-Laws 1910.

(*b*) African biography–autobiographies, funeral sermons, obituaries.

(*c*) Local church histories.

(*d*) Correspondence between missionaries and the Foreign Mission Board copied from the Richmond Headquarters Archives.

(*e*) Periodicals: *The Dawn*, 1916–17; *Nigerian Baptist*, 1924–36.

II. *United Native African*

1. In the possession of the secretary of the General Committee Minute Books 1891–1963: I consulted Vol. I (1891–1911); Vol. II (1911–21).

2. Papers of Supt. G. A. Oke (National Archives, Ibadan):

(*a*) Contains his official papers only, little prior to 1920.

(*b*) Most important being two papers, one by Oke, the other by M. T. Euler-Ajayi, on the African Communion.

(*c*) Two manuscripts by Superintendent A. O. Ijaoye.

III. *The African Church Organization*

1. Broad Street Archives, Lagos (Bethel Cathedral):

(*a*) Dated back to 1922; full in the 1930s; catalogued B: 1 to B: 33.

(*b*) Correspondence between Divisional Headquarters and the Primate's Office.

(*c*) General Committee, Working Committee, and General Conference Minute Books.

(*d*) Personal files.

(*e*) Letter Books of the General Secretary.

2. Coker Papers:

(*a*) Corresponding secretary's incoming and outgoing correspondence, 1907–22.

(*b*) Minutes A.C. (Salem), vol. ii (1907–14); vol. iv (1915–20).
Minutes A.C. (Bethel), vol. iii (1917–22).

(*c*) Typescript, History of the African Church (incomplete), 1941.

(*d*) Voluminous family correspondence.

(e) Account books, 1906–24.

(f) Correspondence—of Agege Planters Union—with Lagos merchants.

3. Lagos Standard Collection:

Special issue which published thirty-five documents dealing with the schism of 1901.

IV. *West African Episcopal*

1. In the possession of the church:

(a) W.A.E. Minute Book, 1903–39, contains minutes of the General Committee, Annual Conference, Ecclesiastical Board. Also deputation reports, Anniversaries, the missionary journeys of J. G. Campbell, autobiographies of clergy, and correspondence relating to the setting up of the Gold Coast Patriarchates, 1918–24.

2. J. G. Campbell Papers:

Relates mainly to the activities of the Christ Army Church of the Niger Delta.

V. *United African Methodist (Eleja)*

Archives in the vestry of Eleja Church, 40 John Street, Lagos. Minute Books of the Executive Committee and class books. Some correspondence, 1929–63.

VI. *National Archives (Ibadan)*

1. C.M.S. Records. *C.M.S. (Ibadan)*:

Local correspondence to and from the local secretary. One file of correspondence regarding schism of The Evangelist Band, 1920.

2. Methodist Records. *W.M.M.S. (Ibadan)*:

All correspondence regarding the schism of 1917 has been removed. Correspondence on comity with C.M.S. was useful.

3. Government Records:

The thirteen volumes of the 'Native Service Record Books' (1873–1929) C 502/13 for biographical material on churchmen.

4. High Court Records:

(a) Cases involving the African churches. St. Jude's property case, 1902–4. Native Baptist Church *vs.* Mojola Agbebi, 1903; Cases relating to the African Church crisis, 1905–9.

VII. *Inscriptions*

Forty-two memorial inscriptions from the walls of seven African churches in Lagos. Tombstone inscriptions from Lagos cemeteries.

VIII. *Interviews*

Fifty formal interviews with thirty-five different groups connected with seven African churches.

IX. *Others*

1. Herbert Macaulay Papers, University of Ibadan Library. One file marked 'Church' contains correspondence with Negro churches in America.

2. J. E. Bruce Papers, Schomberg Collection, New York Library. Correspondence between Bruce and Agbebi regarding assistance from American Coloured to Africa.

X. *Publications Relating to Missionary Societies of Western Nigeria:*
C.M.S. Press, *The Church and Native Customs*, Lagos, 1914.
COLE, M. S., 'The Attitude of the Church to Native Customs', *Synod Reports 1912–14*, Appendix six.
Constitution and Bye-laws, Yoruba Baptist Convention, Lagos, 1914.
CUST, R. N., *Evangelization of the Non-Christian World*, London, 1894.
Diocese of W.A.E., *Resolutions Adopted by a Conference of Bishops of the Anglican Communion*, Lagos, 1906.
Sister, His, *Letters of H. H. Dobinson*, London, 1899.
Minutes of Conference of the Methodist Church, 1884–1921.
PINNOCK, S. G., *Yoruba Baptist Association Year Book*, Lagos, 1915.
Proceedings of the Church Missionary Society, 1876–1917.
Proceedings of the Southern Baptist Convention, 1884–8; 1890–3; 1896–7; 1899; 1901–2; 1904–7; 1909–20.
W.M.M. Society Reports, 1891–1921.

Mission Periodicals:
Church Missionary Outlook, selected years.
C.M.S. Gazette, 1911–12.
Dawn, 1923–7.
Foreign Field of the Wesleyan Methodist Church, 1904–21.
In Leisure Hours, 1920–30.
Intelligencer, 1889–1902.
Niger and Yoruba Notes, 1897–1904.
Nigerian Baptist, 1923–36.
Wesleyan Missionary Notices, 1890–1904.
Western Equatorial Africa Diocesan Magazine, 1904–25.
Work and Workers in the Mission Field, 1892–1904.
Yoruba Church Missionary Gleaner, 1893.

XI. *Official Publications of the African Churches*
1. General:
African Bethlehem Church 1907–57, Lagos, 1957.
African Church Lectionary, Lagos, 1961.
African Church Salem 1908–58, Lagos, 1958.
*CAMPBELL, J. G., *Origin of the Thirty-Six Articles of Faith and the Constitution of the W.A.E. Church*, Lagos, 1945.

* Material so marked should be classed as secondary sources, but I believe there is a decided advantage in keeping African Church publications together in one list. The same applies to the publications of individual African Churchmen.

CAMPBELL, J. G., *Report of the Churches within the W.A.E. Communion*, Lagos, 1924.

Constitution for the General Government of the African Church, Lagos, 1907.

Constitution of the Shanu Mission Church Organization, Lagos, 1924.

Constitution of the U.A.M. (Eleja) Organization, Lagos, 1951.

Directory and Almanack, Lagos, 1933, 1945, 1954, 1961.

HUGHES, D. A., *Charge Delivered to the General Conference*, Lagos, 1922.

Proceedings of the Ninth General Conference, A.C. (Salem) 1916, Lagos, 1917.

Report of the Conference of Delegates of the African Church April 28– May 5, 1907, Lagos, 1909.

Report of the Proceedings of the African Church Organization for Lagos and Yorubaland 1901–8, Liverpool, 1910.

Revised Constitution of the African Church, Lagos, 1951.

Revised Constitution of the U.N.A. Church, Lagos, 1919.

Revised Constitution of the U.N.A. Church, Lagos, 1921.

Thirtieth Anniversary Report, Lagos, 1921.

Twenty-ninth Anniversary Report, Lagos, 1920.

U.A.M. (Eleja) *Compendium of Regulations*, Lagos, 1930.

U.A.M. (Eleja) *Twenty-fifth Annual Report*, Lagos, 1942.

Year Book and Report, The Baptist Church and Mission and the Christian Army of the Gold Coast, London, 1913.

2. Periodicals:

African Church Chronicles, 1934–39; 1950–?

African Hope (U.N.A.), 1919–24; 1945–7.

The Dawn (Native Baptists co-operating with the Mission Society), 1916–17.

3. Newspapers Owned or Edited by Churchmen:

African Herbal Messenger Health Review, 1922.

Eko Akete, 1922–53.

Eko Igbehin, 1926–7.

Eleti Ofe, 1923–53.

Lagos Standard, 1895–1920.

New Age Herald and Herald Alore, 1910–14.

Nigerian Chronicle, 1908–18.

Nigerian Daily Telegraph, 1927–31.

Times of Nigeria, 1910–24.

Yoruba News, 1924–45.

XII. *Publications of African Churchmen Available*

ABOYADE-COLE, A., *Adura Ebe* (African Church Litany), Lagos, 1927.

ADESOLA, 'On Yoruba Terms and Names', *Nigerian Chronicle*, 21 July, 1911.

ADESOLA, 'Burial Customs of the Yoruba Country', serialized in six issues of the *Nigerian Chronicle*, Sept.–Oct. 1909.

——, 'Life of Yoruba Warriors Series', *Eko Akete*, June 1923.

AGBEBI, MOJOLA, *An Account of Mojola Agbebi's Work in West Africa*, New Calabar, 1904.

——, *The Christian Handbook*, New Calabar, 1903?

*——, 'The West African Problem', in G. Spiller, *Papers on Inter-Racial Problems*, London, 1911, pp. 341–8.

*AJALA, AYO, *A Critical Review of the Egba Native Authority Question*, Lagos, 1938.

——, *Atona Esin* (U.N.A. Litany), n.d.

*——, *The Status of Women in Egbaland*, 2nd ed., n.d.

——, 'The African Communion: Its Aims and Objects', *The African Church Chronicle*, Jan.–Mar. and Apr.–June 1936.

AJISAFE, A. K., *Abeokuta Centenary and Its Celebrations*, Lagos, 1931.

——, *Aiye Akamara*, Lagos, 1921, 2nd ed., 1929.

——, *Akanse Adura, Fun Orile-ede enia Dudu papa Iran Yoruba*, 1922, 2nd ed., 1923.

——, *Enia Soro Lagos*, 1921, revised 1931.

*——, *History of Abeokuta*, Suffolk, 1924 (also 1921 and 1931 editions).

——, *Iwe Igbadun Aiye*, 1923.

——, *Kil'e p'oyinbo se?*, Lagos, 1921.

——, *Orunmila*, Lagos, 1923.

——, *Oyel 'Agbaiwo*, Lagos, n.d.

——, *Ogorun Odun Lori Ilu Abeokuta ati re Ajoyo re*, Lagos, 1931.

——, *Tan' t'Olorun*, Lagos, 1921.

——, *The Errors and Defeat of Ladipo Solanke*, Lagos, 1931.

*——, *The Laws and Customs of the Yoruba People*, Lagos, 1924.

AKINSOWAN, AKIDELE (B. A. Coker), 'Life of King Tofa', *Lagos Standard*, 26 Feb. 1908.

*——, *Iwe Itan Ajase* (History of Porto Novo), 1914.

BEYIOKU, AKIN FAGBENRO (H. A. Williams), *Education and the Press*, Lagos, 1919.

*——, *Orunmilaism, The Basis of Jesuism*, Lagos, 1943.

CAMPBELL, J. G., *Lagos Awake on the Election Question*, Lagos, 1923.

——, *Observations on Some Topics During the Administration of Lugard*, Lagos, 1918.

CAULCRICK, H. A., 'Views of Some Native Christians . . . on . . . Polygamy', *Payne's Almanack*, 1894, p. 69.

COKER, J. K., *Polygamy Defended*, Lagos, 1915.

——, *The African Church*, Lagos, 1913.

COKER, S. A., *The Rights of Africans to Organize and Establish Indigenous Churches*, Lagos, 1917.

——, *Three Sermons on the Christian Ministry*, London, 1904.

COLE, J. AUGUSTUS (ABAYOMI), *The Revelations of the Secret Orders of Western Africa*, Dayton, Ohio, 1886.

DAWODU, T. O., *Awo Oruko (Kristian) Onigbagbo ati Itumo Won* (Christian Names and their Yoruba Meanings), Lagos, 1929.

*DENIGA, ADEOYE, *African Leaders*, Lagos, 1919.

EPEGA, D. O., *The Mystery of the Yoruba Gods*, Lagos, 1932.

EULER-AJAYI, M. T., *Polygamy*, Colwyn Bay, after 1890.

——, *The Practical Yoruba Grammar*, before 1899.

——, *Key of the Koran*, before 1900.

——, *The First Step in Theology* (in Yoruba), Lagos, 1913.

——, Bible Concordance, completed, not published.

——, M. T. (Jr.), compiler, *Iwe Orin Isin Olorun* (U.N.A. Hymnal), Lagos, 1939.

*IYALLA, N. B., *The Most Reverend J. G. Campbell*, Lagos, 1945.

LIJADU, E. M., *Ifa*, London, 1897.

——, *Iwe Keji Awon Arofo-Orin ti Sobo Aro-Bi-Odo*, Lagos, 1914.

——, *Iwe Irohin ati Ile Isura Eko ti Egbe Awon Olufe Ile-Ibi Won Li Abeokuta 1884–5*, Lagos, 1886.

*——, *Kekere Iwe Orin Aribiloso*, Exeter, 1910.

——, *Orunmala*, Nottingham, 1907.

——, *The Effects of Foreign Literature and Science Upon the Natives of the Yoruba Country*, Lagos, 1887.

*——, *The Words of Ode-Gaga, Native of Ilujugbe*, Lagos, 1904.

OBASA, D. A., 'Yorubanizing Christianity', *The Dawn*, Oct. 16.

——, *Iwe Kinni ti Awon Akewi*, Ibadan, 1927.

——, *Iwe Keji ti Awon Akewi*, Ibadan, 1933.

——, *Iwe Oriki ti Awon Orile Yoruba*, Ibadan, 1934.

*OGUMEFU, M. I., *Yoruba Legends*, London, 1929.

——, *Yoruba Melodies*, London, 1929.

*——, *The Staff of Oranyan and other Yoruba Tales*, London, 1930.

——, *Tales of Tortoise*, London, n.d.

OGUNBIYI, A. I., *Iwe Iko-omo-Jadi ati Lati Owo* (order of service for a naming ceremony), Lagos, 1926.

OJO-COLE, JULIUS, 'To Moriamo', W.A.S.U., Sept. 1927.

——, 'Personal Worship', *African Church Chronicle*, Jan.–Mar. 1935.

——, *Collection of Yoruba Thoughts*, Lagos, 1931.

*OKE, G. A., *A Short History of the U.N.A. 1891–1903*, Lagos, 1918.

*——, *A Short History of the U.N.A. 1904–1924*, Lagos, 1936.

——, *Iwe Eto Isin Litani ati Majemu*, Lagos, 1930.

OKE, S. A., *The Ethiopian National Church: A Necessity*, Ibadan, 1923.

OLUBI, J. C., *The Rubber Industry of Lagos Province*, Ibadan, 1911.

TAYLOR, OTHNIEL, *The African Church: Necessity for a Standard Policy*, Lagos, 1932.

*THOMAS, I. B., *Herbert Macaulay*, Lagos, 1947.

*WINFUNKE, N. A., *The Cause of the Establishment of Indigenous African Churches in Nigeria*, Lagos, 1957.

XIII. *Publications of African Churchmen (Unfound)*

ABIODUN, S. M., *Okojo Oruko Olorun*, 1919.

——, *Ranti ma Gbagbe*, 1916.

ADEBAYO, J. B., *The Duties of the Educated Natives to the B.W.A. Conference*, Lagos, 1919.

AGBEBI, MOJOLA, *Africa and the Gospel*, 1890.
——, *Feu de Joie*, ?
——, *Intoned Prayers*, 1899.
——, *Iwe Alo*, 1885.
——, *Secret Societies*, 1899.
——, *Ides of March*, 1887.
——, *View of Lagos from the Sea*.
——, *People Should Talk of You*.
——, *Voice of Sorrow*.
——, *Dahomey*.
——, *Pe mi ni Mara*.
BEYIOKU, AKIN, F., *Ifa Brochure*.
——, *Iwe Kini Agbonniregun*.
——, *Origin of Ijo Orunmila*.
CAMPBELL, J. G., *Bilingual Reader*.
——, *The Congress Movement and Herbert Macaulay*, Lagos, 1921.
——, *The First Conference of Africans of B.W.A.*
——, *The Policy of the White Race Examined*.
——, *Our West African Governors*, Lagos, 1921.
——, *Short History of Uhape*.
——, *Some Thoughts of Abeokuta*.
——, *What Nigeria Requires of Sir Hugh Clifford*.
COKER, S. A., *African Church Secessions*.
——, *Special Sermon on the Raising of Rev. A. I. Hart to the Presbyterate*.
DENIGA, A., *A Defence of Native Customs*.
DENIGA, A., *Blyden, The African Educationalist*, 1923.
——, *Church and Politics*, 1922.
——, *Marriage and the Church*, 1916.
——, *Monogamy and the Church*.
——, *Necessity for a B.W.A. Conference*, 1919.
——, *What is Religion?*, 1912.
——, *Yoruba Titles and Their Meanings*, 1921.
——, *Aribiloso*.
——, *Kilopo?*
——, *Memoirs of the Crowned Heads of Lagos*.
——, *Odunlami*, 1919.
——, *Ode to Lagos*, 1909.
HAYFORD, M. C., *West Africa and Christianity*, London, 1900.
ODUMOSU, JOSEPH, *Iwe Egbogi*, 1905.
ODUMOSU, *Iwe Iwosan*, 1907?
——, *Pamphlet on Principal Events in Lagos*.
OSHODI, J. A., *Reasons for the Founding of the U.A.M. (Eleja) Organization*, 1918.
OKEKANMI, CHIEF O., *Native Drugs*.
——, *An Analysis of the Ogboni Society*.
——, *On the Adubi Riots*.
WINFUNKE, B. A., *Awon Owe Yoruba*, Lagos, 1941.

P

XIV. *Newspapers Consulted*

Advanced Opinion, 1924.
African Messenger, 1921–3.
African Times, 1899–1914.
Eagle and Lagos Critic, 1888.
Iwe Irohin Eko, 1890.
Lagos Observer, 1886–9.
Lagos Times and Gold Coast Advertiser, 1891.
Lagos Weekly Record, 1904–21.
Nigerian Law Journal, 1922.
Nigerian Pioneer, 1914–21.
The Mirror, 1888.

C. SECONDARY SOURCES

I. *Select Bibliography*

ADEYEMI, M. C., *Iwe Itan Oye Ile ati Oyo, Isisiyi abi Ago-D'Oyo*, Ibadan, before 1917.
ALLEN, ROLAND, *The Spontaneous Expansion of the Church*, London, 1949.
BAETA, C. G., *Prophetism in Ghana*, S.C.M., 1962.
BENSON, A. C., *The Life of Edward White Benson*, vol. ii, London, 1899.
BLYDEN, E. W., *The Return of the Exiles and the West African Church*, London, 1891.
BOUQUET, A. C., *The Christian Faith and Non-Christian Religions*, London, 1958.
BOWEN, T. J., *Adventures and Missionary Labors in Several Countries in the Interior of Africa 1849–1856*, Charleston, 1857.
CAMPBELL, ROBERT, *A Pilgrimage to My Motherland 1859–1860*, London, n.d.
C.M.S. Press, *The Life and Death of Bishop Oluwole*, Lagos, 1932.
COLE, A. N., *A Century of Wesleyan Methodist Missions 1813–1914*, Lagos, 1915.
COLEMAN, J. S., *Nigeria: Background to Nationalism*, University of California, 1958.
DAVIES, H., *Christian Deviations*, London, 1954.
DELANO, I. O., *One Church for Nigeria*, London, 1945.
DUVAL, L. M., *Baptist Missions in Nigeria*, Richmond, 1928.
Encyclopedia of the Southern Baptists.
EPELLE, E. M. T., *The Church in the Niger Delta*, Port Harcourt, 1955.
FAULKNER, R. E., *Joseph Sydney Hill*, London, 1895.
FREND, W. H. C., *The Donatist Church*, Oxford, 1952.
FYFE, C., *A History of Sierra Leone*, Oxford, 1962.
GOLLOCK, G. A., *Sons of Africa*, London, 1928.
GRAY, G. F. S., *The Anglican Communion*, London, 1958.
GREEN, C. S., *Southern Baptists at Work in Africa*, Richmond, 1936.
GREENSLADE, S. L., *Schism in the Early Church*, London, 1953.
GROVES, C. P., *The Planting of Christianity in Africa*, vols. i–iv, London, 1954.

HODGKIN, T. L., *Nationalism in Colonial Africa*, Muller, 1956.

HUGHES, W., *Dark Africa and the Way Out*, London, 1892.

HUTCHINSON, E., *The Lost Continent, Its Re-discovery and Recovery*, London, 1879.

ILESHA DISTRICT COUNCIL, *Iwe Itan Ogorun Odun ti Isin Kristi ni Ile Ijesha 1857–1957*, Ijebu Ode, 1956.

INGHAM, E. G., *Sierra Leone After a Hundred Years*, London, 1894.

JOHNSON, T. S., *The Story of a Mission*, London, 1953.

JORDAN, A. W., *The A.M.E. Church in Africa*, . . ., 1961.

KNIGHT, W., *Memoirs of Henry Venn*, London, 1882.

LUCAS, J. O., *History of St. Pauls Breadfruit, 1852–1945*, Lagos, 1945.

MACAULAY, HERBERT, *History of Missionary Work in Nigeria with Special Reference to the U.N.A.*, Lagos, 1942.

MACMILLAN, A. (compiler), *The Red Book of West Africa*, London, 1920.

MADDRY, C. E., *Day Dawn in Yoruba Land*, Nashville, 1936.

NEILL, S., *Anglicanism*, London, 1958.

OBISEAN, A., *Who Will Deliver Jacob From the Power of His Enemies?*, Ibadan, 1921.

OGUNBIYI, T. A. J., *Awon Serafu*, Lagos, 1926.

PHILLIPS, S. C., *The Heathen Cult Called Reformed Ogboni Society*, Ibadan, 1956.

PINNOCK, S. G., *The Romance of Missions in Nigeria*, Richmond, 1917.

PLATT, W. J., *From Fetish to Faith*, London, 1935.

RANSOME-KUTI, J. J., *Yoruba Sacred Songs*, Lagos, 1925.

SADLER, G. W., *A Century in Nigeria*, Nashville, 1950.

SHEPPERSON, E., and PRICE, T., *Independent African*, Edinburgh, 1958.

S.P.C.K., *Proceedings of the Pan-Anglican Conference, 1908*, vols. v and vi, London, 1908.

S.P.C.K., *The Six Lambeth Conferences*, 1867–1920, London, 1929.

STOCK, E., *The History of the Church Missionary Society*, vols. i–iv, 1899, 1916.

STONE, R. H., *In Afric's Forest and Jungle or Six Years Among the Yorubans*, Edinburgh and London, 1900.

SUNDKLER, B., *Bantu Prophets in South Africa*, Oxford, 1961.

——, *The Christian Ministry in Africa*, Uppsala, 1960.

TUPPER, H. A., *A Decade of Foreign Missions 1880–1890*, Richmond, 1891.

WALKER, F. D., *A Hundred Years in Nigeria 1842–1942*, London, 1943?

WELBOURN, F. B., *East African Rebels*, S.C.M. Press, 1961.

II. *Theses*

ADERIBIGBE, A. A. B., 'The Expansion of the Lagos Protectorate 1861–1900', Ph.D., London, 1959.

AJAYI, J. F. A., 'Christian Missions and the Making of Nigeria 1841–1891', Ph.D., London, 1958.

BAETA, C. G. K., 'Prophetism in Ghana', Ph.D., London, 1959.

FLORIN, H. W., 'The Southern Baptist Foreign Mission Enterprise in Western Nigeria: An Analysis', Ph.D., Boston, 1958.

HERSKOVITS, JEAN F., 'Liberated Africans and the History of the Lagos Colony to 1886', D.Phil., Oxford, 1960.
HOWELL, E. MILFORD, 'Nigerian Baptist Leaders and Their Contribution', Th.D., Southwestern Baptist Seminary, 1956.
KNIGHT, C. W., 'A Study of the Expansion of Evangelical Christianity in Nigeria', Th.D., Southern Baptist Seminary, Louisville, 1959.

Index